VAMPIRE
MOVIES

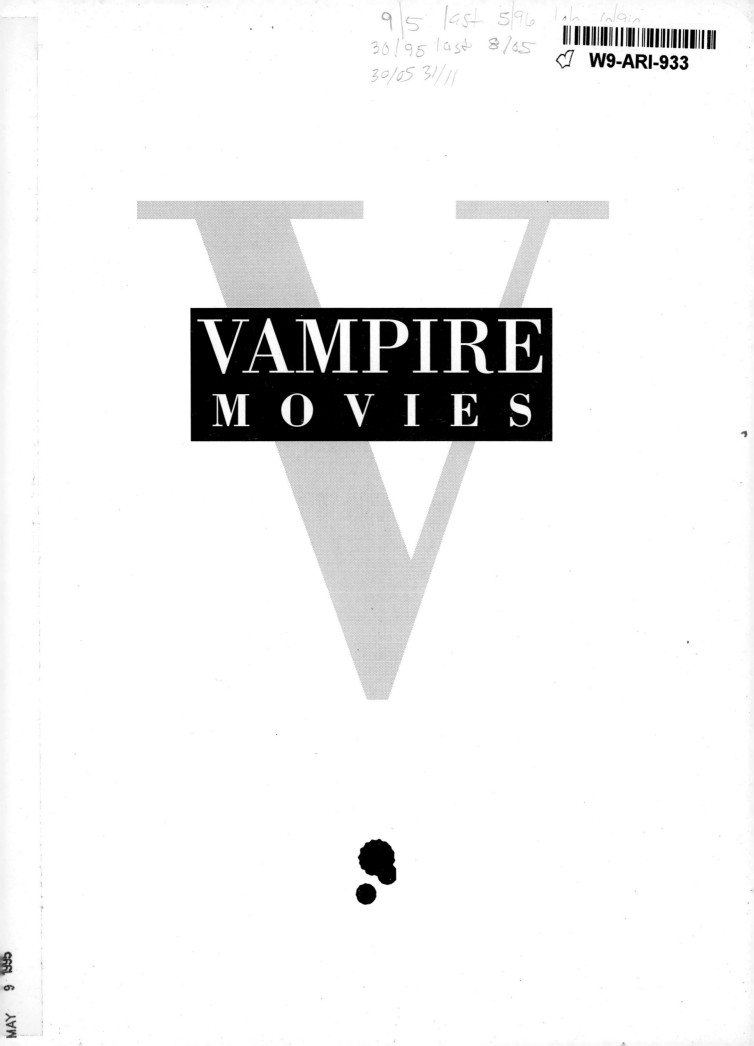

VAMPIRE
M O V I E S

KEY WEST, FLORIDA

Photo Credits

Page 2: Scream, Blacula, Scream (1972)
Page 5: Fright Night (1985)
Page 6: Taste the Blood of Dracula (1969)

Cover Design and Book Layout by Chidsey Graphics

Published by Fantasma Books
419 Amelia Street
Key West, Florida 33040

Queries regarding rights & permissions should be addressed to Fantasma Books, 419 Amelia Street
Key West, Florida 33040

ISBN 0-9634982-3-1
Library of Congress Catalog Card Number: 94-94390

Manufactured in the United States of America

ACKNOWLEDGEMENTS

I am especially grateful to Kat Scodder who was very instrumental in assisting me with photo illustrations. I would also like to thank Mr. Al Shevy of "World of Fandom" Magazine for his kind assistance as well as Alejandro Prince, H. Arthur Taussing and a special thanks to Mr. James Balzano!

TABLE OF CONTENTS

INTRODUCTION

Back in 1992, when I wrote the book *Dracula - the Vampire Legend On Film*, I concluded the book by promising that I would update the journal within two years. As promised, I hereby deliver **Vampire Movies** - the most complete, up-to-date and authoritative reference guide to cinematic vampires. The book covers vampire films and films that feature vampire-related characters from 1922 to 1994.

Since 1992, there have been many additions to this highly popular genre. But first, it is my duty to report that I have changed my published opinions on several films since the least book, primarily Tod Browning's classic DRACULA (1931) and Hammer's TASTE THE BLOOD OF DRACULA (1969).

In 1992, when my review of Browning's DRACULA was published, I received much criticism in the form of letters, faxes and even phone calls (all of which I always welcome), compelling me to take another look at this vintage film. As a result, I have altered my opinion slightly from before. I also changed my comments towards TASTE THE BLOOD OF DRACULA - another fine but overrated vampire film, as well as with Universal's DRACULA 91979) and SALEM'S LOT (1979) and many other films which got a second or third viewing since 1992. The point is, one views films differently with each additional viewing: the film either becomes better or worse.

I have also added numerous new selections since 1992, many of which are obscure older titles

Facing page: FRIGHT NIGHT II (1988)

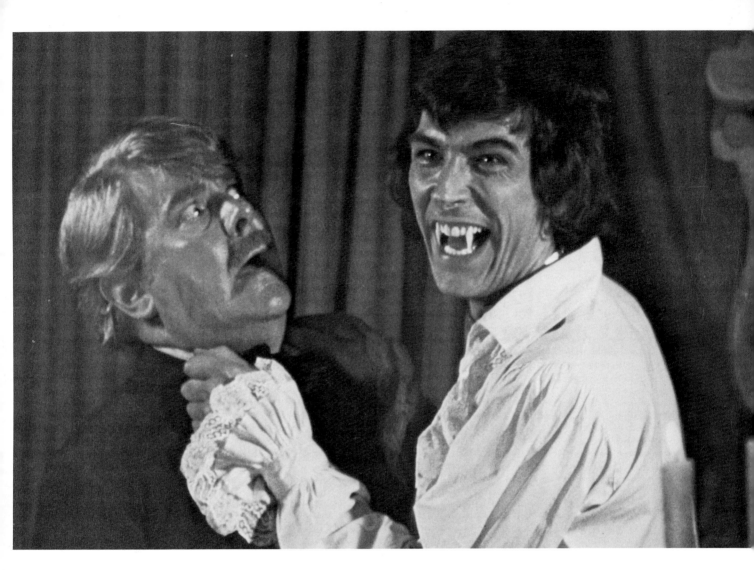

that have failed to go unnoticed or simply forgotten over the years. Although most of these films are awful, some of them, such as CONDEMNED TO LIVE (1933), for example, are gems. Connoisseurs of the vampire movie genre will especially appreciate these additions, some of which included titles as SHE WAS A HIPPY VAMPIRE (1966), THE BLOOD DRINKERS (1966), BLOOD BATH (1966), BLOOD OF DRACULA'S CASTLE (1969), THE HOUSE THAT DRIPPED BLOOD (1970), VIRGINS AND VAMPIRES 91972), SPERMULA (1975) and A POLISH VAMPIRE IN BURBANK (1990).

Also, since 1992, several new vampire movies have been produced. Topping the list, of course, is Francis Ford Coppola's BRAM STOKER'S DRACULA (1992), a $40 million extravaganza on the Dracula legend and one of the most highly awaited horror films in the history of film. Equally impressive, though, are Ted Nicolau's SUBSPECIES films, particularly the first two, both of which are bound to become modern horror classics for their innovative style. Naturally, whenever big budget horror films prevail, so does Roger Corman. Corman's moderately successful (on video) vampire film DRACULA RISING (1992) was produced quickly and relatively cheaply during the production of BRAM STOKER'S DRACULA to capitalize on that film's larger promotional campaign and box

Above: Count Mitterhouse attacks Thorley Walters in VAMPIRE CIRCUS (1971).

"Dracula" (Michael Pataki) goes to the dogs in DRACULA'S DOG (1975).

Clockwise from top left:

THE HOUSE THAT DRIPPED BLOOD (1970)
DRACULA A.D. (1971)
HOUSE OF DARK SHADOWS (1970)
VAMP (1986)
DRACULA A.D. (1971)

office success. And finally, John Landis struck back with INNOCENT BLOOD (1992), his mildly successful but superior contribution to the vampire genre, produced much in the same style as his previous cult classic AN AMERICAN WEREWOLF IN LONDON.

It is obvious in this book that much attention is paid towards Coppola's BRAM STOKER'S DRACULA, and rightfully so. To begin with, the film is the mot expensive and elaborate horror movie ever made. Secondly, the film is genuinely great, with incredible visuals and sets and fantastic special effects. The film is a milestone, and furthermore, BRAM STOKER'S DRACULA is responsible for putting the "zing" back into the horror film; something that it has lacked since the late 1970's and early 1980's. It's multimillion dollar price tag (the largest next to JURASSIC PARK, TERMINATOR II: JUDGEMENT DAY and TRUE LIES) has inspired a new wave of horror movies with big budgets and even bigger stars! Just look at what has resulted from the success of Coppola's *Dracula* movie: Anthony Hopkins is returning as Hannibal Lector in SILENCE OF THE LAMBS II; Robert DeNiro will be seen as the Frankenstein Monster in Coppola's big budget horror film MARY SHELLEY'S FRANKENSTEIN; Jack Nicholson and Michelle Pfieffer starred in WOLF; an American Godzilla movie is schedule for release sometime in 1995; there are rumors of a big budget remake of THE MUMMY; and, of course, superstar Tom Cruise will star during the Fall of 1994 in Anne Rice's INTERVIEW WITH A VAMPIRE! Thanks to Coppola's BRAM STOKER'S DRACULA and its numerous Academy Award nominations and wins, the horror genre is coming back bigger than ever.

Moviegoers, especially those who have a fond admiration towards horror films, almost always criticize big-budget horror films. And they should. There have been many times in the past when Hollywood has let the public down, usually because of bad scripting. In the case of BRAM STOKER'S DRACULA, and Universal's DRACULA of 1979, fans either felt the film suffered from too much romanticism and less horror or from a lack of "groovy" special effects. In the case of the upcoming $50 million dollar vampire film INTERVIEW WITH THE VAMPIRE, it seems that fans loyal to the genre are already bashing the film's producer David Geffen of massacring the well received, highly popular novel of the same title by Anne Rice. As with most screen adaptations, the movie is usually not as good as the novel. Can this be the "big" flaw with INTERVIEW WITH A VAMPIRE? Or will it be Tom Cruise's Lestat characterization?

Chances are slim that the film will turn out to be a great movie, but if it does, it won't matter whether or not the film is a faithful adaptation of the novel. Big studios' and stars' determination to turn good books into terrible movies borders on compulsive. The fact that the film sports a $50 million budget and the box office presence of Tom Cruise will not make a difference here. What will make the difference is a good screenplay. Furthermore, those expecting to see a traditional-style vampire patterned after the familiar cliche mannerisms of Max Schreck and Bela Lugosi will be disappointed. The film, if it is at all faithful to the novel to some degree, will be larded with highly sexual imagery and animalistic passion.

Another factor that will determine whether INTERVIEW WITH A VAMPIRE flies or flops

Fangs of terror from Hammer's LUST FOR A VAMPIRE (1971).

Dracula (Michael Pataki) savagely attacks in GRAVE OF THE VAMPIRE (1972).

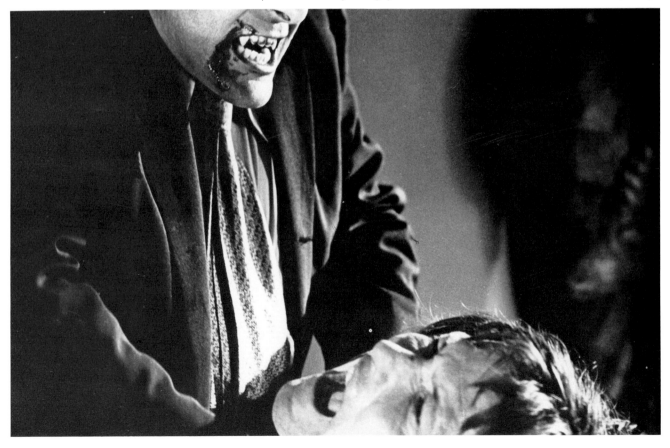

is Tom Cruise. Originally, Anne Rice had envisioned Jeremy Irons or John Malkovich as Lestat. The author was very unhappy when producer Geffen chose Cruise. In fact, she was furious! Hopefully the combination of Tom Cruise, a big budget and a well-written screen adaptation will push this film over the top. Once again, as in 1992 with the pre-release of BRAM STOKER'S DRACULA, we find ourselves in anticipation of another vampire movie extravaganza. Perhaps INTERVIEW's big budget and potential box office returns will put some more "zing" into the horror genre.

But as we all know, it takes more than big bucks and Academy Awards to make a good vampire movie. You need fangs, blood, shape-shifting, and sultry females with fangs down to their arm pits... Well, you simply need fangs! However, for the purists, a good vampire film must have a strong central vampire character such as Count Dracula or even Barnabas Collins. I would rather think as Count Dracula in the person of Mr. Christopher Lee as the most powerful and striking central vampire figure on film. Of course, this is strictly opinion, and everyone is entitled. However, Lee's characterization of Dracula in HORROR OF DRACULA seems to be the favorite of most aficionados worldwide, judging by the numerous letters and comments received since I wrote *Dracula - The Vampire Legend On Film*. And rightly so, HORROR OF DRACULA is a masterpiece.

In any case, the vampire film is undeniably the most popular of all the horror films, stretching from 1922 and the silent classic NOSFERATU to 1994 and INTERVIEW WITH A VAMPIRE. These films, from the best to the worst to the most obscure, have provided generations with a brand of terror that only one can find in a vampire movie. Being an addict to such films, I now, very proudly present to you *Vampire Movies*, an entire book devoted to cinematic vampires. In the great words of Bela Lugosi in DRACULA (1931), "*I bid you welcome*!" Turn the pages and enjoy!

Inevitably, I shall offend some readers by not devoting enough coverage to a "favorite" film, as is often the case. But don't despair — a new volume will be out in a couple of years — so those of you who feel I have overlooked a film still have time to write me.

Robert Marrero
Author

CHAPTER ONE

The 1920's

NOSFERATU, A SYMPHONY OF TERROR
1922; Prana (Germany) (B&W); Director: F.W.
Murnau; Screenwriter: Henrik Galeen, based on the
novel by Bram Stoker; Camera: Fritz Arno Wagner
& Gunther Krampf.

This silent masterpiece of the horror film is the first "true" screen adaptation of Bram Stoker's famous novel, *Dracula*, published in 1897, however, there are rumors that a Hungarian version of the novel entitled DRAKULA was made in 1921 and directed by Karoly Lajthay.

NOSFERATU was directed by one of Germany's greatest filmmakers, F. (Friederich) W. (Wilhelm) Murnau, who, at the time, was a young director of the German school of expressionism. Murnau, along with Fritz Lang, who directed METROPOLIS (1926), is one of the greatest directors from the classic period of silent films. NOSFERATU was clearly Murnau's masterpiece, following the success of his earlier film DER JANUSKOPF (1920), based on Robert Louis Stevenson's *The Strange Case of Dr. Jekyll and Mr. Hyde.*

Murnau did not take the most ethical approach in adapting Stoker's *Dracula* to the screen. *Dracula* was still in copyright in 1921 when the film went into production. Unlike other filmmakers who acquired the rights to adapt the story onto the screen from Stoker's widow, Murnau simply proceeded to make his film, disregarding copyright laws, which were somewhat slack at the time. The film was adapted to the screen by Henrik Galeen. Galeen had co-scripted with Paul Wegener the first version of DER GOLEM (1914), and later went on to script Paul Leni's WAXWORKS (1924). The script written by Galeen was quite faithful to the novel, however, Murnau took several precautions in the making of his bootlegged version. To avoid paying royalties to the copyright owners of *Dracula*, (Stoker's widow), Murnau changed the name of the script from *Dracula* to *Nosferatu*. He also altered the names of the characters and the film's setting. Transylvania became Germany and Bremen was substituted for London. Count Dracula became Count Orlock; Jonathan Harker became Waldemar Hutter; Professor Van Helsing became Professor Bulwer; and Renfield was changed to Knock.

Despite the name and setting changes, the premise

Facing page: Lon Chaney, Sr., as the pseudo-vampire in LONDON AFTER MIDNIGHT (1927).

The destruction of Count Orlock in F.W. Murnau's NOSFERATU (1922).

remained relatively the same as the novel and, in fact, the screenplay by Henrik Galeen is more faithful to the Stoker novel than the Universal and Hammer versions that followed.

The most drastic difference from the Stoker novel and this film is the vampire's physical appearance. Count Orlock, portrayed superbly by actor Max Schreck as a hellish demon, appears as a bald, human rodent-type creature; a monster that appears to have just risen from its foul smelling grave. Unlike Stoker's mysterious and handsome noble character, Orlock wore no tuxedo or cloak, nor did he bid fair maidens welcome. Instead, he preyed upon innocent victims like a bubonic plague, satisfying his unquenchable thirst for human blood. Schreck's Orlock was and still is the most hideous vampire ever to prowl the screen. With pointed ears, a pale face, razor sharp teeth and claws, the hellish demon leads his legions of rats from the subterranean levels of Germany and sails to

Bremen where a terrible plague strikes the town. The demon vampire is eventually destroyed when the film's heroine sacrifices her own life and soul to the vampire. She keeps Orlock occupied until sunrise by allowing the foul creature of the night to slowly drain her blood. In the morning, Orlock perishes from exposure to the sun's lethal rays.

NOSFERATU was never given wide distribution. The film's faithfulness to the Stoker novel forced it out of circulation because of copyright infringements enforced by Florence Stoker. Murnau was ordered to withdraw the film in July 1925. The court also ordered that all negatives and prints of the film be destroyed, but obviously, NOSFERATU survived (luckily), and the film was screened in London three years afterwards, followed by its first American screening in 1929. Today, NOSFERATU is considered by film historians as one of the greatest silent horror films ever made.

NOSFERATU was apparently remade in Italy in 1971 as HANNO COMBIATO FACCIA (THEY CHANGED FACES), directed by Corrado Farina for Garigliano Films. The film follows the same plot of NOSFERATU, only gangsters are substituted for vampires (sounds much like INNOCENT BLOOD made in 1992). A more faithful remake was made in color in 1979 with Klaus Kinski as Count Dracula rather than Count Orlock.

LONDON AFTER MIDNIGHT
1927; MGM (B&W); Director: Tod Browning; Screenwriter: Waldemar Young from an original story by Tod Browning; Camera: Merritt Gerstad.

During the mid 1920's, American film companies became more involved with the growing genre of horror films, mainly as a result of many superior and commercially successful German pictures such as DER GOLEM (1914, 1916 & 1920), THE CABINET OF DR. CALIGARI (1919), DER JANUSKOPF (1920), NOSFERATU (1922) and several others. Actor Lon Chaney, Sr. was the leading horror film star in America at a time, several years before Bela Lugosi and Boris Karloff rose to fame. The actor was most famous for his monstrous movie characterizations in THE HUNCHBACK OF NOTRE DAME (1923) and THE PHANTOM OF THE OPERA (1925).

In 1927, the actor played a pseudo vampire in the first American vampire film, LONDON AFTER MIDNIGHT. The film was based on the story *The Hypnotist* by Tod Browning, who also directed the film.

For years, there had been much discussion about this film and how it compared to its remake, MARK OF THE VAMPIRE (1935), which Browning also directed and which starred Bela *"Dracula"* Lugosi. However, because LONDON AFTER MIDNIGHT is virtually a lost film (although there seems to be a rumor that a print may exist in a private collection in England), it is therefore impossible to compare the two films equally and fairly.

Supposedly LONDON AFTER MIDNIGHT, like its remake, leads the viewer to believe that there really is a vampire (played by Chaney) running around an old castle, when really the vampire is later revealed as being a police detective in disguise during the film's climax. The vampire trappings were staged throughout the film to frighten a murderer into disclosing his involvement with a killing. Chaney assumed both the roles of the detective and the vampire, and the audiences of 1927 were subject to the hoax.

Despite the prank, Chaney's vampire is quite impressive, and the supernatural elements prior to the revelation of the hoax are quite effective. As with his highly memorable and distorted creations in both THE HUNCHBACK OF NOTRE DAME and THE PHANTOM OF THE OPERA, the actor delivers a frightening characterization of a movie vampire, complete with formal wear, top hat and a set of rigid fangs that cover his entire mouth.

By 1927, Chaney was the undisputed master of the American horror film. Unfortunately, Chaney passed away in 1930 just before production began on Universal Pictures' version of Stoker's novel. One can only wonder how Chaney's Count Dracula would have been depicted had he portrayed the character in the Universal classic that followed in 1931. Many have speculated, but chances are his Dracula would not have been the suave nobleman that Bela Lugosi's Count Dracula is today.

Above: Lon Chaney and his bride attack in LONDON AFTER MIDNIGHT (1927).

19

CHAPTER TWO

The 1930's

DRACULA

1931; Universal Pictures (B&W); Producer: Carl Laemmle, Jr.; Director: Tod Browning; Screenwriters: Garrett Fort & Dudley Murphy from the play by Hamilton Deane and John L. Balderston and from the novel Dracula by Bram Stoker; Camera: Karl Freund.

Lon Chaney, Sr. died in 1930, and so did his golden opportunity to portray Bram Stoker's legendary vampire, Count Dracula. Universal was basically up a creek without a paddle, so-to-speak.

Studio executives considered Conrad Veidt, who was Germany's greatest silent horror film star who had been in DER JANUSKOPF (1920), THE CABINET OF DR. CALIGARI (1919), WAXWORKS (1924), and THE HANDS OF ORLAC (1925). Veidt was actually the logical choice, since he had just completed Universal's THE MAN WHO LAUGHS (1927), an incredibly successful film based on Victor Hugo's novel. Unfortunately the actor had other previously arranged obligations elsewhere. Paul Muni of SCARFACE (1932) fame was also considered, as well as actors William Courtney and Ian Keith, the latter would later go on to play a vampire in Republic

Pictures' VALLEY OF THE ZOMBIES (1946). The role, as everyone knows, went to Hungarian-born actor Bela Lugosi, who had starred in the stage version of *Dracula* around the same time.

With the exception of several minor roles in major films during the silent era, including F.W. Murnau's DER JANUSKOPF (1920) and Tod Browning's THE THIRTEENTH CHAIR (1929), Lugosi was virtually an unknown actor; unknown in America, until March 27, 1931, after the release of DRACULA. As a result of the film's enormous box office success, Lugosi became a superstar of the horror film from that moment onward.

To this day, no other actor is most associated with the name Count Dracula than Bela Lugosi. Lugosi is indisputably the epitome of the classic movie vampire, possessing the handsome, suave and debonair charm of an aristocratic nobleman. Lugosi's Dracula is cunning and clever and very resourceful with centuries of knowledge at his disposal. His vampire is both mysterious and romantic; a polished gentlemen turned into a nondescript living monster.

Browning's film is not a faithful and strict adaptation of Stoker's novel. The film was actually

Facing page: Bela Lugosi as Dracula in Tod Browning's DRACULA (1931).

based more on Hamilton Deane's play. The majority of DRACULA is virtually a photographed stage play, with few close-ups and a less-than-normal fluid camera by Karl Freund, an excellent cinematographer from the vintage movie years, responsible for the luminous, stylized and often theatrical photography of such films like THE GOLEM (1920), FAUST (1926), METROPOLIS (1926) and DR. JEKYLL AND MR. HYDE (1932). It is obviously in the film's stagey style wherein lies the movie's greatest disappointment to many modern-day viewers. The scenes are static, cold, and often uninteresting and boring, and the climax is far from thrilling for this type of vehicle. In addition, the vampire trappings are totally obsolete. However, though the film is an overall disappointment to many modern viewers, primarily those seeing the film for the first time, DRACULA offers some of the most atmospheric sets and moments in a horror film, especially the ghostly sets of both Castle Dracula in Transylvania and Carfax Abbey in London, created by Universal set designers with impeccable detail and style. Technically speaking, DRACULA is a superior piece of filmmaking, although it's special effects, which were once considered innovative, are dated by today's standards.

Despite its unfaithfulness, DRACULA follows the story line of Bram Stoker's novel relatively close, beginning with Renfield's arrival at Castle Dracula in Transylvania. Count Dracula naturally devours the Englishman's soul, as he has done with most of his countrymen, and sets sail to England, where he begins sinking his teeth (off screen) into the necks of Englishmen and seducing young maidens with his mysterious charm. As the vampire carries out his evil doings, he is eventually revealed as an inhuman monster by his arch nemesis Professor Van Helsing (played by Edward Van Sloan). The exchange in dialogue and the confrontations between the two foes is well written for its time, but less than thrilling for today's sophisticated moviegoer, who demands much more than theatrical dialogue and mundane special effects..

The entire film in general is breathtaking, and is undoubtedly one of the greatest horror films ever to

Professor Van Helsing (Edward Van Sloan) confronts Dracula (Bela Lugosi) in DRACULA (1931).

Lionel Atwill and Fay Wray in a scene from VAMPIRE BAT (1933).

come out of Universal's early stockade of horrors.

DRACULA is a relic of an era long vanished and one of cinema's true masterpieces, one that modern viewers and connoisseurs of classic horror films can appreciate, like good bottle of wine - *for those who drink wine!*

DRACULA
**1931 Universal Pictures (Spanish Version) (B&W);
Producer: Carl Laemmle, Jr.; Director: George
Melford; Screenwriters: Garret Fort and Dudley
Murphy from the script written for the 1931 version,
based on Bram Stoker's novel.**

With the enormous success of DRACULA (1931), Universal produced a Spanish version of the film directed by George Melford. The film, currently made available on videocassette, stars Carlos Villarias as Count Dracula. Villarias has an uncanny resemblance to Bela Lugosi, and like his counterpart, he makes an effective Dracula. Lupita Tova is equally convincing as the heroine, and Dracula's intended victim.

DRACULA was filmed at the same time as the Bela Lugosi version was being made, using the same sets and the same script (in Spanish, of course). There is one difference, however, this version is thought to be more frightening and visually appealing than its English counterpart. Since the film is readily available on video, fans should decide for themselves.

Fans should look out for the one and only scene of Bela Lugosi in this Spanish version. Apparently, Browning scrapped the scene of the vampire walking in London from the original version. The edited scene was latter picked-up by director George Melford, who felt that Lugosi bore an uncanny resemblance to Carlos Villarias, thus he inserted the sequence secretly.

Bela Lugosi and Carroll Borland as pseudo-vampires in
MARK OF THE VAMPIRE (1935).

VAMPYR

**1931/1932; (German/French) (B&W); Producer:
Baron Nicholas De Gunzburg; Director: Carl
Theodor Dryer; Screenwriters: Dryer & Christen
Jul, suggested by Sheridan le Fanu's novella**
Carmilla; **Camera: Rudolf Mate.**

In addition to being the first sound vampire film,
beating Universal's DRACULA into release,
VAMPYR is also the very first of many vampire films
to be based upon the novella *Carmilla* by Sheridan le
Fanu. VAMPYR is regarded as one of the true
masterpieces of the golden era of the horror film,
but, like DRACULA, the film is considered to be very
dated and a bit on the boring side for modern viewers.

Atmospherically photographed by cameraman
Rudolph Mate for director Carl Dreyer, the film very
subtlety tells the story of a man's (played by Julian
West, who also produced the film under the name of
Baron De Gunzburg) journey to a small village that
is plagued by an old female vampire (played by
Henriette Gerard). Dreyer uses strong symbolisms

to establish the film's mood by the simplest means,
such as a chilling nightmare sequence in which the
hero imagines himself buried alive in a coffin and the
vampire lady peering at him through the lid's transom.
This scene is still most frightening, even today, as the
camera replaces the actor's position in the casket,
allowing the viewer the uncomfortable feeling that
they too are trapped alive inside the coffin. This is the
single most important element of the film; the
uneasiness created by such foreboding scenes.
Interestingly, this rather disturbing scene most
probably served as a predecessor to many of those
"buried alive" sequences in the later Edgar Allan Poe

horror films. Photographer Mate shot the entire film through a special gauze lens to create the film's dreamlike effect and Dreyer only filmed during dusk and dawn. Mate's polished cinematography in films such as this would later contribute to his long film career in America, where he directed the visually stunning sci-fi classic WHEN WORLDS COLLIDE.

VAMPYR, like NOSFERATU (1922), was given a very limited release in America. American distributors felt that audiences would not appreciate the subtle qualities of the film after having enjoyed such traditional horror films such as Universal's DRACULA and FRANKENSTEIN (Both 1931). In hindsight, the distributors were correct.

VAMPIRE BAT
1933; Majestic (B&W); Producer: Phil Goldstone; Director: Frank Strayer; Screenwriter: Edward T. Lowe.

Directed by Frank Strayer on a low budget, that is, compared to Universal's DRACULA (1931), FRANKENSTEIN (1931), MURDERS IN THE RUE MORGUE (1932) and THE MUMMY (1932), VAMPIRE BAT stars Lionel Atwill as mad scientist Otto Von Niemann. The film tries hard to imitate many of the earlier sound horror Universal films. In fact, if we did not know any better, one would actually believe that they were watching a Universal picture. The similarities are obvious. To begin with, Lionel Belmore repeats his burgomaster role in Universal's FRANKENSTEIN and Dwight Frye's lunatic batkeeper named Herman Gleib resembles his Renfield performance from Universal's DRACULA. Even the mood and atmosphere is highly reminiscent of the old Universal horrors.

In the film, Atwill perpetrates the hoax that a vampire is killing the townspeople when, in actuality, it is he who is draining the blood of the villagers to keep his experiment alive. Atwill's henchman-servant Emil Borst (played by Robert Fraser) is sent out for victims by Atwill to nourish a blob of living tissue he keeps alive in a tank. In the film, Emil wears a flowing cloak as he seeks his victims at night, thus first creating the image of a vampire and second panic and paranoia. Atwill controls his servant's mind by way of some hocus pocus telepathic control. Meanwhile, Atwill tries to pin the crimes on lunatic Frye, and naturally, the villagers already suspect the poor bat-keeper. After a chase through the countryside, the townspeople trap him in a cave and kill him. Fay Wray (who, by this point, had already starred opposite Lionel Atwill in three horror films) is the heroine while Melvyn Douglas (star of both THE OLD DARK HOUSE and GHOST STORY) is the hero who saves Wray from the clutches of Atwill.

VAMPIRE BAT, a low budget programmer, did not fare well next to Universal's DRACULA and FRANKENSTEIN, two big budget productions. Because of the vast differences in production values, VAMPIRE BAT should therefore not be judged too harshly. In fact, the film should not be compared to the Universal pictures, nor is it fare to compare the film to Atwill's previous horror films (DR. X, THE MYSTERY OF THE WAX MUSEUM and MURDERS IN THE ZOO). When viewed today, VAMPIRE BAT appears as a very dated exploitation movie, mainly because of its obvious budget restrictions, its shoddy, but familiar borrowed sets, and its typical formula script by Edward T. Lowe, normally an imaginative screenwriter who would later script Universal's formula monster movies HOUSE OF FRANKENSTEIN (1944) and HOUSE OF DRACULA (1945). But Frye is excellent once again as a lunatic and Atwill is ideal as the mad scientist, delivering his lines with sinister glee.

CONDEMNED TO LIVE
1935; (B&W); Director: Frank Strayer.

This very rarely seen, hardly known mild horror film is directed by Frank Strayer, the director of THE VAMPIRE BAT.

In the film, Ralph Morgan and his wife Maxie Doyle seem like your average European couple, but this is far from the case. Morgan is a full-fledged vampire who has been concealing his sanguine secret from Doyle. Naturally, she finds out, and in the process, she falls in love with Russell Gleason, learning to never jilt a vampire.

For nourishment, Morgan's dwarf hunchback assistant commits ghastly murders (DR. X-style) and conceals the evidence. Very rare!

MARK OF THE VAMPIRE
1935; MGM (B&W); Producer: E.J. Manix; Director: Tod Browning; Screenwriters: Guy Endore & Bernard Schubert; Camera: James Wong Howe.

With the success of DRACULA (1931) and FREAKS (1932) behind him, director Tod Browning set out to remake his previous pseudo-vampire classic LONDON AFTER MIDNIGHT (1927). MARK OF THE VAMPIRE is indeed a remake of the Lon Chaney classic, however because it offers many of the characteristics of Universal's DRACULA, primarily because both films feature Bela Lugosi as their principal vampire, in this case he portrays Count Mora the pseudo vampire. Because of Lugosi's presence, MARK OF THE VAMPIRE closely resembles DRACULA in both mood and style. Lugosi's part in this film is rather small, but quite effective, as he and twenty-one year old Carroll Borland as his daughter-vampire Luna pretend to be vampires when really they are merely actors hired by Inspector Neumann (Lionel Atwill) to trick some criminals into believing the house is haunted by the undead.

Universal's DRACULA had not yet been produced when LONDON AFTER MIDNIGHT was released, therefore the original has a style and mood all of its own, whereas MARK OF THE VAMPIRE was produced under the influence of DRACULA, to capitalize on its success. Like the original, MARK OF THE VAMPIRE uses its vampire trappings to disclose a murderer. The entire scheme works on film, but the hoax, however, does not. By 1935, audiences were spoiled by the likes of real monsters and their "true" supernatural elements as in DRACULA, FRANKENSTEIN (1931), THE MUMMY (1932) and THE WEREWOLF OF LONDON (1935). These monsters were not a hoax, at least, not on film. In 1935, the climax of MARK OF THE VAMPIRE was considered a let down when the vampires are revealed merely as actors, and therein lies the film's major flaw. However, prior to that moment, MARK OF THE VAMPIRE is a superior piece of horror film, actually superior to DRACULA in many ways (technically speaking). Browning delivers some very eerie moments that actually surpass many of the trappings used in DRACULA, therefore the film should not be judged so harshly when compared to other classic horror films. MARK OF THE VAMPIRE is a first rate Gothic thriller right up to the hoax and although he does not deliver any dialogue, Lugosi is instrumental in establishing the mood of the film.

DRACULA'S DAUGHTER
1936; Universal (B&W); Producers: E.M. Asher & Carl Laemmle, Jr.; Director: Lambert Hillyer; Screenwriter: Garrett Fort, based on *Dracula's Guest* by Bram Stoker.

Universal was very good at making sequels to its original horror films, and DRACULA'S DAUGHTER is actually a very competent sequel to DRACULA, even though the film lacks the key personality of such horror superstars as Bela Lugosi and Boris Karloff. DRACULA'S DAUGHTER is smoothly directed by Lambert Hillyer, the director of THE INVISIBLE RAY (1936) from a good, solid script written by Garrett Fort. And even though the film was produced on a lower than normal budget for a Universal picture made during the first cycle of sound horror movies, DRACULA'S DAUGHTER appears to be as expensive a film as DRACULA, FRANKENSTEIN or THE MUMMY.

Cast in the title role is the beautiful actress Gloria Holden. As Countess Marya Zaleska, the ill-fated daughter of Count Dracula who seeks a cure to her unholy condition, Holden delivers a modest but restrained performance. In the film, she is tempted by the film's real villain, her evil manservant Sandor (played by Irving Pichel), complete with a pale face and hair parted straight down the middle. Sandor influences the Countess to perform acts of vampirism because he fears that she will not fullfil her promise of making him immortal.

With DRACULA'S DAUGHTER, Universal has managed to produce a beautifully atmospheric, well-mounted vampire tale that offers both continuity with the original film and interesting new characters to satisfy the viewer's appetite for fresh material. Actor Edward Van Sloan, who in between DRACULA and this film starred in both Universal's FRANKENSTEIN (1931) and THE MUMMY (1932), reprises his role as Professor Van Helsing while co-star Otto Kruger is convincing as the film's skeptical hero and fearful-at-times vampire killer.

The film clearly represents and documents the end of an era of quality horror films produced by Universal Pictures during the early to mid 1930's. Once the studio was purchased from the Laemmles, Universal would never make another Gothic horror film quite as technically good as DRACULA'S DAUGHTER (discounting SON OF FRANKENSTEIN made in 1939 under Universal's new regime). The change became evident following SON OF FRANKENSTEIN with the studio's formula-style

A rare scene in which Bela Lugosi appears in the Spanish version of DRACULA (1931).

horror vehicles that followed, such as FRANKENSTEIN MEETS THE WOLFMAN (1943), HOUSE OF FRANKENSTEIN (1944) and HOUSE OF DRACULA (1945), to name just a few.

THE RETURN OF DR. X
1939; Warner (B&W); Producer: Bryan Foy; Director: Vincent Sherman; Screenwriter: Lee Katz.

Humphrey Bogart starred in only one horror picture during his entire career: THE RETURN OF DR. X. Apparently, Bogart was forced into the picture as part of a multi-film contract with Warner. The actor hated the idea of sitting in a make-up chair for two hours prior to filming and an additional two hours after to apply and remove the make-up that made his character appear as one of the undead. The make-up

for Bogart's vampire was created by make-up artist Perc Westmore.

Bogart's lack of enthusiasm shows in his bland performance as the vampiric undead, electrocuted to death for committing murder restored to life by Dr. Xavier (John Litel). Now Boggie, the living dead, runs around with a scalpel because he needs blood!

THE RETURN OF DR. X, directed by Vincent Sherman, was, in the opinion of many, an entire waste of Boggie's talents, as well as a waste of actors Wayne Morris, Dennis Morgan and Rosemary Lane's time, because the film did not really enhance any of their careers in the horror genre let alone their careers in general. The film was nothing more than a simple-minded programmer. Furthermore, the misleading title suggests that the film is a sequel to the classic Warner horror film DR. X (1932) with Lionel Atwill. This is not true. In actuality, the same play that inspired the original DR. X inspired a much later film entitled THE INVISIBLE MENACE with Boris Karloff. THE RETURN OF DR. X, a more traditional, formula-style horror film reminiscent of Boris Karloff's THE WALKING DEAD (1936), was in no way a sequel or a remake, and certainly John Litel's stodgy performance as Dr. Xavier cannot hold a candle to Lionel Atwill's original characterization. In addition to resembling THE WALKING DEAD, THE RETURN OF DR. X offers many similarities to both MAN MADE MONSTER (1941) and THE INDESTRUCTIBLE MAN (1956).

George Melford prepares to sink his fangs into the neck of Lupita Tova in the Spanish version of DRACULA (1931).

In this scene from DRACULA'S DAUGHTER (1936), Gloria Holden is impaled with a wooden arrow.

CHAPTER THREE

The 1940's

SON OF DRACULA

1943; Universal Pictures (B&W); Producer: Ford Bebe; Director: Robert Siodmak; Screenwriter: Eric Taylor from an original story by Curt Siodmak.

During the late 1930's and the early 1940's, Universal Pictures launched a new series of monster movies beginning with SON OF FRANKENSTEIN (1939), as well as a new horror film star to alter its tired and old image. The studio began by grooming Lon Chaney, Jr. as Bela Lugosi and Boris Karloff's replacement in a series of horror films that included MAN MADE MONSTER (1941), THE WOLFMAN (1941), GHOST OF FRANKENSTEIN (1941), and THE MUMMY'S TOMB (1942), in which the actor portrayed the title monsters.

Chaney was given the opportunity over Bela Lugosi to portray the new Count Dracula in the studio's latest vampire outing SON OF DRACULA. However, the studio made an unwise decision in choosing Chaney over Bela Lugosi, for Chaney was too awkward and brute an actor to take control of the suave and debonair Count Alucard (Dracula spelled backwards) in this long-awaited sequel to

DRACULA'S DAUGHTER. The role should have been given to Bela Lugosi, or even to actor John Carradine, who would later don the cloak and name of Dracula for Universal in HOUSE OF FRANKENSTEIN (1944) and HOUSE OF DRACULA (1945).

In any case, Chaney's awkward performance as the Count is overcome by the fast-paced and entertaining direction of Robert Siodmak, whose only concern at the time was to inject thrills and excitement into an otherwise dull series. Thus, the film relies heavily on the special effects of John P. Fulton rather than the dialogue of Eric Taylor's weak adaptation of Siodmak's story. For the first time, we see the vampire transform into a bat right before our eyes, with the help of Fulton's improved bag of special effect tricks!

The script removes the setting from Transylvania to a southern plantation in America, possibly Louisiana, where the vampire Alucard seduces a very willing hostess (played by Louise Albritton). Meanwhile, the Count is pursued by a Professor Van Helsing-type authority on vampires named Professor Lazlo (played by J. Edwards Bromberg). Horror starlet Evelyn Ankers, who starred in THE

Facing page: Lon Chaney, Jr., as Count Alucard in SON OF DRACULA (1943).

WOLFMAN (1941) opposite Chaney, plays Dracula's next victim, while Robert Paige is the hero.

SON OF DRACULA offers many flaws and inconsistencies with its predecessors, and in fact, many film historians have blasted the film as not being a sequel to DRACULA and DRACULA'S DAUGHTER. However, for those who enjoy the simplicity and cheap thrills these vehicles provided - that good old fashion entertainment that Universal horror films of the 1940's specialized in, then perhaps you can overlook the numerous flaws, the dated trappings and Chaney's awkward performance, as well as the rudimentary script.

RETURN OF THE VAMPIRE
1943; Columbia (B&W); Producer: Sam White; Director: Lew Landers; Screenwriter: Griffith Jay, based on the idea by Kurt Neumann.

While Universal had Lon Chaney as Count Dracula, the Wolfman and the Frankenstein monster, Columbia Pictures launched their own series of "B" horror films beginning with superstar Boris Karloff's mad scientist films and continuing with Bela Lugosi's RETURN OF THE VAMPIRE. The race was on to see who could produce the best and the most successful horror films, which is why Universal objected to Columbia's request for permission to name and call Lugosi's vampire "Dracula" in the film.

Armand Tesla (Lugosi) is a student of the occult turned into a vampire. With the aide of his werewolf servant Andreas (played by Matt Willis), the vampire sets out to kill the ancestors of those who destroyed him a century ago. However, whenever you have two monsters in the same room, there's bound to be trouble, and as predicted, both monsters fall in love with beautiful Nina Foch. The monsters battle each other for her love. In pursuit of the vampire are Miles Mander and Frieda Inescort the latter runs an asylum in the film.

RETURN OF THE VAMPIRE is directed by Lew Landers in a style that is reminiscent of the Universal horror films of the time, especially FRANKENSTEIN MEETS THE WOLFMAN (1943) in which the title monsters battle each other during the climax. The teaming of movie monsters seemed to be the profitable thing to do during the 1940's and RETURN OF THE VAMPIRE was produced to capitalize on the multi-monster craze of that era, primarily the success of Universal's

FRANKENSTEIN MEETS THE WOLFMAN (1943), as well as on the name of fading horror film star Bela Lugosi.

Lugosi was afforded plenty of rich dialogue for his character and received several major close-ups. The actor, who had not had a good role since his performance as Ygor in GHOST OF FRANKENSTEIN (1941), once commented in an interview as to how pleased he was with the project and with his "new" vampire role. Lugosi was paid a mere $3,500 for his role in a film that cost Columbia $75,000 to produced. RETURN OF THE VAMPIRE grossed nearly $500,000 during its first run.

Despite the film's low production values, RETURN OF THE VAMPIRE does offer some effective moments as a horror film, primarily the scene in which Lugosi's vampire claws his way out of his grave after a World War II German bomb hits the cemetery in which he is buried. The film is,

J. Edwards Bromberg feels the wrath of the Count in SON OF DRACULA (1943).

Vampire Bela Lugosi is confronted by werewolf Matt Willis in RETURN OF THE VAMPIRE (1943).

nevertheless, the better of the many "B" vampire films that emerged from the 1940's and early to late 1950's prior to Hammer's colorful HORROR OF DRACULA (1958).

As a notation for horror fans, the film's director, Lew Landers, was originally known as Louis Friedlander, and he had also directed THE RAVEN (1935) with both Bela Lugosi and Boris Karloff for Universal.

DEAD MEN WALK
1943; PRC (B&W); Producer: Sigmund Neufeld; Director: Sam Newfield; Screenwriter: Fred Myton.

Producers Releasing Corp. (PRC) was a poverty-

row studio like Monogram and Allied, followed later by the likes of American International Pictures in the 1950's, that specialized in turning out mass-manufactured creature "cheapies" that were often deliberately humorous. This runty collection of films included the likes of such classic programmers as THE CORPSE VANISHES (1942) and THE APE MAN (1943) with Bela Lugosi, and KING OF THE ZOMBIES (1941) and THE INVISIBLE GHOST (1941). These films or "programmers," as they were often called, delighted and capitalized on mimicking the otherwise "respectable" horrors of Universal and Columbia's "B" pictures. Normally, many of these poverty-row films would be produced on a minuscule budget, and then rake in thousands, while the Universal films would cost four to five times the amount to produce. Very rarely would a poverty row film rise to the technical excellence of a "studio" film.

Actor Dwight Frye was excellent as demented dwarfs, lunatics and grave diggers in classic horror films such as DRACULA (1931), FRANKENSTEIN (1931) and THE VAMPIRE BAT (1933). In DEAD MEN WALK, Frye gives another Renfield-type performance, this time as Zolar, the hunchback servant of George Zucco's vampire. Zucco is the film's real star, an actor who rose out of the 1940's Universal horror film to become a leading star in many of the poverty-row horrors of the 1940's. In DEAD MEN WALK, Zucco plays a vampire who menaces his twin brother Dr. Clayton (also Zucco).

The film was PRC's first and only vampire film, and as typical of these films, there is no atmosphere, no character development, cheap sets and very little budget. The film was directed without any style by Sam Newfield, the director of PRC's THE MAD MONSTER (1942), also with Zucco. PRC went out of business in 1947, and actor Dwight Frye died in 1944 of a heart attack.

HOUSE OF FRANKENSTEIN
1944; Universal (B&W); Producer: Paul Malvern; Director: Erle C. Kenton; Screenwriters: Curt Siodmak & Edward T. Lowe from an original story by Siodmak; Camera: George Robinson.

Writers Curt Siodmak and Edward T. Lowe had exhausted every conceivable original idea for a new horror film before coming up with the "sensational" notion of combining the studio's most famous movie monsters into one feature film. FRANKENSTEIN

MEETS THE WOLFMAN (1943) was the first of these films, opening to good reviews and record-breaking profits as a result of Universal's enormous and skillful marketing campaign. The film's success encouraged studio officials to further tap into the multi-monster movie market and instead of using two monsters the studio thought, *"how about five monsters for the price of one?"* Guess what, it worked! Once again, Universal raked in the dough! Although the premise is a bit rudimentary and "old-hat" by today's standards, the film is considered a moderate "B" classic that is still enjoyable nonetheless.

In the film, the Frankenstein Monster (Glenn Strange), the Wolfman (Lon Chaney, Jr.), the Mad Scientist (Boris Karloff), the hunchback assistant (J. Carrol Naish) and Count Dracula (John Carradine) have a field day with their victims. Count Dracula is revived from his skeletal remains when Karloff removes a stake that once sent the vampire king into limbo. Now fully revived, Dracula is promised victims by Karloff in return for doing the mad scientist's evil bidding. Dracula disguises himself as Baron Latos and eventually begins working for himself, meaning, he's out for blood and bride (how typical of these bloodsucking fiends!). The vampire seduces and abducts actress Anne Gwynne with intentions of making her his mistress and an undead creature of the night like himself. In a fast-paced cross country chase with the police staged during the early part of the film, the vampire becomes a victim of the sun's powerful rays. Count Dracula's frantic attempt to reach the safety of his coffin before the sun rises is to no avail; the undead creature begins to decompose before he can reach his coffin.

In reality, HOUSE OF FRANKENSTEIN is directed in a hurried, unstylish fashion by Erle C. Kenton, who also directed ISLAND OF LOST SOULS (1932) for Paramount. Siodmak and Lowe's script uses the Dracula legend to link the other monsters into the film. In fact, Carradine's Dracula is but a memory by the time Chaney transforms into a werewolf. The real star of this film and these type of vehicles is the Frankenstein Monster, but Carradine's Dracula makes a great and lasting impression with his deep, authoritative voice, his gray-streaked hair, small mustache and gaunt features. Carradine was perfect for the role of Count Dracula. In fact, physically, he resembled Bram Stoker's description of the vampire king more so than Bela Lugosi's 1931 characterization. One can only wonder how better or worse a film HOUSE OF FRANKENSTEIN could have been with Boris Karloff as the Mad Scientist, Lon Chaney Jr. as the Wolfman and Bela Lugosi as Count Dracula. The only answer to this speculation is to contemplate another ABBOTT AND COSTELLO MEET FRANKENSTEIN vehicle without the comedy antics.

Also starring in this all-star horror extravaganza are George Zucco as Professor Lampini and Lionel Atwill as the police inspector. HOUSE OF FRANKENSTEIN was intended to be Universal's final monster movie, however, it is "sequeled" by both HOUSE OF DRACULA (1945) and ABBOTT AND COSTELLO MEET FRANKENSTEIN (1948), the latter stars Bela Lugosi as Count Dracula for the very last time.

HOUSE OF DRACULA
1945; Universal (B&W); Producer: Paul Malvern; Director: Erle C. Kenton; Screenplay: Edward T. Lowe; Camera: George Robinson.

Unexpectedly, Universal, pleased with the profits from HOUSE OF FRANKENSTEIN immediately made this superior and direct sequel in which actor John Carradine returns to the role of Count Dracula. In the film, Dracula announces himself again as Baron Latos and uses Mad Scientist Onslow Stevens to find a cure to his vampiric condition, however the vampire's plans go haywire when Stevens gives most of his attention to curing Lon Chaney Jr.'s werewolf condition and reviving the Frankenstein Monster (played once again by Glenn Strange). To make matters worse, Stevens inadvertently turns himself into a Jekyll-Hyde monster after a failed blood transfusion with Dracula.

Once again, Count Dracula perishes at the mercy of the sun's lethal rays. Although Carradine's Dracula was given more footage in HOUSE OF DRACULA, the film was Universal's shortest running horror film and a final farewell to their monstrous creations. The film ended a generation of monster movies that once dominated the screen. As for John Carradine, the actor would not don the cloak again until BILLY THE KID VS. DRACULA in 1966.

John Carradine and Onslow Stevens in
HOUSE OF DRACULA (1945).

THE VAMPIRE'S GHOST

1945; Republic (B&W); Producer: Rudy Abel; Director: Lesley Selander; Screenwriter: Leigh Brackett & John K. Butler.

Republic Pictures typically produced "B" exploitation horror and western films during the 1940's, and THE VAMPIRE'S GHOST is a typical example of how the studio would exploit a genre. In the film, actor John Abbott is a centuries-old vampire, an underworld leader in the west coast of Africa. Abbott's vampire did not sleep in a coffin as did his traditional ancestors. Instead, he carried a miniature casket with some native soil. By day, the vampire sports around with dark sunglasses, doomed by an ancient curse to roam the Earth throughout eternity since Elizabethan times.

The film just does not have the budget nor the time (59 minutes) to develop any type of atmosphere and uses cheap thrills to satisfy its audience. The screen treatment by Leigh Brackett is weak and Lesley Selander's direction is aimed towards action and suspense rather than toward the characters and the plot. More superior were Columbia's low budget "B" films, mainly RETURN OF THE VAMPIRE (1943) and CRY OF THE WEREWOLF .

ABBOTT AND COSTELLO MEET FRANKENSTEIN

1948; Universal-International (B&W); Producer: Robert Arthur; Director: Charles T. Barton; Screenwriters: Robert Lees, Frederic I. Rinaldo & John Grant; Camera: Charles Van Enger.

The horror film cycle had virtually ended for Universal with HOUSE OF DRACULA, but the old monsters were called upon one last time to chill audiences alongside the studio's then top box office draw: Bud Abbott and Lou Costello.

ABBOTT AND COSTELLO MEET FRANKENSTEIN cleverly combines the comedy antics of Abbott and Costello with the horrors created by the Frankenstein Monster (Glenn Strange), The Wolfman (Lon Chaney, Jr.) and Count Dracula (Bela Lugosi).

Yes, poor Bela Lugosi was finally given a break by the big studio, and his actual performance as Count Dracula some seventeen years after DRACULA (1931) is as mysterious and fascinating as his original characterization. Lugosi, donning his famous black cape and tuxedo, as the vampire king once more, has fiendish plans of reviving the Frankenstein Monster. Although the plot is feeble in how the monsters are used, the story is quite entertaining, though dated, and Bela gives a distinguished farewell performance as the Count Dracula.

The massive box-office success of ABBOTT AND COSTELLO MEET FRANKENSTEIN actually saved the declining careers of Bud Abbott and Lou Costello, at the expense of the "monsters." Unfortunately, the film's success was not enough to save the old horror monsters from the new horizon of upcoming horror films.

The new horror comedy was actually a blessing for most of the veteran horror actors, with the exception of Boris Karloff, who was enjoying a successful later career in first rate horror films at RKO Pictures. Many of the original horror stars were hired, finding salvation in their declining and quickly fading careers, most of whom had been dropped from the studio rooster after HOUSE OF DRACULA. Bela Lugosi rightfully won the role of Count Dracula over John Carradine, while Lon Chaney and Glenn Strange were given their roles back as the Wolfman and the Frankenstein Monster. But for the three actors, this was basically the end of the road to stardom; all three actors would be subjected to staring in obscure, moderately successful poverty-row horrors until each of their demises; indeed a sad story in itself that should someday be explored, researched and written about.

John Abbott as the centuries-old vampire in THE VAMPIRE'S GHOST (1945).

Poster from *ABBOTT AND COSTELLO MEET FRANKENSTEIN* (1948).

Bela Lugosi as Count Dracula and Glenn Strange as the Frankenstein monster in ABBOTT AND COSTELLO MEET FRANKENSTEIN (1948).

CHAPTER FOUR

The 1950's

OLD MOTHER RILEY MEETS THE VAMPIRE
1952; Renown Pictures (Great Britain) (B&W);
Producer: George Minter; Director: John Gilling;
Screenwriter: Val Valentine

Known also as MY SON, THE VAMPIRE, VAMPIRE OVER LONDON and THE VAMPIRE AND THE ROBOT, this film is not as bad as it sounds. In England, comedian Arthur Lucan had been playing an Irish washer-woman named Old Mother Riley in a series of comedies since the 1930's. His career was quickly fading, and producer George Minter and director John Gilling came up with a brainstorm: If Bela Lugosi's presence in ABBOTT AND COSTELLO MEET FRANKENSTEIN could actually save the careers of fading American comedians, then could it be possible that he could do the same for Lucan's career. "*Yes,*" they thought, "*Lugosi can help us save our drag act!*" The rest, as they say, is history.

The film was eventually sold to an American distributor, Jack H. Harris, who tried to sell the film as CARRY ON VAMPIRE. Harris was legally stopped by the producers of that series, and retitled the film MY SON, THE VAMPIRE. Unfortunately, the film did poorly in America, overshadowed by the current *Abbott and Costello meet "the monsters"* movies from Universal.

Director John Gilling's tale about a mad scientist named Von Husen (played by Bela Lugosi) who tries to control the world by creating an army of lethal robots has really nothing to do with the vampire legend. In fact, the word vampire in the title is explained away in the script as Von Husen's fantasies. In the film he sleeps in a coffin and expresses his desire for human blood, an obsession of being a reincarnation of an infamous ancestor (Dracula?). Lugosi does manage to wear his black tuxedo and Dracula cape, but this is all a ploy to develop his character's deranged image.

Poor Lugosi was paid only a mere $5,000 for his role in this film. Shortly after the film, the actor became ill, however, he still made five more films before his untimely death in 1959.

Gilling would go on to direct and write successful horror films like FLESH AND THE FIENDS, PLAGUE OF THE ZOMBIES, THE REPTILE and THE MUMMY'S SHROUD for Hammer Films in England.

Facing page: Francis Lederer falls to his death in a scene from THE RETURN OF DRACULA (1958).

Dracula (Francis Lederer) rises from his coffin in THE RETURN OF DRACULA (1958). (see page 45)

DRAKULA IN ISTANBUL

1953; And Films (Turkey) (B&W); Producer: Turgut Demirag; Director: Mehmet Muhtar; Screenwriter: Umit Deniz, based upon the novel *Dracula* by Bram Stoker and the novel *Kasigli Voyvoda* by Ali Riga Seifi.

This Turkish version of the Bram Stoker novel and the novel *Kasigli Voyvoda* by Ali Riga Seifi directed by Mehmet Muhtar is quite impressive. The film stars Atif Kaptan as a bald and grey Drakula baring unusually long fangs.

The plot generally follows that of the Stoker book. An accountant named Amzi journeys to Castle Drakula in the Carpathian Mountains to become the nobleman's personal secretary. Amzi is greeted by the Count's hunchback assistant and at sunset, he meets Drakula himself. He discovers that Drakula is a vampire when he locates the fiend slumbering in a coffin. Amzi manages to flee the castle, but Drakula soon follows him to Istanbul and begins to terrorize his family, enticing his fiance and transforming her into a vampire too. Accompanied by a Turkish version of Van Helsing, Amzi locates Drakula's secret resting place and the heroic duo drive a wooden stake through the creature's heart. According to the legend established in this Turkish film, they must then behead the Count to finally destroy him, a legend that would survive into later films as recent as BRAM STOKER'S DRACULA (1992).

EL VAMPIRO

1956; Cinematografica (Mexico) (B&W); Producer: Abel Salazar; Director: Fernando Mendez; Screenwriters: Ramon Obon & Javier Mateos; Note: Released in America by K. Gordon Murray.

This Mexican-made vampire film is the one that started it all for Mexico! Directed by Fernando Mendez, EL VAMPIRO (THE VAMPIRE) stars actor German Robles as Count Lavud, a carbon copy of Bela Lugosi's Dracula image. In addition, the Count is also equipped with a set of fangs and dressed in a tuxedo and cape with a royal medallion hung over his chest.

A young girl named Marta (Ariadna Welter) visits a farm owned by her two elderly aunts. She soon discovers that one of them is under the spell of the mysterious Count Lavud who, at the beginning of the film, goes under the name of Mr. Duval (another backwards spelling and an effort to mimic the familiar Alucard spelling from the Universal film SON OF DRACULA). Soon after, the other aunt mysteriously dies, drained of all her blood, and soon Marta is at risk. Later, Marta discovers that her undead but very much alive aunt casts no reflection. As she becomes suspicious, the aunt slips Marta a drug that gives her the semblance of death. Marta is nearly buried alive when a kind doctor saves her, resulting in yet another attack by the master vampire. During the climax, the doctor and the vampire engage into a battle with one another, leading to a stake driven into the heart of Count Lavud.

Considering the film's low production values, director Mendez's pleasing Gothic style and atmosphere is to be commended. The film is almost worthy of many of the American-made films of the same era, primarily Columbia's RETURN OF THE VAMPIRE and United Artists' RETURN OF DRACULA. The film is unquestionably Mexico's best vampire entry from its era.

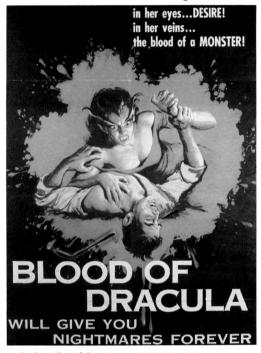

in her eyes...DESIRE!
in her veins...
the blood of a MONSTER!

BLOOD OF DRACULA
WILL GIVE YOU
NIGHTMARES FOREVER

THE DEVIL'S COMMANDMENT
1956; RCIP (Italy) (B&W); Producers: Ermanno Donati & Luigi Carpentieri; Director: Riccardo Freda; Screenwriters: Piero Regnoli & Rik Sjostrom; Camera: Mario Bava.

A mad doctor uses the blood of humans to restore and maintain the youth and beauty of an evil countess.

As the grandaddy of Italian horror films, THE DEVIL'S COMMANDMENT was imported to America with added scenes of violence and nudity (mild by today's standards), which gave it an adults-only rating at the time.

NOT OF THIS EARTH
1956; Allied Artists (B&W); Producer & Director: Roger Corman; Screenwriters: Charles Griffith & Mark Hanna; Camera: John Mescall.

Roger Corman was hired by Allied Artists to make two pictures, one of which was ATTACK OF THE CRAB MONSTERS, the other, this film about alien vampires.

In the film, actor Paul Birch stars as an anemic alien vampire who hires horror starlet Beverly Garland to give him blood transfusions. In the meantime, Birch transports street bums and drunks to his home planet for their nourishment.

The film moves at a rapid pace, with great action, humorous touches and flying, head-crushing bat critters, which would later reappear in IT CONQUERED THE WORLD!

Thirty-two years later, Corman authorized filmmaker Jim Wynorski to produce a color remake of this film, with Traci Lords and Arthur Roberts.

THE VAMPIRO'S COFFIN
1957; Cinematografica (Mexico) (B&W); Producer: Abel Salazar; Director: Fernando Mendez; Screenwriters: Ramon Obon & Javier Mateos.

Salazar's EL VAMPIRO (THE VAMPIRE) was so successful in Mexico that producers were extremely interested in a follow-up with Fernando Mendez directing again. The film was played in America on a double bill with THE ROBOT VS. THE AZTEC MUMMY (1959), for which Salazar wrote the screenplay.

In this film, a mad scientist and his assistant steal the impaled corpse of Count Lavud and accidentally remove the stake to steal the vampire's medallion. The removal of the wooden stake revives the creature who is now determined to recapture his Marta (again played by Ariadna Welter) from the first film. During the film's climax, Count Lavud manages to transform into a bat to escape the doctor's silver blade, but the good doctor does manage to pin the bat against the wall with one thrust of a javelin. The vampire regains his human form, still pinned to the wall, where he dies slowly.

Like its predecessor, THE VAMPIRO'S COFFIN offers some impressive shadow photography, and the confrontation between the film's savant (el doctor) and the vampire is as impressive as their previous clashes in the first film, which is totally surprising since often these Mexican-made horror films decline in production values with each succeeding entry. Don't allow the fact that this is a sequel fool you. The film is both consistent and stylishly photographed.

THE VAMPIRO'S COFFIN ended the series of Count Lavud films from Mexico, but actor German Robles would go on to portray cinematic vampires in various Mexican productions, most of which never reached a level above mediocrity.

BLOOD OF DRACULA
1957; AIP (B&W); Producer: Herman Cohen; Director: Herbert L. Strock; Screenwriter: Ralph Thorton; Camera: Monroe Askins.

During the mid to late 1950's, filmmaker Herman Cohen started a sensation by producing low budget horror films that used teenagers as the film's focal monsters. Naturally, these films were marketed toward the nation's youth and included such

John Beal in THE VAMPIRE (1957).

memorable titles as I WAS A TEENAGE WEREWOLF (1957), I WAS A TEENAGE FRANKENSTEIN (1957), THE BLOB (1959) and many others.

BLOOD OF DRACULA was Cohen's teenage version of the vampire legend. In fact, the film is really Cohen's vampire remake of his own I WAS A TEENAGE WEREWOLF. The film should have really been called I WAS A TEENAGE VAMPIRE, but Cohen felt that he needed the name of *"Dracula"* somewhere in the title, regardless of how misleading a selling device it would be. *"Dracula"* and *"Frankenstein"* were still BIG box office! Cohen knew this, thus he set out to produce a series of low budget films that clearly capitalized on the *"old"* horrors of a decade past.

The film is misleading in that neither Dracula nor his blood is ever featured anywhere throughout this film. In fact, the teenage vampire in the film was not even from Transylvania nor was she a descendant of the infamous vampire. Sandra Harrison plays a neurotic Nancy Perkins, who enrolls into an all girls school. There she is coerced into wearing a centuries-old medallion that once belonged to a very powerful vampire (Dracula?) by a suspicious old chemistry teacher. The amulet causes the teenager to transform into a bloodthirsty human vampire with long bushy eyebrows and two elongated fangs, as created by make-up artist Philip Scheer. The film should have been called DRACULA'S MEDALLION, but somehow BLOOD OF DRACULA sounds much more enticing. Ads for the film read, *"In her eyes - Desire! In her veins - the blood of a monster!"*

THE VAMPIRE
1957; United Artists (B&W); Producers: Arthur Gardner & Jules Levy; Director: Paul Landres; Screenwriter: Pat Fielder.

In THE VAMPIRE from producers Jules Levy and Arthur Gardner, actor John Beal undergoes a transformation into a bloodthirsty vampire when a scientist subjects him to a new kind of pill. Whenever the moon rises, Beal becomes a puffy-faced monster who disposes of his victims in a furnace.

The low budget thriller was directed by Paul Landres, who would later direct RETURN OF DRACULA, a superior effort, the following year. The film was also released as MARK OF THE VAMPIRE.

BLOOD OF THE VAMPIRE
1958; Universal (Great Britain) (Color); Producers: Robert S. Baker & Monty Berman; Director: Henry Cass; Screenwriter: Jimmy Sangster.

Between Hammer's CURSE OF FRANKENSTEIN and HORROR OF DRACULA, Jimmy Sangster took time out to write the screenplay for this rather obscure but fairly good vampire tale starring future Hammer starlet Barbara Shelley as the heroine. In the film, Shelley and her husband (played by Vincent Ball) are terrorized by Dr. Callistrastus (played by Sir Donald Wolfit), a doctor who was executed but returns to life to run an insane asylum and torture chamber. In order to survive, the "good" doctor requires human blood, so he kills and tortures the inmates of the asylum with the aide of his crippled servant Carl (played by Victor Maddern).

Wolfit's vampire is highly reminiscent of Bela Lugosi's vampire image, with bushy, upturned eyebrows, pointed sideburns, and a streak of white in his hair. Of course, this fashionable Lugosi-style image, which lasted from 1931 to 1958, diminished when Christopher Lee gave new life to the Count in Hammer's HORROR OF DRACULA, released the same year as this film.

THE CASTLE OF THE MONSTERS
1957; Sotomayor (Mexico) (B&W); Director: Julian Soler.

In the tradition of Universal's ABBOTT AND COSTELLO MEET FRANKENSTEIN (1948), comes this Mexican-made version that features a shoddy Frankenstein Monster (known as Frentestein), the Creature From The Black Lagoon, the Wolfman, the Mummy and the Gorilla. Of course, leading the group of ghouls is the infamous Count Dracula (played by German Robles, Mexico's answer to Bela Lugosi) dressed in black formal attire and cape.

When a newlywed couple (played by comedians Clavillazo and Evangelina Elizondo) are forced to stay the night in a haunted old mansion, they encounter its creepy and monstrous inhabitants. The film was later mimicked by another Mexican film, FRANKENSTEIN, EL VAMPIRO AND COMPANY in 1961.

Robles also starred in EL VAMPIRO and THE VAMPIRO'S COFFIN.

Poster from BLOOD OF THE VAMPIRE (1958).

Christopher Lee reprimands his vampire bride in this classic moment from HORROR OF DRACULA (1958).

RETURN OF DRACULA (1958)

1958; United Artists (B&W); Producers: Jules V. Levy & Arthur Gardner; Director: Paul Landres; Screenwriter: Pat Fielder.

More traditional than THE VAMPIRE (1957) is Levy, Gardner and Landres' RETURN OF DRACULA. The film stars handsome Czechoslovakian actor Francis Lederer as a curly-haired Count Dracula. The vampire drains the blood of a fellow country-man named Bellac Gordal, who prepares to leave to America for the very first time to meet his relatives in contemporary southern California. Dracula assumes Bellac's identity and travels to southern California where he "vampirizes" the poor dead man's relatives, who, throughout most of the film, believe Dracula to be their European cousin.

For those who have not yet seen this film, Francis Lederer is refreshing as Dracula, though obviously influenced by Lugosi's Dracula. The plot is quite original and still undated by today's standards, however, the vampire trappings are far from thrilling.

The theme of transplanting Dracula from centuries-old Transylvania to the American Midwest works much better here than in Universal's SON OF DRACULA (1943). Lederer's vampire is much more satisfying than Chaney's, therefore the film works much smoother with less awkward moments. Unlike Lugosi's Dracula, however, who usually wore a formal and conspicuous tuxedo, Lederer's Dracula wore a standard business suit, a hat and an overcoat that slightly resembled a cape. Still, even though Lederer's Dracula is presented as a much more contemporary fiend, his vampire is reminiscent of Lugosi's to a small degree.

The vampire's destruction in which Dracula falls into a deep pit and onto a wooden shaft is quite effective, but somehow this very good film seems anemic next to Hammer's classic HORROR OF DRACULA, which was released the same year.

HORROR OF DRACULA

1958; Hammer Films (Great Britain) (Color); Producer: Anthony Hinds; Director: Terence Fisher; Screenwriter: Jimmy Sangster, based on the novel *Dracula* by Bram Stoker; Camera: Jack Asher.

By the late 1950's, the traditional movie monsters that were once worshipped at the Universal lot during the previous two decades, were quickly becoming fond memories in the minds of horror cinema-goers. All hopes of resurrecting the traditional horrors of Universal seemed faint after the emergence of such films as I WAS A TEENAGE WEREWOLF, BLOOD OF DRACULA and other silly teenage horrors. In 1957, Hammer Films began filming Gothic horror movies in color, bringing life and popularity back to the vintage monsters of the golden age of cinema. What Universal had once concealed in atmospheric shadows or in characters reacting to off-screen supernatural occurrences, Hammer exposed in full light and in vivid and colorful close-ups. The effect was stunning. Actually, the effect on moviegoers was overwhelming. Hammer would successfully use generous helpings of red color in their films to create a mood. They would also add loads of blood, sex and nudity (all of which are considered very tame by today's carefree standards) as well as violence. In short, Hammer's horror films of the early 1950's offered the same impact that THE EXORCIST had on the public in 1973, or HALLOWEEN in 1977, or THE HOWLING IN 1981 and finally films like FRIDAY THE 13TH and NIGHTMARE ON ELM STREET during the 1980's and 1990's, all of which owe their successes to Hammer, the company that started the movement towards splatter horror.

In 1957, the studio made CURSE OF FRANKENSTEIN, a color remake of the 1931 Universal classic. The film raked in big bucks at the box office; the film's success was noticed around the world. As a result, executive producer James Carreras commissioned screenwriter Jimmy Sangster to write a new script based on Bram Stoker's *Dracula*. Sangster's main objective was to focus on the physical characteristics of Dracula, as portrayed convincingly in this film by British actor Christopher Lee.

Lee's Dracula was incredibly deceiving: he was handsome but also totally evil and corrupt - a sinister nobleman with only one thing on his mind, human blood! This Dracula was dynamic instead of subtle, colorful instead of gray, and very much "alive!" This Dracula was a cunning creature of the night, a fiend both alluring and irresistible to women, yet gruesome and fearful. In fact, Lee's Dracula, dressed completely in black formal wear with a red-lined black cloak, is the most fiendish and powerful vampire the screen had ever witnessed up until that point.

HORROR OF DRACULA was stylishly directed by Terence Fisher. The film follows the Stoker novel faithfully, to a degree. In the film, Jonathan Harker (John Van Eyssen) is sent to Castle

John Van Eyssen in an electrifying moment from
HORROR OF DRACULA (1958).

Dracula in Transylvania by Professor Van Helsing (Peter Cushing). Harker poses as a British librarian who arrives to the castle to apply for the opening of Dracula's librarian position (this was probably Dracula's way of luring fresh victims to his castle from faraway places). Harker meets a horrible and ghastly death when he tries to destroy the Count. Soon after, Professor Van Helsing arrives to discover that his friend has suffered a horrible fate that is worse than death: "undeath!" Dracula next travels to London and hides in the catacombs of a large estate where he makes the move on Harker's fiance.

The climax of HORROR OF DRACULA is one of the greatest and most breathtaking sequences ever filmed in a vampire movie. After Van Helsing locates Dracula's lair, the vampire races back to his castle with his future mistress. The final battle between good and evil is staged in Castle Dracula, where Van Helsing and the Count feverishly battle each other to the finish. Van Helsing forces the vampire into the sun's early morning rays with a crucifix fabricated from two candlesticks. Like a laser beam, the sun's rays rip right through the vampire's flesh, who painfully decomposes into a pile of dust. The climax is still an incredible finish to a spectacular vampire movie.

As a result of the fast-paced graphic action,

HORROR OF DRACULA was an immediate success world-wide and rolled-in handsome profits for Hammer Films. The film launched a long series of Dracula movies with Christopher Lee in the title role and reshaped the face of the horror film forever because of its colorful, graphic style, which, up until that point in movie history, had not been witnessed. As a result, the film, together with CURSE OF FRANKENSTEIN, firmly reestablished the Gothic horror formula. The monsters of Universal that were once near final extinction had been given a new lease on life in the world of movies, one that, thanks to Hammer, would last straight up into the 1990's with films like DRACULA RISING, FRANKENSTEIN UNBOUND, THE MONSTER SQUAD, BRAM STOKER'S DRACULA, WOLF, INTERVIEW WITH A VAMPIRE and Francis Ford Coppola's FRANKENSTEIN.

HORROR OF DRACULA is a masterpiece of

horror, a classic with an impact that has not diminished even with time. The film is perhaps one of the best Dracula movie ever made and undeniably one of cinema's most influential horror films.

HORROR OF DRACULA was once criticized for its graphic style. Fans and critics found themselves comparing the film to Tod Browning's DRACULA (1931), which was and still is unfair, since both films were made nearly three decades apart. Director Terence Fisher publicly admitted that he had neither sought to duplicate nor draw upon the earlier film in any way. What we have is a film, based on the literary workings of Bram Stoker, that stands mostly upon its own merits and virtually has very little to do with the Universal classic of 1931.

The London Daily Worker said about the film, *"This film disgusts the mind and repels the senses!"* Exactly what a good horror film is suppose to do. Right?

American critics, however, were much more tolerant and appreciative. Variety said, *"......the Jimmy Sangster screenplay has ably preserved the sanguinary aspects of the Bram Stoker novel...."*

Not bad for a film produced on a £200,000 budget. HORROR OF DRACULA inspired seven sequels, and it is there wherein lies the film's success: the ability to create big box office single-handedly, let alone through several equally successful sequels that are all technically appealing.

CURSE OF THE UNDEAD
1959; Universal (B&W); Producer: Joseph Gershenson; Director: Edward Dein; Screenwriters: Edward & Mildred Dein.

A young cowboy named Don Drago Robles (played by Michael Pate, dressed in black, of course) is hired by the film's heroine, a feisty rancher-cowgirl (played by Kathleen Crowley), to hunt down the man responsible for killing her father and brother. Little does she know Drago is a bloodsucker who drinks warm human blood. The vampire gunslinger helps out the young girl, but finds himself falling in love with her. He then puts her under his spell, then his bite and drinks her blood until a local preacher realizes

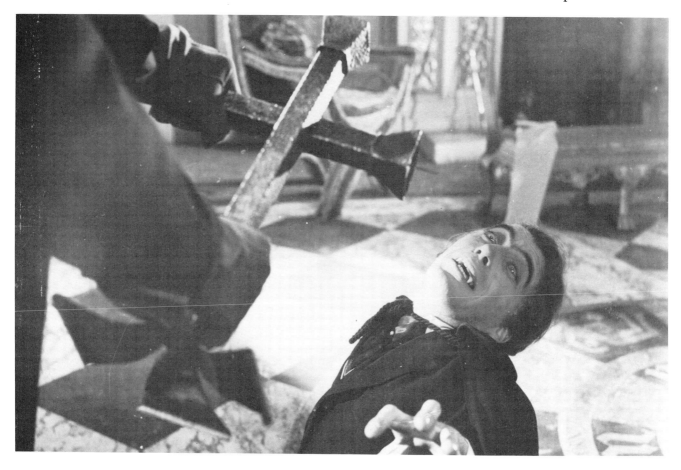

Dracula (Christopher Lee) meets his death in the spectacular climax of HORROR OF DRACULA (1958).

Drago's secret and kills him with a silver crucifix. CURSE OF THE UNDEAD, also known as THE UNEARTHLY, was the first film to feature a vampire in the wild, wild west, but it was certainly not the last!

Bela Lugosi as mad scientist/pseudo-vampire in John Gilling's OLD MOTHER RILEY MEETS THE VAMPIRE (1952), also known as MY SON, THE VAMPIRE. (see page 39)

Vampire Michael Pate tries to make Kathleen Crowley his latest victim in CURSE OF THE UNDEAD (1959).

Beverly Garland and Paul Birch in Roger Corman's NOT OF THIS EARTH (1956).

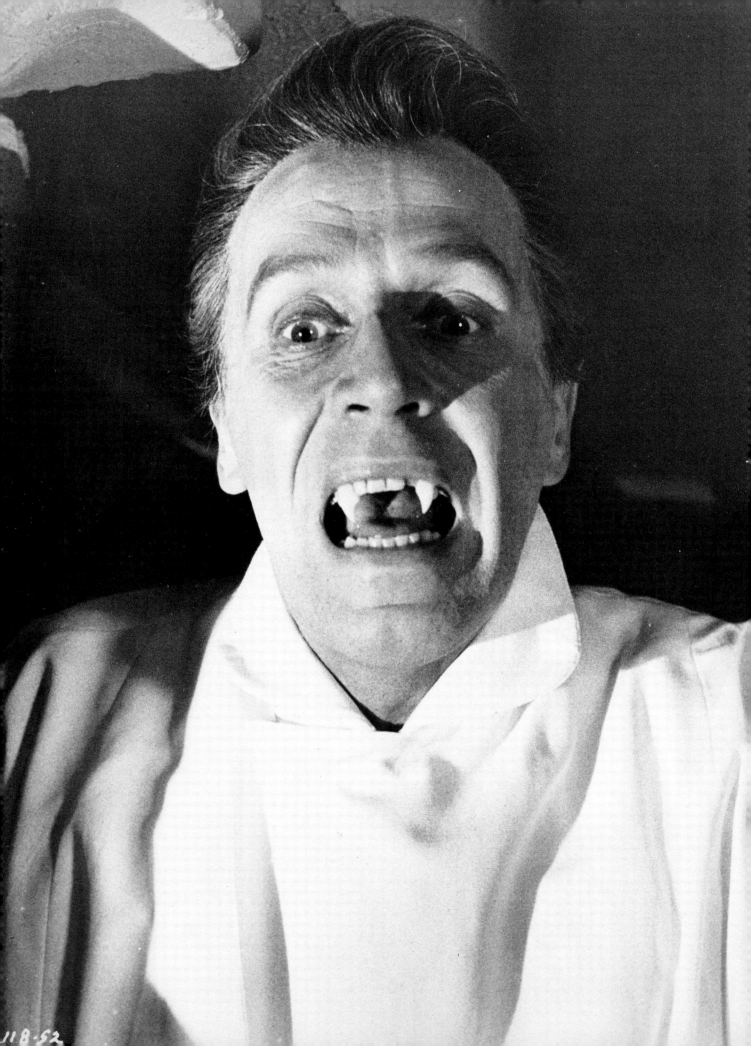

CHAPTER FIVE

The 1960's

BRIDES OF DRACULA

1960; Hammer Films (Great Britain) (Color); Producer: Anthony Hinds; Director: Terence Fisher; Screenwriters: Jimmy Sangster, Edward Percy & Peter Bryan; Camera: Jack Asher.

Next to HORROR OF DRACULA, BRIDES OF DRACULA is perhaps Hammer's greatest film. One word describes this vampire film: Brilliant! Call this author bias, but I have every reason to be when it comes to this sensational vampire "epic." The screenplay, after several rewrites by Jimmy Sangster, is well conceived and evokes a dreamlike mood, while Terence Fisher's stylish direction creates a strong atmosphere of Gothic horror that parallels a Gothic fairy tale. In fact, BRIDES OF DRACULA is Fisher's signature film, possessing all the characteristics that make a great Terence Fisher horror film: strong emphasis on style and mood rather than content, which the later Hammer/Dracula films would overlook in order to achieve commercially appealing cheap thrills. Many of these films would rarely rise to the standard of excellence set forth by both HORROR OF DRACULA and BRIDES OF DRACULA. It is very difficult to say which film is better out of the two, therefore for arguments sake, it should be safe to say that both films are equivalent.

Christopher Lee was originally intended to return to the role of Count Dracula while Peter Cushing was asked to reprise his Professor Van Helsing role. At the time, the project was called DRACULA II and later changed to THE MARK OF DRACULA. However, Lee, who, by this point was already identified with the role of Dracula in the minds of moviegoers, was unable to don the cloak so soon in his career after appearing in three horror films: CURSE OF FRANKENSTEIN (1957), HORROR OF DRACULA (1958) and THE MUMMY (1959) in fear that he would become typecast as a horror actor. Furthermore, Lee did not want the character resurrected. In addition, the dilemma of resurrecting Dracula after his very memorable disintegration in HORROR OF DRACULA also proved to hamper plans. As a result of Lee's decision, Sangster, with the aid of writers Edward Percy and Peter Bryan, had to redraft the script; thus focusing not on reviving Dracula, but centering on one of his many vampirized disciples. Elements from Sangster's original screen treatment would later appear in DRACULA -

Facing page: Noel Willman bares his fangs in the Hammer classic KISS OF THE VAMPIRE (1963). (see page 61)

PRINCE OF DARKNESS (1964), the official sequel to HORROR OF DRACULA.

Actor David Peel was cast in the place of Christopher Lee, but not as Count Dracula. Instead, Peel portrayed Baron Meinster, a very devious, sinister and cunning vampire. Peel was about forty years old at the time the film was made, but Hammer's chief make-up artist Roy Ashton transformed the middle aged actor into a handsome blonde, boyish-looking vampire. Because neither Dracula nor his brides really appear in this film, unless, of course, you consider the baron one of his brides therefore hinting to a homosexual subplot, the title is thus misleading. To avoid lack of continuity, Sangster added a narrative read by the voice of Peter Cushing during the film's prologue explaining that Baron Meinster was simply one of Dracula's many disciples. In addition, the film offers several dramatic confrontations between Professor Van Helsing (Cushing) and Baron Meinster, an incestuous sub-plot between Meinster and his Baroness mother (brilliantly played by Martita Hunt), who must suffer from the moral dilemma of supplying her vampire-son with the blood of young maidens,

and, of course, another great Hammer climax, in which the vampire is destroyed symbolically when he is forced upon the shadow of a gigantic cross created from the reflection of a windmill vane against the moonlight.

This dynamic and enthusiastic film is well crafted and should be regarded as a hallmark vampire movie worthy of all the best. BRIDES OF DRACULA is undoubtedly Hammer and Fisher's masterpiece, hands down!

BLACK SUNDAY

1960; AIP-Galatea (Italy) (B&W); Producer: Massimo De Rita; Director: Mario Bava; Screenwriters: Ennio Deconcini, Mario Bava, Marcello Coscia & Mario Seranore; Camera: Ubaldo Teranzo & Mario Bava.

The German title for this Italian horror film was THE HOUR WHEN DRACULA COMES. The film was also known as THE MASK OF THE DEMON in Italy and in England as REVENGE OF

David Peel as Baron Meinster in Hammer's BRIDES OF DRACULA (1960).
Above right: Arturo Dominici as the Satanic prince Javutich in Mario Bava's atmospheric horror classic BLACK SUNDAY (1960).

THE VAMPIRE.

BLACK SUNDAY was director Mario Bava's (a former camera-man) debut as a filmmaker, and what a frightening, technically lavish film for a rookie filmmaker. Though not really a Dracula film, BLACK SUNDAY stars horror starlet Barbara Steele in the dual role of an evil vampire witch named Princess Asa and as her mortal descendant Katya. Asa is found guilty of vampirism and witchcraft and as her sentence, she is bound to a large cross and executed by a spiked mask which is nailed onto her face. The Dracula character in the film (to which the German title refers to) is apparently her lover Prince Javutich (Arturo Dominici), whose appearance resembles that of many screen Draculas, primarily an uncanny resemblance to Christopher Lee's vampire. The prince is given the same grisly death as Asa.

Before Asa dies she swears to return from the grave for vengeance, and she does! That is, centuries later, when a doctor and his assistant inadvertently splatter the blood of a huge bat over the ashes of her corpse. It is now Black Sunday, the day Satan walks the Earth every hundred years, and the prince of a nearby castle fears that his ancestor might return from the grave. Asa, now fully revived, summons Prince Javutich to rise with her, and together they plan to destroy their descendants. However, Asa has plans of her own which include taking the place of Katya, a descendant (also played by Steele) who is physically identical. No one would ever know!

During the climax, the young doctor who inadvertently revived Asa in the first place, kills the prince during a fierce duel, but when he reaches the tomb of Asa he finds two identical women claiming to be Katya. The doctor is about to mistakenly impale the real Katya with a wooden shaft when he notices her crucifix. Realizing he's about to kill the wrong person, he pulls Asa's cloak away to reveal the rotting ribs of a corpse. The rotting vampiress is taken away by the villagers, burned at the stake and damned to an eternal death.

BLACK SUNDAY is certainly one of Italy's most supreme Gothic horror films, mostly due to Bava's stylish photography in black and white and the film's many ghostly and haunting images. Barbara Steele, in her first of many horror films, is illuminative as the vampire witch. As a result of her performance in this film, Steele was imported to America by AIP to star in THE PIT AND THE PENDULUM with Vincent Price. As for Mario Bava, the filmmaker went on to make many genre films, some of which are BLOOD AND BLACK LACE (1964), DANGER:

DIABOLIK (1968), HATCHET FOR A HONEYMOON (1968), BARON BLOOD (1972), BEYOND THE DOOR II (1979).

THE WORLD OF THE VAMPIRES
1960; Cinematografica (Mexico) (B&W); Producer: Abel Salazar; Director: Alfonso Corona Blake; Screenwriter: Ramon Obon.

Producer Abel Salazar and his film company Cinematografica were very busy making vampire films during the late 1950's and 1960's, first with EL VAMPIRO in 1957 and THE VAMPIRO'S COFFIN the same year. There would be more to come.

In this film directed by veteran filmmaker Alfonso Corona Blake, a vampire named Count Subotay rules over a horde of cloaked vampires who reside beneath an old house. Subotay uses a large pipe organ composed of human bones to control his cult of vampires with whom he plans to use to exterminate mankind. The vampires are destroyed when the film's hero plays a specialized musical tune on Subotay's organ. As for Count Subotay, he is destroyed during a fierce battle with the hero when he his pushed into a pit of stakes.

Despite the bizarre plot, THE WORLD OF THE VAMPIRES was perhaps one of Mexico's better vampire movies, that is, in terms of atmosphere and photography.

CREATURE OF THE WALKING DEAD
1960/1965; A.D.P. Productions (Mexico) (B&W); Producer: (U.S. Version) Jerry Warren; Director: Fernando Cortes; Screenwriters: Fernando Cortes & Alfredo Varela, Jr.

Originally released in 1960 as MARK OF THE DEAD, this film tells how a scientist revives the body of his dead grandfather. Now alive, the walking dead kills for blood to stay alive and strong.

American footage was added with actors Katherine Victor and Bruno Ve Sota, but this does not really matter, since, chances are, the viewer will not be able to make any sense of this film within a film.

THE VAMPIRE'S LAST VICTIM
1960; Nord Film/Fanfare (Italy) (B&W); Producer: Tiziana Longo; Director & Screenwriter: Piero Regnoli.

Released in the United States as THE PLAYGIRLS AND THE VAMPIRE and also as CURSE OF THE VAMPIRE, this Italian-made pseudo-nudie fright film directed by Piero Regnoli stars Walter Brandi in a dual role as Count Gabor Kernassy and his twin brother, who just happens to be a vampire living in an underground tomb. When a group of sexy show girls dressed in skimpy "nighties" stay the night at Castle Kernassy, the vampirized brother makes his move. Before long, lots of lovely female vampires sporting long fangs are chained up in the tomb.

The film plays more towards its sexual content rather than serious horror. THE VAMPIRE'S LAST VICTIM is not a film that would please the masses of horror and vampire film enthusiasts, but admirers of pornographic films should be pleased. Brandi went on to star in THE VAMPIRE'S LOVER (1961), which is better known as THE VAMPIRE AND THE BALLERINA.

CRY OF THE VAMPIRE
1960-1962; Pao International (Italy) (B&W); Director: Theodora Fec.

This Italian-made vampire film features a handsome and distinguished looking Baron who preys on fine Italian women during the midnight hours. The vampire figure is made up to look much like Christopher Lee's Dracula and he also perishes much like Lee's vampire in HORROR OF DRACULA (1958). The film was directed with strong atmosphere by Theodora Fec. Not much is ever heard or seen from this obscure film.

BLOOD AND ROSES
1960; E.G.E. Films/Paramount (France/Italy) (Color); Producer: Raymond Eger; Director Roger Vadim; Screenwriters: Vadim, Roger Vailland, Claude Brule & Claude Martin from the novel *Carmilla* by Sheridan le Fanu; Camera: Claude Renoir.

Roger Vadim, a French filmmaker who would later direct BARBARELLA(1968), directs this elegant and slow-moving tale of lesbianism and vampirism based on the seductive story *Carmilla*.

Playing Carmilla Von Karnstein is Vadim's beautiful blonde wife Annette Vadim (he would later wed Jane Fonda and Brigette Bardot). In the film, Carmilla is possessed by the spirit of ancestor Mircalla, a long-entombed vampire. While under Mircalla's influence, Carmilla seduces Georgia Monteverdi (Elsa Martinelli), her aristocratic cousin's fiance, slowly draining the young girl's blood (the American version omitted all references to lesbianism, which virtually ruined this otherwise sensual film).

During the conclusion, Carmilla, now completely possessed by Mircalla, returns to her grave, during which she inadvertently stumbles upon a wooden shaft that destroys her as it penetrates her heart.

To most American viewers, Vadim's version of the le Fanu story is blatant in its lesbian elements, but the film does offer some good dream sequences and strong atmospheric photography. BLOOD AND ROSES is undoubtedly Vadim's best picture, and it

should be noted that the film is the only serious (faithful) attempt to adapt le Fanu's *Carmilla* onto the screen. Vadim's style is more of uneasiness rather than fright. The film is a grotesque fairy tale of sorts. Vadim's use of color helps create the strong dream-like effect that makes this film so unique.

BLOOD AND ROSES was the first screen adaptation of the le Fanu novel since Carl Dreyer's VAMPYR (1932).

THE CURSE OF NOSTRADAMUS
1960; Cinematografica/AIP (Mexico) (B&W); Producer: Victor Parra; Director: Frederick Curiel; Screenwriters: Charles Toboada & Alfred Ruanova.

Actor German Robles's death as a vampire in THE VAMPIRO'S COFFIN did not end the actor's career in vampire movies. Instead, Robles went on to star in four Mexican films chronicling the adventures of the vampire Nostradamus, a descendent of the

Elsa Martinelli in the classic nightmare sequence of BLOOD AND ROSES (1960).

original Nostradamus who made his famous predictions.

As Nostradamus, Mexico's new vampire sensation, Roble's new vampire is cloaked all in black with a Satanic mustache and beard.
Nostradamus, a totally evil and ruthless fiend will stop at nothing to establish a vampire cult. He is aided by a ludicrous hunchback assistant named Leo. Unlike most movie vampires, Nostradamus is a creature who must sleep in his coffin containing the ashes of his long-dead ancestors (usually, the vampire must sleep in his coffin filled with the native soil of his ancestral land). This vampire can only be destroyed by platinum bullets, therefore making it a bit more expensive to eliminate.

In the film, Nostradamus threatens the film's savant Dr. Dolan (Domingo Soler) by telling him that he will claim the lives of thirteen unlucky people unless he cooperates with his plans of creating the ultimate vampire utopia. Nostradamus's plans are temporarily halted when he is trapped in a tunnel cave-in.

The *"Nostradamus"* series was produced on a shoe-string budget and from scripts that resembled the old serial thrillers from the 1940's and 1950's. In fact, Cinematografica originally made the *Nostradamus* films as a ten-part serial, later re-edited and dubbed into four feature films for American television.

NOSTRADAMUS & THE DESTROYER OF MONSTERS
1960; Cinematografica/AIP (Mexico) (B&W); Producer: Victor Parra; Director: Frederick Curiel; Screenwriter: Charles Toboada.

This sequel to CURSE OF NOSTRADAMUS, also directed by Frederick Curiel, tells how the infamous Mexican vampire Nostradamus (German Robles) returns from his previous entrapment to enslave a condemned murderer, who ultimately assists the vampire in his revenge against Dr. Dolan. Meanwhile, the good-hearted doctor develops an electronic device that uses sound waves to torment vampire bats into a frenzy, which results in the extinction of the human vampires in a climax similar to Hammer's KISS OF THE VAMPIRE (1962).

NOSTRADAMUS - THE GENIUS FROM THE DARK
1960; Cinematografica/AIP (Mexico) (B&W); Producer: Victor Parra; Director: Frederick Curiel; Screenwriters: Charles Toboada & Alfred Ruanova.

In this, the third feature installment in the four film series involving the vampire Nostradamus, the vampire's ashes are scattered in the wind when Dr. Dolan and a group of villagers storm his tomb.

This segment of the serial-turned-feature series is not nearly as good as the previous films, which is not really saying much for this movie, since all of these films seem to be alike and indistinguishable.

THE BLOOD OF NOSTRADAMUS
1961; Cinematografica/AIP (Mexico) (B&W); Producer: Victor Parra; Director: Frederick Curiel; Screenwriters: Charles Toboada & Alfred Ruanova.

Considered to be the best (if you can believe?) and the last of the *Nostradamus* series, THE BLOOD OF NOSTRADAMUS reveals that the famous vampire substituted his ancestral ashes in his coffin with the ashes of his victims. A hoax?

The ruthless Nostradamus is eventually chased by police and destroyed forever (really forever this time!) with the timeless stake through the vampire's heart, thus concluding the series of the legendary Mexican vampire played by German Robles.

ATOM AGE VAMPIRE
1961; Lion/Topaz Films (Italy) (B&W); Producer: Mario Fava; Director & Screenwriter: Anton Giulio Masano

First there was THE ATOMIC KID (1953), then THE ATOMIC MAN (1956) followed by THE ATOMIC RULERS OF THE WORLD (1956) and THE ATOMIC SUBMARINE (1959). But an "Atomic Vampire?"

Also released under the unfamiliar title of SEDDOK, this Italian-made low budget science fiction horror film features a scientist (Alberto Lupo) who experiments with tissue transplants on Hiroshima bomb victims.

In the film, he restores a young woman's (Susan Loret) horribly scarred face which was the result of a bad car accident. Naturally, he falls in love with her, and in order to keep her looking young and beautiful,

Vampire Alberto Lupo attacks in ATOM AGE VAMPIRE (1961).

he must kill other women for their glands.

ATOM AGE VAMPIRE is a very confusing film, primarily due to bad dubbing. Being the confusing film that this feature is, it is never explained why the scientist occasionally transforms into a horrible reptile-faced creature. Is he suffering from a lack of glands too? Is he a refuge from THE ALLIGATOR PEOPLE (1959)? Is he the "Atom Age Vampire" that transforms into a hideous beast that requires human blood to maintain his existence? Who knows?

The film, dubbed for America and directed by Richard McNamara, is actually, if one can bare the thought, one of the better combinations of science fiction and vampirism from its era.

FRANKENSTEIN, THE VAMPIRO AND COMPANY
1961; Cinematografica (Mexico) (B&W); Director: Benito Alazaraki.

This obvious Mexican remake of Universal's ABBOTT AND COSTELLO MEET FRANKENSTEIN (1948) is directed by Benito Alazaraki with less style than its American counterpart of thirteen years prior. In addition, unlike the Abbott

and Costello picture, the vampire of this film is never really referred to as Dracula.

The plot is quite simple and feeble. Two wax figures of the Vampire and the Frankenstein Monster are assigned to an express agency in the care of comedians Paco and Agapito. They are employed to deliver the wax figures to a spooky old mansion where they actually come to life. The Vampire has plans of giving the Frankenstein Monster the brain of Agapito and then use the Monster to conquer America. The unexplained sudden appearance of the Wolfman interrupts the operation, and both the werewolf and the Vampire battle each other until they are destroyed in a fire. The Frankenstein Monster is left to sink in a bog. Sounds quite familiar?

THE VAMPIRE OF THE OPERA
1961; NIF (Italy) (B&W); Producer: Bruna Bolognesi; Director: Renato Polselli.

You've all heard of THE PHANTOM OF THE OPERA, based on the famous Gaston Leroux novel. But chances are, many of you have never heard of *The Vampire of The Opera*!

Renato Polselli, who also co-wrote and directed THE VAMPIRE'S LOVER (1961), directed this Italian-made vampire film about a vampire (Giuseppe Addobati) who is devoted to the opera. The film, set in and around an opera house, is a combination of DRACULA and THE PHANTOM OF THE OPERA.

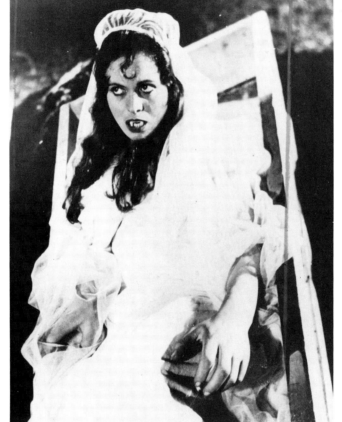

A ghost warns a theatrical group at the opera house about a vampire, but when they do not take the warning serious, the vampire begins attending rehearsals and attacking various performers. The film's hero tries to destroy the vampire by burning his portrait, but he only succeeds at burning the vampire's skin. The vampire is eventually trapped on the stage and set on fire by the performers.

THE VAMPIRE'S LOVER
1961; CIF/United Artists; (Italy) (B&W); Producer: Bruno Bolognesi; Director: Renato Polselli; Screenwriters: Renato Polselli, Ernesto Castaldi & Giuseppe Pellegrini.

Better known as THE VAMPIRE AND THE BALLERINA, this film tells how two female members of a ballet troupe are caught in a rainstorm in the woods and how they are forced to stay the night in a castle inhabited by two vampires, the Contessa (Maria Luisa Rolando) and her cloaked servant (Iscaro Ravajoli), the latter has a rotted, leathery face. The Contessa sends her servant to drink the blood of her female guests. She then oddly drinks the stolen blood from the neck of her servant, a nontraditional method of drinking human blood that would later be touched on in NEAR DARK (1987). As she drains off his stolen blood, her servant reverts back to a rotted, withered old man.

Inspired by the climax of HORROR OF DRACULA (1958), the film's hero fabricates a cross from two candlesticks and drives the vampires into the burning sunlight. The film concludes with their ashes blowing away in the wind.

THE BAD FLOWER
1961; Sunglim Film (South Korea) (B&W); Director: Yongmin Lee.

This Korean remake of the classic Hammer Dracula film HORROR OF DRACULA (1958) stars Chimi Kim as Dracula and Yechoon Lee as Van Helsing - Korean style, that is. The film, very rarely seen in America, supposedly blends Oriental mysticism with the Dracula legend less stylishly than Hammer's THE LEGEND OF THE SEVEN GOLDEN VAMPIRES (1974). However, this remains to be seen. Unfortunately, it is unknown where one can obtain a print of this film for viewing.

The film's correct Korean title is AHKEA KKOTS.

Above: Maria Luisa Rolando in THE VAMPIRE'S LOVER (1961) also known as THE VAMPIRE AND THE BALLERINA.

THE BLOODY VAMPIRE
1961 Tele-Talia/AIP (Mexico) (B&W); Producer: Rafael Perez Grouas; Director & Screenwriter: Miguel (Michael) Morata.

This very atmospheric Mexican production rises to a level that slightly resembles the cinematic work of famous Italian filmmaker Mario Bava, but never reaches the superior level of Bava's BLACK SUNDAY (1960) in terms of atmosphere.

The film begins very promisingly, with a cloaked skeleton driving a coach through the fog in slow motion. Unfortunately, the story and atmosphere are not consistent with the opening reel, as Count Frankenhausen (Carlos Agosti) rises from his coffin-like trunk and goes to great length to transform his wife into a vampire. Meanwhile, Count Cagliostro, a Mexican Van Helsing-type, disguises his own daughter as a servant to gain entrance into the home of the vampire. Quite risky - wouldn't you think? In any event, the vampire in this film survives!

The poorly scripted and directed film was also released as EL V A M P I R O SANGRIENTO and, if you can believe, actually influenced a sequel entitled INVASION OF THE VAMPIRES (1962).

SANTO VS. THE VAMPIRE WOMEN
1961; Corona Panamerica/AIP (Mexico) (B&W); Producer: Luis Garcia DeLeon; Director & Screenwriter: Alfonso Corona Blake.

During the 1960's, Mexico produced several vampire and horror films in which wrestlers were depicted as heroes against monsters, often werewolves, mummies and even vampires. The most popular of the Mexican masked wrestlers and super-heroes was Santo, and in this "famous" Mexican picture, Santo must wrestle several masked vampires in the ring. In the film's one and only memorable scene, Santo unmasks one of his opponents to reveal the face of a snarling werewolf! The monster then transforms into a bat and flies away.

During the climax of the film, Santo battles several male vampires, keeping them occupied until the sun rises, during which they are reduced to dust, which is really what should have happened to this film!

SANTO VS. THE VAMPIRE WOMEN is also known as SAMSON VS. THE VAMPIRE WOMEN in America.

UNCLE WAS A VAMPIRE
1961; Maxima/Embassy (Italy); (B&W); Producer: Mario Cecchi Gori; Director: Stefano Steno; Screenwriters: Eduardo Anton, Dino Verde & Sandro Continenza; Camera: Marco Scarpelli.

UNCLE WAS A VAMPIRE was originally produced and released in Italy in 1959 by Maxima as HARD TIME FOR VAMPIRES. The film features the talents of Christopher Lee, in his first of many European horror films, as a fanged and cloaked Count Dracula-type vampire named Baron Rodriguez. The actor had just received critical acclaim for his portrayal of Count Dracula in Hammer's HORROR OF DRACULA (1958), therefore he was freshly acquainted with the mannerisms of playing a vampire. Lee's vampiric Baron is virtually a carbon copy of his own Count Dracula characterization, and although the film is basically a comedy, Lee maintains a serious

Vampire bats kill in the stunning climax of Hammer's KISS OF THE VAMPIRE (1963).

Vincent Price as the only surviving human on earth, must confront zombified vampires during the night in THE LAST MAN ON EARTH (1964).

portrayal of his Baron vampire throughout much of the film.

The film showcases the cinematography of Marco Scarpelli and the stylish direction of Stefano Steno resulting in some rather fine, atmospheric footage of Chris Lee prowling the rooftops of his castle with his cape majestically flowing in the wind.

Despite the low production values (in comparison to Hammer's HORROR OF DRACULA and BRIDES OF DRACULA), director Steno is successful in both delivering a well-mounted genre film and combining horror with comedy.

In the film, Baron Oswald (played by Renato Rascel, Italy's top comedian at the time) looses his fortune and is forced to sell his castle. To the Baron's dismay, the castle is turned into a hotel, and he is forced to take a job as a bellboy. Baron Rodriguez, Oswald's cousin, arrives on the scene and begins attacking the women guests at the hotel, resulting in chaos and panic in the Gothic structure. Eventually, Rodriguez puts the bite on Baron Oswald too.

THE AWFUL DR. ORLOFF
1962; Sigma III (Spain/France) (B&W); Producer: Serge Newman; Director & Screenwriter: Jesse Franco.

Jesus Franco's ground-breaking film is awful, but fans will enjoy watching Howard Vernon as the title character steal human blood to recreate his daughter's horribly disfigured face. As Dr. Orloff, Vernon must kidnap pretty females in order to perform skin graft operations on his daughter. But there's more. Dr. Orloff has an accomplice, his brother Marius (played by Ricardo Valle), a blind human zombie-like creature who commits most of the vampire-like murders.

THE AWFUL DR. ORLOFF, originally co-billed with THE HORRIBLE DR. HICHCOCK, is a variation on the theme created way back in the early 1930's with films like DR. X and THE VAMPIRE BAT.

Right: A scene from Mario Bava's classic PLANET OF THE VAMPIRES (1965).

INVASION OF THE VAMPIRES

1962; Tele-Talia/K. Gordon Murray Productions (Mexico) (B&W); Producer: Raphael Grovas; Director & Screenwriter: Miguel (Michael) Morayta.

A sequel to THE BLOODY VAMPIRE (1960) in which Count Frankenhausen (Carlos Agosti) returns with plans of invading the world (AGAIN?) with an army of vampires under his royal command. A Van Helsing-like scientist named Dr. Ulises opposes the vampire with a mysterious flower from a plant called the Mandagora. The plant itself has a toxic effect on the undead.

The vampire, who escaped death in the first film, is finally staked and destroyed in his bat form (Thank God!) in this sequel, and all of his victims return to their original life form and live happily ever after. How sweet! There's only one problem; the victims still have stakes protruding from their chests.

The only moment in this film worthy of honorable mention is the scene in which we are able to visit the vampire's cavern- a mist-filled cave crammed with huge vampire bats and coffins containing the vampire's victims.

INVASION OF THE VAMPIRES marked the final film in which Count Frankenhausen would be seen.

SLAUGHTER OF THE VAMPIRES

1962; CIF/Pacemaker (Italy) (B&W); Producer: Dino Sant'Ambrogio; Director & Screenwriter: Roberto Mauri.

Another version of both DRACULA (1931) and HORROR OF DRACULA (1958), this time from Italy.

Two vampires, one resembling Dracula and the other his bride, are pursued by angry villagers. The female vampire (played by sexy Graziella Granata) is impaled by a pitchfork, but the Dracula-like vampire escapes. The film then proceeds to tell how the vampire replaces his mistress with a new woman. Her husband seeks the aide of a Van Helsing-type vampire killer and together they hunt the fiend down. The vampire is destroyed when the spikes of an iron gate penetrate his chest.

SLAUGHTER OF THE VAMPIRE was simply another carbon-copy Italian vampire film that offered nothing original to the legend that viewers had already been exposed to.

The film was also released under the commercial title CURSE OF THE BLOOD GHOULS.

KISS OF THE VAMPIRE
1963; Hammer Films (Great Britain) (Color);
Producer: Anthony Hinds; Director: Don Sharpe;
Screenwriter: John Elder.

Ironically, KISS OF THE VAMPIRE, one of Hammer's most superior vampire tales, was unfortunately a failure at the box office compared to Hammer's more successful HORROR OF DRACULA (1958) and BRIDES OF DRACULA (1960). The reasons for the film's commercial failure are quite simple. To begin with, the film lacked the presence of a key personality or major horror film celebrity such as Christopher Lee or Peter Cushing. Secondly, KISS OF THE VAMPIRE was a more subtle and artistic vampire film, which, right from the start, eliminated half of the horror movie fans who only wanted to see another bloody and violent horror film that dove straight for the throat in a typical Hammer fashion. Finally, the vampires in this film are not exactly the most dynamic of species. Instead, they are very subtle about their identities and their nocturnal practices. Still, despite the vast differences, the script, written by John Elder is one of the finest vampire tales ever written for the screen, and there lies its major asset.

The tale is evenly and smoothly written, moving slowly and carefully to establish its mood as we are introduced to the film's main characters and their unfortunate involvement with the vampires. It all seems dream-like, yet simple and non-threatening, until its tastefully savage final.

Director Don Sharp, a brilliant filmmaker with a taste for the lavish, lacks the knack and the enthusiastic approach that Terence Fisher would have normally injected into such a film. Had Fisher directed KISS OF THE VAMPIRE, the result would most probably have been a more colorful, dramatic and savage film right from the start. The dark grays and muted colors and the mystery would have been replaced with fangs, violence, blood, and a tint of red to make it all horrifically marvelous, resulting in what would had been another HORROR OF DRACULA or BRIDES OF DRACULA. This is not meant to be taken as an insult, since both of these Fisher-made films are superior in their own light. It would be unfair to compare KISS OF THE VAMPIRE with Fisher's films since they offer many vast differences and since each filmmaker possesses a distinct style. It would be much like comparing a Steven Spielberg film with a Roger Corman movie. If anything, one can actually compare KISS OF THE VAMPIRE with Roger

Andrew Keir and monks prepare to release Barbara Shelley from her affliction in this tense moment from DRACULA - PRINCE OF DARKNESS (1965).

Vadim's BLOOD AND ROSES or even Roman Polanski's THE FEARLESS VAMPIRE KILLERS; Polanski was obviously strongly influenced by this film.

The film is evenly paced and the story is quite interesting. A vacationing young couple (Edward De Souza and Jennifer Daniel) encounter a vampire cult headed by a nobleman named Count Ravna (played in a restrained fashion by Noel Willman). The Count invites the couple to his chateau for dinner. They later learn that their host is a vampire.

There is an elegant and fascinating masquerade ball for the vampires, but the film's highlight is its most savage moment in which the vampire cult is destroyed by vicious vampire bats in a crazed frenzy.

Willman's vampire, not as dynamic as Christopher

Lee's Dracula, is, if anything, convincing and very mysterious, and Clifford Evan's vampire killer is actually superb and often more powerful than and superior to Peter Cushing's performances as Professor Van Helsing. The lavish sets of Bernard Robinson are also fabulous.

Unfortunately, Americans were never privileged to see the superior, uncut version of this film, containing many of the original film's best scenes. KISS OF THE VAMPIRE was released in America as KISS OF EVIL.

TERROR IN THE CRYPT
1963; Hispaner Films/AIP (Italy/Spain) (B&W); Producer: William Mulligan; Director: Thomas Miller - English scenes (also Camillo Mastrocinque); Screenwriters: Maria Del Carment, Jose L. Monter & Martinez Roman from the novel *Carmilla* by Sheridan le Fanu; Camera: Julion Ortas.

In this faithful and fascinating screen adaptation of Sheridan le Fanu's *Carmilla*, Christopher Lee portrays Count Ludwig Karnstein in what was the actor's only involvement on screen with the classic novel (Lee never played in neither of Hammer's three colorful films based on *Carmilla*, which are THE VAMPIRE LOVERS, LUST FOR A VAMPIRE and TWINS OF EVIL).

In the film, Count Ludwig's evil housekeeper summons the spirit of Mircalla, an evil witch vampire and the descendant of Count Karnstein, executed centuries ago. The blond vampire slowly takes revenge on the Karnstein family until she is eventually staked in her crypt.

The film is often dull in blood and action next to the more colorful Hammer versions, but the black and white atmospheric photography of Julion Ortas is quite impressive. A much better rendition of the novel is Roger Vadim's BLOOD AND ROSES(1960).

TERROR IN THE CRYPT was released in Spain as THE CURSE OF THE KARNSTEINS. The film is also known as CRYPT OF HORROR.

THE BLACK SABBATH
1964; AIP (Italy) (Color); Producer: Salvatore Billitteri; Director: Mario Bava; Screenwriters: Marcello Fondato, Alberto Bervilacqua & Mario Bava.

THE BLACK SABBATH is another brilliant Mario Bava horror film, with strong atmosphere, great cinematography and well-written dialogue. The film consists of three stories: "*The Drop of Water*," "*The Telephone*" and "*The Wurdalak*," the latter about a hunter (Boris Karloff) who becomes a vampire and must prey upon his own loved ones.

Karloff's first victim is his grandson, who returns from the dead and cries out to the remaining family members to lure them to Karloff. "*The Wurdalak*" is the most chilling of the three segments, and quite an impressive tale of vampirism that will literally scare the pants off of first-time viewers, even today!

THE LAST MAN ON EARTH
1964; AIP (Italy) (B&W); Producer: Robert L. Lippert; Directors: Ubaldo Ragona/ Sidney Salkow (U.S. Version); Screenwriters: Logan Swanson & William P. Leicester, from the Richard Matheson story *I Am Legend.*

This rather unique Vincent Price horror vehicle combines elements of vampirism with elements of an end-of-the-world thriller. The film, which has been given a bad rap, has always been hated by Matheson for reasons unknown. The film was later remade with Charlton Heston as THE OMEGA MAN in the early 1970's, and is quite obviously the inspiration behind George Romero's NIGHT OF THE LIVING DEAD.

In the film, Vincent Price portrays Morgan, the only surviving human on the face of the earth. The other inhabitants of this planet are either dead corpses or zombified vampires who spend most of the nighttime hours trying to break into Morgan's suburban home hideaway. During the day, these pasty-face ghouls retreat, allowing Morgan to wander the streets in search of garlic. The rest of his time is spent sharpening stakes, which he uses against the ghouls of the night!

THE LAST MAN ON EARTH has found its way into this book because of the fact that the creatures in this rather obscure film crave human blood as well as human flesh. The fact that they also cannot stand sunlight or garlic constitutes a connection to the vampire myth. There is a fine line that separates this film from non-vampire films like NIGHT OF THE LIVING DEAD, DAWN OF THE DEAD, DAY OF THE DEAD and RETURN OF THE LIVING DEAD, all of which feature human zombies who either crave human flesh or human brains.

PLANET OF THE VAMPIRES
1965; AIP (Italy/Spain) (Color); Producer: Fulvio Lucianso; Director: Mario Bava; Screenwriters: Catillo Cosulich, Antonio Roman, Alberto Bevilacqua, Mario Bava, Rafael J. Salvia (American version written by Ib Melchior & Louis M. Heyward), from the novel *Una notte di 21 ore* **by Renato Pestriniero; Camera: Antonio Rinaldi.**

A year before QUEEN OF BLOOD and years before LIFEFORCE (1985), PLANET OF THE VAMPIRES was the first full blown science fiction vampire film, and what a colorful and exciting film to watch. Mario Bava, the acclaimed director of BLACK SUNDAY (1960), delivers another visually lush horror film. Despite the film's commercial title, suggesting that it is another low budget PLANET OF THE DINOSAURS or something, PLANET OF THE VAMPIRES is one of Bava's better films.

Actor Barry Sullivan leads a space expedition to the distant planet of Aura. No sooner have they landed on the mysterious planet's surface before the crew begins to act homicidally. Three corpses are buried, only to rise out of their body bags in what is one of the film's most electrifying sequences. Somehow, they are transformed into vampirized zombies. We later learn that they are possessed by alien life-forms from the planet Aura. The Auranians plan to sabotage the American spacecraft and leave their dying planet for Earth, where they will rule supremely.

The "vampiric" aliens manage to escape during the film's climax, which was probably AIP's idea of leaving possibilities open for a sequel had this film taken-off at the box office. Amazingly, PLANET OF THE VAMPIRES did not take-off as planned and quickly faded from the box office scene as just another poorly dubbed foreign genre film.

The film is also known as DEMON PLANET.

DRACULA - PRINCE OF DARKNESS
1965; Hammer Films (Great Britain) (Color); Producer: Anthony Nelson Keys; Director: Terence Fisher; Screenwriter: John Samson (Jimmy Sangster).

Originally, elements from this film were conceived way back in 1959 by Hammer screenwriter Jimmy Sangster for the film BRIDES OF DRACULA (1960). What was not used later became part of a project known as DRACULA'S REVENGE, also scripted by Sangster, which later became DRACULA - PRINCE OF DARKNESS (Hammer should have considered the word "revenge" in the film's title since the remaining Hammer Dracula films from this point onward would revolve around the unimaginative and often misplaced theme of revenge).

DRACULA - PRINCE OF DARKNESS is actually a very good, well mounted vampire film. True, the film has several if not many flaws, but the overall production was quite clever and original during its initial release.

Christopher Lee returned to the role of Count Dracula eight long years after HORROR OF

DRACULA, which was great. However, by the time the studio got around to making this film, the actor had become a high paid star. Hammer simply could not afford Sangster's original script in which Lee was to deliver some meaty dialogue. As a result, the screen treatment was entirely redrafted, and the vampire's dialogue was entirely deleted from the script. The changes disappointed fans, still, the overall effect of Chris Lee's Dracula hissing and emerging from shadows is not as bad as proclaimed by arrogant aficionados who often judge films harshly just for the sake of doing so, especially when one views the film today retrospectively or for the first time. Back in 1965, screenwriter Jimmy Sangster did not see it that way. Outraged, Sangster removed his name from the credits and replaced it with the fictitious name of John Sansom. Director Terence Fisher was not all too pleased with the changes as well, however he was forced to comply with the studio's demands. One can only wonder how much of a greater film DRACULA - PRINCE OF DARKNESS could have been had Lee delivered the lines originally written for him by Sangster.

The film opens with footage of Dracula's memorable destruction from the climax of HORROR OF DRACULA. Now that continuity has been established, the film proceeds to tell a new story. Four travelers inadvertently arrive at Castle Dracula. One of the couples quickly fall prey to the master vampire and his evil servant Klove; the husband is destroyed and his blood is used to revive Dracula, while the wife (played by Barbara Shelley) is transformed into Dracula's evil vampirized mistress. Together, Dracula and his new mistress torture the lives of the second couple (Francis Matthews and Suzan Farmer). Farmer becomes Dracula's next intended bride after his current mistress is destroyed by a Van Helsing-like monk (played brilliantly by Andrew Keir), who drives a wooden stake through her heart. This scene is perhaps one of filmdom's better vampire-staking scenes ever.

The climax is most brilliant. Dracula is dramatically destroyed when he becomes trapped beneath layers of ice that surround his castle.

The Sangster script introduced a new addition to the vampire movie folklore. According to this film, a

John Carradine as the villainous Count Dracula in the low badget William Beaudine western/horror vehicle, BILLY THE KID VS. DRACULA (1966).

vampire cannot cross running water. Furthermore, running water can actually destroy a vampire upon contact, thus, when Dracula falls beneath the ice in the climax, he is supposedly destroyed.

Though not the best entry in the Hammer series, DRACULA - PRINCE OF DARKNESS is still an exciting film. Fisher makes good use of the well constructed, spacious sets (borrowed from RASPUTIN - THE MAD MONK). If anything, the film is a perfect example of Hammer's trademark style of turning a low budget horror film into an expensive-looking epic.

The success of DRACULA - PRINCE OF DARKNESS prompted Hammer to immediately begin production on their next and most successful Dracula film in the series, DRACULA HAS RISEN FROM THE GRAVE (1968).

SANTO VS. BARON BRAKULA
1965; Corona-Panamericana/AIP (Mexico) (B&W); Producer: Alberto Lopez; Director: Alfonso Corona Blake; Screenwriters: Fernando Galiana & Julio Porter.

How many screenwriters does it take to write a "Santo" movie? Two "too" many, obviously. This inferior sequel is a direct rip-off of HORROR OF DRACULA, but then again, how many low budget films made in the late 1950's and early 1960's were not? Think about it.

Santo - the masked wrestler returns to the screen to battle vampire Baron Brakula in this film labeled as a Mexican remake of Hammer's HORROR OF DRACULA (1958) with Santo substituting as Van Helsing. Brakula (A poor man's Dracula) attacks a female victim, who is later saved with blood transfusions. Soon after, the vampire, grinning with bloody fangs, reclaims his victim, and digs a grave for her, until Santo arrives on the scene and the two nemesis engage in a fierce battle. Hmmm; sounds very familiar! I'm sure Hammer Films loved the producers of this film!

THE DEVILS OF DARKNESS
1965; 20th Century-Fox (Great Britain) (Color); Producer: Tom Blakely; Director: Lance Comfort; Screenwriter: Lynn Fairhurst.

A cult of Devil worshippers in modern-day Brittany are lead by the vampire Count Sinistre (played by Hubert Noel). The count poses as an artist, but really enjoys sacrificing young female tourists to Satan in their secret underground crypt. Our vampire also enjoys sex orgies with a snake dancer.

William Sylvester plays the film's hero, who in the film goes up against both the Count and Satan himself.

THE DEVILS OF DARKNESS can be seen on late night television from time to time.

BILLY THE KID VS. DRACULA
1966; Embassy (Color); Producer: Carroll Case; Director: William Beaudine; Screenwriter: Carl K. Hittleman.

"The West's Deadliest Gunfighter! The World's Most Diabolical Killer!" Advertisements for movies, especially the low budget sector, are often misleading, as in the case of BILLY THE KID VS. DRACULA. The ads for this film promised the viewer an action-packed film. Naturally, as evident by the final production, Embassy failed to deliver, unless, of course, you were a juvenile at the time the film was released.

Director Beaudine, who directed over one hundred and fifty films (mostly westerns), filmed this one in *"Shockorama" ala* William Castle - style! The unintentionally funny dialogue and the film's low production values simply do not help this hopeless horror film.

Actor John Carradine, who was already sixty years old at the time, won the part of Count Dracula. Dracula now sported a satanic-like mustache and beard and a bright red ascot. Carradine's performance here has always been ridiculed as being unenthusiastic and even non-existent. Perhaps the actor had very little regard for this film during production, as evident in his one-dimensional, uninspired performance.

Although BILLY THE KID VS. DRACULA was produced on a very low budget and although Carradine delivers a dismal performance as Dracula, director Beaudine does manage to deliver a good old-fashion cowboy film marketed towards the Saturday "Kiddie Matinee" of 1966. In its original time and intended market, the film works. You have a good guy, a heroine and a villain - the three standard ingredients for a western film. The hero is dressed in white, while the villain is cloaked in black. It's all a very standard and familiar formula, but it works. However, in order to appreciate the film, you must teleport yourself back to 1966 and alter your mind to the age of ten years old. Once outside of its market, this obscure film (and this is one of Hollywood's most obscure horror outings) is viewed as nothing more than absurd, escapist entertainment that sinks to the lowest intellectual level thought possible to exist. But then again, compared to PLAN 9 FROM OUTER SPACE (1959), this film is not half bad.

Naturally Dracula is the villain, who begins his evil by attacking a young Indian girl in bat form. He then massacres the occupants of a passing stagecoach and assumes the identity of one of his victims. Next, the vampire in disguise sets his sights on the film's heroine (Melinda Plowman), but Billy the Kid (Chuck Courtney), now turned into a hero for this film, destroys the vampire with a surgeon's scalpel, reducing Dracula to a pile of what appears to be cigarette ashes.

Carradine, now older since his days as Dracula in Universal's HOUSE OF FRANKENSTEIN (1944) and HOUSE OF DRACULA (1945), has the ability to transform himself into a vampire bat. Furthermore, his vampire does not cast an image in a mirror. However, being the quickly-made low budget "epic" that it is, BILLY THE KID VS. DRACULA offers many flaws. For one, and the most obvious, the vampire is seen parading around in the sun-light. An oversight perhaps? Secondly, the fact that the vampire is never called Dracula throughout the entire film raises yet another question as to whether this film is actually a legitimate Dracula movie or not. It is a fact, however, that the name "Dracula" is very present in the Carl K. Hittleman script. A flaw or just another oversight? Finally, the fact that Dracula, or the vampire, cast a reflection is quite contradictory, considering that we are told otherwise in the very same film.

In retrospect, BILLY THE KID VS. DRACULA, though not the atrocity that it has been labeled, is one of filmdom's most obscure offerings and certainly not one of the genre's better vampire movies. Carradine has done better. But then again, he's also done far worse.

THE EMPIRE OF DRACULA
1966; Filmica-Vergara (Mexico) (B&W); Director: Federico Curiel.

Also known as THE WOMEN OF DRACULA, this Mexican-made vampire film portrays Count Dracula as a handsome, dynamic and athletic figure played by Lucha Villa.

Dracula, surrounded by beautiful vampire women, terrorizes the Mexican countryside, leaping onto moving carriages and attacking unsuspecting victims at he blink of an eye. The film offers lesbian aspects in which women victims are bitten by female vampires, as well as several dramatic moments such as when the fanged vampire is fought in his own coffin by a man wielding a crucifix.

Mexico has always been famous for producing some very fast paced, rigid and action packed vampire films, and THE EMPIRE OF DRACULA is, without a doubt, a by-product of this sub-genre.

CARRY ON SCREAMING
1966; Audio Film Center (Great Britain) (Color); Producer: Peter Rogers; Director: Gerald Thomas; Screenwriter: Talbot Rothwell.

This rather obscure title tells how the recently revived Dr. Watt (played by Kenneth Williams) and his vampirized, *femme fetale* sister (played by Fenella Fielding) create twin Frankenstein Monsters called Oddbod! And if that weren't enough, the Mummy and Dr. Jekyll join in the fun!

ISLAND OF THE DOMMED
1966; Allied Artists (Spain/W. Germany) (Color); Producer: George Ferrer; Director: Mel Welles; Screenwriter: Stephen Schmidt.

Originally released in Spain as THE ISLAND OF THE DEAD, this film stars Cameron Mitchell as Baron Von Weser, a mad botanist who creates a vampire-tree that sucks human blood with its tentacle-like branches. Eventually, Mitchell ends up strangled at the "hands" of his own mutant creation.

The film is also known as THE MAN EATER OF HYDRA and simply as BLOODSUCKERS. The film was obviously inspired by Allied's DAY OF THE TRIFFIDS (1963).

DR. TERROR'S GALLERY OF HORRORS
1966; American General Pictures (Color); Producers: David L. Hewitt & Ray Dorn; Director: David L. Hewitt; Screenwriters: David Prentiss, Gary Heacock & Russ Jones.

Christopher Lee as the vampire Lico in Mario Bava's
HERCULES AND THE HAUNTED WORLD (1966).

A scene from Roman Polanski's classic spoof
THE FEARLESS VAMPIRE KILLERS (1967).

Made fast and cheap to capitalize on the very successful anthology horror films that were being made in Great Britain at the time (primarily led by the successful DR. TERROR'S HOUSE OF HORROR), DR. TERROR'S GALLERY OF HORRORS is comprised of five short story segments of horror. Two of these segments are vampire tales.

The first vampire segment is entitled *King Vampire,* in which a vampire in Nineteenth Century London is revealed to be the female secretary of the police inspector investigating mysterious vampire-like murders.

The second vampire segment is entitled *Count Alucard.* The title role was originally intended for John Carradine, who was occupied with BILLY THE KID VS. DRACULA. The role of Count Alucard went to actor Mitch Evans (Carradine did play the narrator and warlock of *The Witches Clock* segment of this film).

The tale adheres to the opening chapters of Bram Stoker's *Dracula* with Jonathan Harker journeying to Castle Alucard to sell him the Carfax property in London. Evans delivers the expected dialogue quite nicely and Harker is attacked by a female vampire, who is later destroyed by angry villagers. Harker returns to castle Alucard and accuses the Count of being a vampire and just when we think Harker is about to become mince meat at the hands of the Count, the Englishman unexpectedly transforms into a werewolf and kills the vampire. Talk about surprise endings.

DR. TERROR'S GALLERY OF HORRORS is amateurishly directed by David Hewitt and is inferior to other horror anthology films made during that time, primarily because of the film's shoddy script and low production values. Still, the Count Alucard segment is worth a look and the better of the stories in the film.

The other segments include *Monster Raid,* and *Spark of Life,* the latter starred Lon Chaney, Jr. as a mad doctor who brings to life the corpse of a dead murderer.

THE HAND OF NIGHT
1966; Schoenfeld Films (Great Britain) (B&W); Producer: Harry Field; Director: Frederic Goode; Screenwriter: Bruce Stewart.

Better known as THE BEAST OF MOROCCO, this low-budget vehicle tells the story of how actor William Sylvester, who would later star in THE DEVILS OF DARKNESS, flees his troubles in America by running off to Morocco to visit in archaeologist friend. There he falls in love with a beautiful woman who turns out to be a vampire queen.

This mild but entertaining film is very rarely seen.

QUEEN OF BLOOD
1966; AIP (Color); Producer: George Edwards; Director & Screenwriter: Curtis Harrington.

How did producer George Edwards and director Curtis Harrington manage to assemble an all-star cast (John Saxon, Dennis Hopper, Basil Rathbone, and Forrest J. Ackerman) for a film with a production budget of $65,000? The answer is quite simple. Horror genre producer and director Roger Corman, who actually had nothing to do with this film, had acquired real-life Soviet footage of spaceships (the same impressive footage would later be used in VOYAGE TO A PREHISTORIC PLANET and VOYAGE TO THE PLANET OF PREHISTORIC WOMEN). Harrington saw the footage and virtually wrote the screenplay around it, which took a mere seven to eight days to film at a cost of $65,000. True, QUEEN OF BLOOD does not offer the award-winning special effects of Kubrick's 2001 A SPACE ODYSSEY or PLANET OF THE APES (filmed two years after), but considering the little film's modest budget, this obscure movie is pretty effective.

This offbeat tale combines science fiction with horror as a space expedition from earth led by Dr. Farraday (Basil Rathbone) arrives near the planet of Mars as a rescue effort to a distress message. They find only one survivor, Velena (played quite effectively by Florence Marly). To the crew's dismay, Velena turns out to be an alien specimen and indeed the Queen of Blood that the title suggests as she seduces the crew one by one and drains them intimately of all their blood. After killing off most of the crew, she engages in a battle with one of the remaining survivors and accidentally cuts herself during the struggle. Since Velena is an alien hemophiliac by nature, she slowly bleeds to death. However, back on Earth, we learn that Dr. Farraday and his assistant (F. J. Ackerman) have managed to smuggle the alien Queen's eggs and await their hatching in a laboratory. Sequels, anyone?

QUEEN OF BLOOD, also known as PLANET OF BLOOD, is perhaps one of filmdom's most unusual efforts, especially for its time. The film is undeniably the forerunner of Ridley Scott's ALIEN (1979) and Tobe Hooper's LIFEFORCE (1985).

TOWER OF THE DEVIL
1966; Hemisphere (Phillipine) (B&W); Director: Lauro Pacheo; Based on the serial *Lagim Komiks* by Nela Morales.

This obscure and totally bizarre Philippine-made film concerns a cult of vampires who attempt to get a strange pregnant woman, who actually sucks the blood of lizards, to give birth to their vampire offspring. The leader of the vampire cult (played by Ramon D'Salva) leads his fellow "vamps" in an attack against some nasty werewolves. The monsters are all destroyed at the mercy of an earthquake. But the lizard-blood sucking woman's offspring carries on their evil heritage.

Good God. Who writes these ridiculous films?

THE BLOOD DRINKERS
1966; Hemisphere (U.S./Philippine) (B&W); Producer: Cirio H. Santiago; Director: Gerardo de Leon; Screenwriter: Cesar Amigo.

Filmed partially in color and tinted black and white, THE BLOOD DRINKERS is an awful entry into the genre of vampire movies.

The story is laid in a small village invaded by a group of vampires led by Marco (played by Ronald Remy), a bald-headed fiend who wears dark sun glasses. Marco is accompanied by Tanya and a dwarf named La Gordo. The reason for Marco's coming to this particular village is that the twin sister of the girl he loves lives there. His lover, Christine (played by Amelia Fuentes), is at the verge of death. It is necessary for Marco to transfer the heart of Christine's twin sister, Charita (also Fuentes), into Christine's body. Christine has been living off blood and has become a vampire. In order to strengthen Christine for her heart transfer, the vampires cause many deaths. The local priest and the police try to combat this evil force, but Marco proceeds with his plans, with the help of a vampire bat that he uses as a carrier pigeon.

All goes according to plan for Marco until a traveler named Victor arrives into town and falls in love with Charita. Victor turns out to be the film's hero, as he leads a group of villagers to Marco's hideout and together, they drive wooden stakes into the hearts of the vampires, ridding the entire village of them, except for Marco, who escapes.

HERCULES AND THE HAUNTED WORLD
1966; Woolner Brothers (Italy) (B&W); Producer: Achille Piazzi; Director: Mario Bava; Screenwriters: Allesandro Continenza, Mario Bava, Duccio Tessari & Franco Prosperi.

The question as to whether or not Christopher Lee plays a vampire in this film has often come up. Technically, the answer is no. However, Florence Marly was not a traditional bloodsucker by definition in QUEEN OF BLOOD. Nor were the alien "vamps" of LIFEFORCE or the closet vampires of SLEEPWALKERS. In film history, there have been many films that have border-lined as being vampire vehicles. This is one of them. However, the ads for this film clearly suggests that Christopher Lee plays a vampire. To further substantiate this movie as a vampire film, its European title was HERCULES VS. THE VAMPIRES.

Christopher Lee plays a supernatural character in the film that requires blood to become immortal. The film's border-line premise, as well as its suggestive advertisements and European title strongly suggest that HERCULES IN THE HAUNTED WORLD is indeed a vampire movie and under such pretenses is this film included in this complete guide of vampire movies.

In the film, Christopher Lee actually plays Lico, an inhabitant of Hades and servant of Pluto. As we have established, Lico needs blood, and in this case, he requires the blood of a beautiful princess to become immortal. Hercules (Red Park) learns that he can save the princess by obtaining a certain mystical plant located deep in the pits of hell. Once there, he must overcome flying vampires (creatures conjured up by Lico?), seas of lava, rock-men and various other supernatural creatures.

During the climax, Hercules battles with Lico himself, who is pinned under a boulder and left to perish when the sun emerges after a lunar eclipse (Who says this guy isn't a vampire?).

HERCULES IN THE HAUNTED WORLD is perhaps the best of the muscle-men epics made in Italy, with lavish sets and strong atmospheric direction by Mario Bava.

The vampire beast prepares to claim another victim in THE VAMPIRE BEAST CRAVES BLOOD (1968).

SHE WAS A HIPPY VAMPIRE
1966; ADP Productions (B&W); Producer, Director & Screenwriter: Jerry Warren.

Chances are, most fans of horror and vampire movies have never heard of this picture. Chances are many of you will never see this film. With a little luck, you might not run into this rather obscure title, originally produced as THE WILD WORLD OF BATWOMAN.

Producer Jerry Warren was sued for using the word "*Batwoman*" in the film's original title. As a result, he changed the title to SHE WAS A HIPPY VAMPIRE, a title that lured millions to the box office. Right! Warren lost a fortune fighting the lawsuit that he never again "blessed" us with another masterpiece!

In the film, actress Katherine Victor plays the "Batwoman" of the title, who leads other batgirls dressed in tight black leotards against Dr. Neon and

Ratfink. The entire premise revolves around some type of hearing aid/atomic bomb combination. How absurd!

BLOOD BATH
1966; AIP (B&W); Producer: Jack Hill; Directors: Jack Hill & Stephanie Rothman; Screenwriter: Jack Hill.

Executive producer Roger Corman fired screenwriter and director Jack Hill during production. He replaced Hill with Stephanie Rothman, gave her old footage of a Yugoslavian vampire movie plus footage shot by Hill and asked her to shoot additional footage around the old stuff and have it make sense. Remarkably, this resulted in what is a confusing but interesting tale about a crazed artist (played by William Campbell) who believes he has become his 15th Century ancestor - a vampire artist who was burned at the stake. Now fully demented, Campbell stalks girls at night, attacks them, kills them and sometimes,

the maniac lures them back to his vault where he drops them into a vat of boiling wax.

The climax is totally unpredictable. Campbell is destroyed when his wax-covered babes return to life and strangle him.

BLOOD BATH is the type of film you would normally see on late-night television, but the film is quite good. The combination of "*Horror-of-the-wax-museum*" and vampire themes really work well. The film also offers some fabulous shadow motifs. Also known as TRACK OF THE VAMPIRE.

A TASTE OF BLOOD
1966 Creative Film Enterprises/Ajay Films; (Color); Producer & Director: Herschell Gordon Lewis; Screenwriter: Donald Stanford.

Producer, director Herschell Gordon Lewis is notorious for producing some of the most gruesome horror films from the 1960's and 1970's; films such as BLOOD FEAST (1963), COLOR ME BLOOD RED (1964), and 2000 MANIACS (1969). TASTE OF BLOOD was his sole effort into the vampire genre.

A man (played by Bill Rogers) receives a mysterious package from Yugoslavia containing rare brandy. Naturally, he drinks it. The liquid causes the man to become nocturnal, sleeping by day and prowling about by night. In visiting his mother country, the man discovers that he is a descendant of Count Dracula and that the brandy was actually his ancestor's blood.

The man returns to America (Miami) as a full-fledged vampire and immediately puts his wife under his spell, as well as claiming a few victims along the way, one of which is a female stripper. The vampire is eventually destroyed in his coffin by Dr. Howard Helsing (Otto Schlesinger), who drives a wooden stake through his heart, but not after some very graphic stakings, stomach-turning mutilations and gory violence - Lewis style.

THEATRE OF DEATH
1967; Hemisphere (Great Britain) (Color); Producer: Michael Smedley-Astin; Director: Samuel Gallu; Screenwriters: Ellison Kadisous & Roger Marshall; Camera: Gilbert Taylor.

Above: Christopher gets the shaft in Hammer's DRACULA HAS RISEN FROM THE GRAVE (1968).

This Grand Guignol horror film takes place in Paris where Christopher Lee as Phillippe Daruas is suspected of committing vampire-style murders.

The film is played as a mystery all the way to its climax, with voodoo dances, stakings and puncture marks on the neck.

THEATRE OF DEATH is also known as BLOOD FIEND. Cinematographer Gilbert Taylor went on to work on STAR WARS years later.

THE VAMPIRE GIRLS
1967; Filmica Vergara/Columbia (Mexico) (B&W); Producer: Luis Enrique Vergara; Director: Federico Curiel; Screenwriters: Adolfo Torres Portillo & Federico Curiel.

John Carradine, in his last of four Mexican horror movies, returns to the role of Count Dracula (again!). This time Dracula is imprisoned behind bars, and his Countess must take over and command a cult of vampire women in an attempt to free her "hubby".

The film's hero is one of Mexico's famous masked wrestlers - he is called "Thousand Masks" (Mils Mascaras). He actually enters the vampire's castle, battles her muscular henchmen and defeats her vampire minions, who are outfitted in tights and ridiculous capped and winged cloaks.

THE VAMPIRE GIRLS is definitely one of Carradine's least memorable horror movies. Chances are, anyone reading this will probably never get to see this obscure foreign "epic!"

THE FEARLESS VAMPIRE KILLERS
1967; Filmways/MGM (Color); Producer: Gene Glitowski; Director: Roman Polanski; Screenwriters: Gerald Brach & Roman Polanski; Camera: Douglas Slocombe.

Roman Polanski firmly established himself as a master filmmaker of the modern horror film with titles such as REPULSION (1965), and ROSEMARY'S BABY (1968) to his credit. Polanski, a genre fan since childhood and a great fan of the Hammer horror films - primarily Hammer's Gothic horror fairy tale BRIDES OF DRACULA (1960), decided to make a Gothic vampire film of his own. The film is not Polanski's best effort, but it is nonetheless a brilliant-at-times genre film that often rises above the normal fare.

Also known as DANCE OF THE VAMPIRES, THE FEARLESS VAMPIRE KILLERS, OR PARDON ME, BUT YOUR TEETH ARE IN MY NECK, is in fact one of the better vampire films ever made. The film offers some striking sets and good use of color photography. Polanski's mixture of comedy and horror works extremely well; there is a Jewish vampire unaffected by the crucifix and even a homosexual vampire who would rather break tradition and put the bite on a male victim. And in the tradition of KISS OF THE VAMPIRE and BLOOD AND ROSES, there is a pre-conquest ball, or dance, in which the vampires rise from their tombs and elegantly dance in a great big castle ballroom that is, without a doubt, a very impressive scene. The incredible mirror scene staged during the lavish ballroom sequence is superbly photographed by Douglas Slocombe. There are also many other chilling and hilarious moments that make this film a gem. Polanski's direction, though not his best here, is highly commendable. Finally, the characters and the actors that portray them are quite interesting and actually amusing to watch.

Count Von Krolock (played by Ferdy Mayne) and his homosexual vampire son lead the nest of the undead, while the bumbling Professor Abronsius (Jack MacGrowran) and his naive, weak-hearted assistant Alfred (played by Polanski himself) play the heroes.

DANCE OF THE VAMPIRES tells the story of vampire hunter Professor Abronsius and Alfred's journey into the Italian Alps (the film was shot on location six thousand feet high in the alps of Italy) to investigate rumors of a community of vampires in Transylvania. Once at Count Krolock's castle, the pair of vampire killers must abort their fumbled mission, but take with them the vampire's mistress-victim (played by Sharon Tate). Both are unaware that she has already been infected by Krolock.

DANCE OF THE VAMPIRES, though offbeat and comical at times, is a vampire film that every fan should watch at least once. It is unfortunate that American producer Martin Ransohoff cut the film by sixteen minutes and re-dubbed many of the actors' voices, thus eliminating their East European accents. Ransohoff also added cartoon caricatures of Krolock, Abronsius and Alfred to accompany the opening credits.

THE VAMPIRE BEAST CRAVES BLOOD
1968 Tigon/Pacemaker (Great Britain) (Color); Producer: Arnold L. Miller; Director: Vernon Sewell; Screenwriter: Peter Byran.

Released as THE BLOOD BEAST OF TERROR, this shoddy film stars Peter Cushing as an inspector who arrives in a fishing village to investigate mysterious murders. We later discover that entomologist Robert Fleming has turned his daughter (played by Wanda Ventham) into a giant moth creature that needs human blood to survive. Cushing's daughter (played by Vanessa Howard) is captured by the moth woman.

Basil Rathbone agreed to play the father, but died before filming starting, thus the role went to Fleming.

SPACE VAMPIRES (1969)
1968; Gemini Films; Producer & Director: Ted V. Mikels; Screenwriters: Wayne Rogers & Ted V. Mikels.

This far-from-terrifying tale about corpse stealers, bug-eyed outer space vampire monsters, mutant brutes and human transplants stars actor John Carradine in one of his worst performances ever. Carradine portrays mad scientist Dr. DeMarco, who works diligently in his basement to develop a superhuman race of Astro-Zombies! But DeMarco needs parts! Body Parts, that is.

This ridiculous film gets even more absurd when secret agents and spies become involved. Even the FBI and special agents of the Chinese government interact in the ghastly events.

SPACE VAMPIRES, to put it simply, is an awful film. Even had this movie been released during the late 1950's amidst the horrible low-budget horror vehicles of that era - for instance, THE GIANT GILA MONSTER or PLAN 9 FROM OUTER SPACE, SPACE VAMPIRES would still have gone unnoticed. There is no doubt, however, that SPACE VAMPIRES belongs to that cheap, sleazy era and the film is certainly a candidate for being one of the worst movies ever made.

This ludicrous horror-sci-fi mish- mash is better known as ASTRO ZOMBIES.

DRACULA HAS RISEN FROM THE GRAVE
1968; Hammer Films (Great Britain) (Color); Producer: Aida Young; Director: Freddie Francis; Screenwriter: John Elder; Camera: Arthur Grant.

DRACULA HAS RISEN FROM THE GRAVE is perhaps the most underrated of all the Hammer-Dracula movies. Ironically, the film is also the studio's most successful Dracula film, commercially speaking.

Christopher Lee returns as Count Dracula. This time around, Lee delivers dialogue in the form of authoritative commands. Director Freddie Francis makes great use of the bumped-up budget, resulting in a larger-than-life and unexpected vampire epic. Francis uses heavy religious symbolism to create a definitive line between good and evil. The premise, based on the familiar theme of revenge, is well written by John Elder (producer Anthony Hind's pseudonym). The film is visually stunning and features some fabulous rooftop sets designed by Bernard Robinson. As for the cast, they are above-average, especially Ewan Hooper as the enslaved priest. Finally, the sweeping music score of James Bernard adds the final touch to this superior Hammer Dracula movie. Next to HORROR OF DRACULA, this is the strongest and best looking entry in the series, with more eroticism and graphic violence than before. DRACULA HAS RISEN FROM THE GRAVE is a true Hammer classic.

The film begins when Dracula is released from the icy prison that once held him captive during the climax of DRACULA - PRINCE OF DARKNESS. A priest (Hooper) accidentally spills some of his own blood into the vampire's mouth. Now free from three years of entrapment, Dracula is unable to enter his own castle because it has been exorcised by a powerful Monsignor. Enraged, the vampire uses the weak-willed priest to locate the Monsignor's family, and then the killing begins. Dracula uses his supernatural powers to destroy the family, but he eventually sets his sites on the niece of the Monsignor (played by the lovely Veronica Carlson). Apparently, screenwriters felt it unimportant to have Dracula take out his revenge on the persons responsible for his death in the previous film. Instead, Hammer executives felt it was more important to center on new characters and events.

In the film, Dracula meets several near deaths, including a spectacular sequence in which he is caught slumbering in his coffin during the pre-dusk hours by both the priest, who has temporarily escaped Dracula's evil spell, and the film's hero, Paul (played by Barry Andrews). Just before the sun begins to set, the two crusaders ram a wooden stake through Dracula's heart, but the fiend jumps out of his coffin and miraculously removes the stake from his own chest. In all the confusion, the vampire manages to escape, but before racing away, the vampire fires the wooden stake like a missile back at his foes.

For this effective scene, Hammer created their own addition to the folklore, which requires certain religious prayers to destroy a movie vampire. Since Paul is portrayed as an atheist in the film and the Priest is still under the Satanic influence of Dracula, their fall from grace, so-to-speak, allows the vampire to remove the stake from his heart and escape. Under normal circumstances, the vampire would have been reduced to a pile of ashes after such an impalement.

The script for this film is loaded with many similar religious symbolism, clever plot twists and exciting moments that elevate this otherwise rudimentary Hammer vehicle above the norm.

An action-packed chase scene follows in which Dracula and Paul battle each other on the front terrace of Castle Dracula. The vampire is inadvertently tossed over the terrace where he is impaled by a silver crucifix below. In a desperate attempt to destroy the vampire, the Priest regains his faith in God and delivers the words of exorcism necessary to send the vampire king back to the world of the undead. Quite spectacular!

THE MARK OF THE WOLFMAN
1968; Maxpar (Spain) (Color); Producer: Maxpar; Director: Enrique L. Equiluz; Screenwriter: Jacinto Molina.

This Spanish-made horror film was the beginning of a series of werewolf and monster movies starring Paul Naschy. The series of horror films would occasionally feature various vampires, including Count Dracula himself. The film was a big hit in Spain, and launched Naschy's career as a horror star in such films as DRACULA VS. FRANKENSTEIN (1969), DR. JEKYLL VS. THE WEREWOLF (1971), DRACULA'S GREAT LOVE (1972), NIGHT OF THE HOWLING BEASTS (1975) and nearly twenty other films.

A frantic Count Dracula (Christopher Lee) in TASTE THE BLOOD OF DRACULA (1969).

MARK OF THE WOLFMAN was released in Asia as THE WOLFMAN OF COUNT DRACULA and in Germany as THE WOLFMAN.....THE VAMPIRE OF DR. DRACULA. In Belgium the film was known as DRACULA AND THE WEREWOLF. The film was released in the United States under the very misleading title FRANKENSTEIN'S BLOODY TERROR by Independent International.

The film never really features Dracula by name, nor does it feature any relatives to the Frankenstein family. However there is a vampire named Dr. Mikelhov whose mannerisms and physical appearance resemble that of Count Dracula's.

The film begins with a scene straight out of Universal's FRANKENSTEIN MEETS THE WOLFMAN (1943) when two gypsies loot the resting place of a man with a silver cross imbedded in his heart. The two greedy men remove the shimmering object only to die at the fangs of a savage werewolf.

Later, young Waldemar Daninsky (Paul Naschy) joins the villagers in a search for his werewolf-father, now set free by the two gypsy men. During the hunt, he is attacked by his own father. Waldemar manages to kill the werewolf with a silver dagger. As a result of his father's death, Waldemar inherits the family curse and now it is he who transforms into a dreaded beast when the moon is full. Both his girlfriend and best friend chain him to the castle cellar and send for the help of occult specialists Dr. Mikelhov and his beautiful wife, both of whom happen to be vampires. The vampires deceive the young couple into thinking that they will cure Waldemar of his inherited curse, but in reality, they have plans of using the powers of the Devil to make

the beast even stronger. In a motion picture first, the werewolf escapes from the cellar and battles with the vampires, who, in the end, burst into flames. Waldemar is eventually shot with a silver bullet. But have no fear! The famous Spanish werewolf returned in the sequel to this film!

Despite the comic book style in which the film is presented and its bad editing style and poor dubbing, MARK OF THE WEREWOLF is an extremely atmospheric and a very exciting entry in the vampire genre, technically speaking. Most English-speaking viewers will find it difficult to keep themselves from being distracted, however.

American distributors gave the film a silly prologue, a misleading title and cut about forty-five minutes of important footage.

SANTO AND THE TREASURE OF DRACULA 1968; Calderon (Mexico) (B&W); Producer: Alberto Lopez; Director: Rene Cardona.

In this episode from the series, Santo goes back in time in a scientific device which allows him to locate Count Dracula, who just so happens to be running loose somewhere in Mexico incognito as Count Alucard. The vampire is destroyed by a wooden stake through the heart, and Santo journeys back to the present to locate Dracula's grave. Once found, Santo proceeds to steal the nobleman's royal ring, which is considered very valuable and powerful.

Later, villains remove the stake from the vampire's heart, and Dracula, now revived, wants his ring. Once again, Santo must battle Dracula, this time in the present. The film ends with another timeless stake

Dracula (Christopher Lee) comes face to face with the powers of goodness in TASTE THE BLOOD OF DRACULA (1969).

driven through Count Dracula's heart.

SANTO AND THE TREASURE OF DRACULA features mindless sex and nude chorus girls as a cheap device used to fill time and appeal to an adult market. In fact, the film was widely known as THE VAMPIRE AND SEX! Are you surprised?

TASTE THE BLOOD OF DRACULA
1969; Hammer Films (Great Britain) (Color); Producer: Aida Young; Director: Peter Sasdy; Screenwriter: Anthony Hinds; Camera: Arthur Grant.

Many film critics still proclaim that TASTE THE BLOOD OF DRACULA is Hammer's most underrated and its most superior Dracula film next to HORROR OF DRACULA. At one time, I too was guilty of stating the same, however, after viewing and reviewing this film several times recently, I have changed my own thoughts slightly; enough so to say that this film is perhaps slightly over-rated. This does not mean to say that the film is an inferior effort by Hammer. Instead, I simply believe that the film is not as great as many proclaim. TASTE THE BLOOD OF DRACULA, like many of these films, has its flaws.

DRACULA HAS RISEN FROM THE GRAVE was so successful that Hammer began making sequels on a yearly basis, which meant that the screenwriters for these pictures were under an enormous amount of pressure, resulting in weak scripts. Thus the reason for the downfall of the Hammer-Dracula series and one of the major flaws of this particular picture. In fact, this was the case with all of the Dracula pictures from Hammer beginning with TASTE THE BLOOD OF DRACULA. John Elder's script delivers several flaws, which are, for the most part, trivial to most aficionados, especially those who proclaim this epic to be one of Hammer's finest.

The one major and obvious flaw is also an aspect of the film that is quite puzzling. In the film, Dracula is revived when three wealthy businessmen finance a ritualistic sacrifice in which a Satanic worshipper, who turns out to be a disciple of Dracula, gives his life to revive the vampire. With this being the case, then why does Dracula enact his revenge against the families of the three businessmen indirectly responsible for his resurrection? Why not go after the persons responsible for destroying him in the previous film? A mystery, no doubt, and one that has yet to be solved. But again, this is nothing more than a trivial flaw, and

obviously one that is often overlooked in favor of other exploits and cheap thrills. There is also the rather ambiguous climax in which Dracula is overcome by the once dormant forces of goodness that suddenly re-inhabit a church.

For the most part, TASTE THE BLOOD OF DRACULA is a well-mounted vampire film and director Peter Sasdy's first. The film did not approach the excellence of HORROR OF DRACULA, nor does it even come close to the superior quality and scripting of BRIDES OF DRACULA. However, technically speaking, the film does surpass DRACULA HAS RISEN FROM THE GRAVE in quality. The film's Victorian setting is near to being authentic as humanly possible for a low budget film, which is an asset. The set of the Gothic church where Dracula dwells throughout most of the film is also impeccably eye-catching. In short, the sets and costumes are breathtaking for such a modest picture as well as the performances. Furthermore, where TASTE THE BLOOD OF DRACULA lacks in consistency with the series it delivers in mood, atmosphere and authenticity.

In the film, Dracula (Christopher Lee), revived by a satanic disciple (Ralph Bates), now seeks revenge against the families of the three businessmen responsible for destroying his loyal servant. In doing so, he manages to destroy everyone except for the film's heroine Lucy (Isla Blair), who the vampire plans on vampirizing in an old desecrated church (this scene was later revamped by screenwriters Sam Hall and Gordon Russell for the climax of HOUSE OF DARK SHADOWS).

In the church, Dracula attempts to destroy Lucy by draining off all her blood. Suddenly, Lucy's boyfriend (Anthony Corlan) arrives in time to save the day. The hero places a crucifix on the church doors to prevent Dracula from escaping. Now trapped in a church and surrounded by righteous and holy symbols that appear out of nowhere, the vampire makes a daring attempt to climb to safety high above the altar, but his efforts are to no avail. The evil of Dracula is totally overcome by the forces of goodness, causing the vampire to fall to his demise. Having fallen onto the altar below, Dracula perishes to dust once again, leaving the heroine embraced in the arms of the handsome and fearless hero.

BLOOD OF DRACULA'S CASTLE

1969; Paragon Pictures (Color); Producers: Al Adamson & Rex Carlton; Directors: Jean Hewitt & Al Adamson; Screenwriter: Rex Carlton; Camera: Laszlo Kovacs.

Next to VOODOO HEARTBEAT, this Al Adamson "Z" film is perhaps one of the worst vampire movies ever made. In fact, it can be said that BLOOD OF DRACULA'S CASTLE is one of the worst horror films ever made. Well, maybe not the worst, but definitely among the top five!

BLOOD OF DRACULA'S CASTLE suffers from a weak script and from low production values resulting in poor sets and horrid performances by its cast. Poor John Carradine doesn't even play Count Dracula; instead, he's George, the vampires' murderous butler and a moonlighting high priest of a selenology cult. The actor is totally wasted in what is probably one of his worst performances.

Count Dracula is portrayed in this film by Alex D'Arcy. In the film, Dracula and his Countess (played by Paula Raymond, star of THE BEAST FROM 20,000 FATHOMS) attempt to conceal their identities by changing their names to Count and Countess Townsend. They sleep in coffins in their bedrooms and drink human blood from - cocktail glasses! Cocktail glasses? In their cellar below are pretty young women whom Carradine and Mango (Ray Young), the latter a half-wit hunchback, tap for blood with syringes. Syringes? Whatever happened to fangs? The blood is then served to the vampires. Occasionally, the young women are sacrificed to the great god Luna! To make matters more confusing, an escaped convict (Robert Dix) arrives to the castle and causes mayhem when he transforms into a werewolf.

The Draculas are destroyed by the sun's rays during the film's climax, but two bat like creatures rise from the ashes and fly away, suggesting that they survived.

Producer Adamson announced a sequel entitled DRACULA'S COFFIN that was never made. Thank your lucky "bats!"

BODY SNATCHERS FROM HELL

1969; Pacemaker (Japan) (Color); Producer: Shochiko; Director: Hajime Sato; Screenwriters: Susumu Tataku & K. Kobayashi.

For the price of admission you get a disaster film, a science fiction movie and a film about alien vampires!

Wow! You can't beat that. After watching this vapid Japanese-made "epic," the only thing that will be on your mind is beating something!

A plane crashes. The survivors become the victims of an alien vampire, who takes over their bodies. The film, also known as GOKE, THE BODY SNATCHER FROM HELL, does offer some interesting special effects sequences obviously patterned after the 1956 classic INVASION OF THE BODY SNATCHERS.

SANTO AND THE BLUE DEMON VS. THE MONSTERS

1969; Cinematografica/AIP (Mexico) (Color); Producer: Alberto Lopez; Director: Gilberto Martinez.

This film in the Santo series has the famous Mexican wrestler Santo teaming up with another popular Mexican wrestler to do battle against an army of monsters headed by The Vampire (David Alvizu). Together with his vampirized bride, The Vampire joins forces with Mexico's version of the Frankenstein Monster, the Wolfman, the Mummy, and the Cyclops to battle the masked heroes.

SANTO AND THE BLUE DEMON VS. THE MONSTERS is the least inspiring entry in the series, lacking much of the atmosphere established in the original B&W series.

The Blue Demon would go on to star in another Santo epic as well as his own horror films, THE SHADOW OF THE BAT (1966) directed by Federico Curiel and Rene Cardona's THE INVASION OF THE DEAD (1972), in which he must go up against Count Dracula (Cesar Silva), the Frankenstein Monster and a zombie.

SANTO AND THE BLUE DEMON VS. DRACULA AND THE WOLFMAN

1969; Calderon/AIP (Mexico) (Color); Director: Miguel M. Delgado.

Santo and the Blue Demon are side by side again bringing justice to the world of the undead. In this vehicle, Dracula is revived when human blood splatters into his coffin and onto his ashy remains. Joining forces, both Dracula and the Wolfman go after friends of Santo and the Blue Demon. Throughout the course of the film, Dracula manages to create a horde of

Right: John Carradine and Ray Young feed Countess Dracula (Paula Raymond) human blood in the obscure Al Adamson film BLOOD OF DRACULA'S CASTLE (1969).

vampire women, while the Wolfman creates a horde of other werewolves to spice up the entertainment level of this juvenile film.

The filmmakers must of had a field day making the climax of this picture in which the heroes must fight all the vampires and werewolves, throwing them into a pit of stakes. Dracula and the Wolfman suffer the same doom.

Santo continued to battle against the undead in several feature films, however, SANTO AND THE VENGEANCE OF THE VAMPIRE WOMEN (1974), a sequel to SANTO VS. THE VAMPIRE WOMEN (1961), was his only other encounter with the vampires of the cinema world.

DRAKULITA
1969; RJF Productions (Philippine) (B&W); Director: Consuelo P. Osorio.

Direct from the Philippines, comes this comical tale of vampirism. The film stars actress Rossana Ortiz as a female vampire known as Drakulita, who terrorizes the comedic cast of this film who are trapped in an old dark house!

DRAKULITA has never been screened in America, nor is it available on video, therefore we can only assume that the film's quality is rather poor. The same holds true for another film from the Philippines entitled THE MEN OF ACTION MEET THE WOMEN OF DRAKULA (1969), directed by Artemio Marquez. The film featured a confrontation between human tumblers and the infamous Count and his vampire women. Not much else is known about these two films.

THE REVIVAL OF DRACULA
1969; Paolessi (Italy) (Color); Director: U. Paolessi; Screenwriter: L. Mauri.

Not much information is available from this picture other than it stars Gabby Paul and Gill Chadwich. It is uncertain whether the film is a comedy or a straight forward horror vehicle.

DRACULA - THE DIRTY OLD MAN
1969; Boyd Productions/Art Films (Color); Producer/Director/Screenwriter: William Edwards.

Much like SPERMULA (1976) and DRACULA SUCKS (1979), this film, made in "Dripping color," deals with the erotic side of Dracula. The film was originally planned as a pornographic sexploitation film but producer, writer, director William Edwards eventually realized that by way of proper editing, this film could be made into a good comedy.

The film offers several bizarre and offbeat characters and Dracula, once again under the pseudonym of Alucard (played by Vince Kelly), runs around seducing young naked virgin girls, quarreling with his mother (literally an old bat) and hypnotizing a man who becomes a werewolf. Dracula also has a servant named Irving Jekyllman, who aids the vampire in kidnapping sweet young female victims.

DRACULA - THE DIRTY OLD MAN is not one of the genre's more respectable efforts.

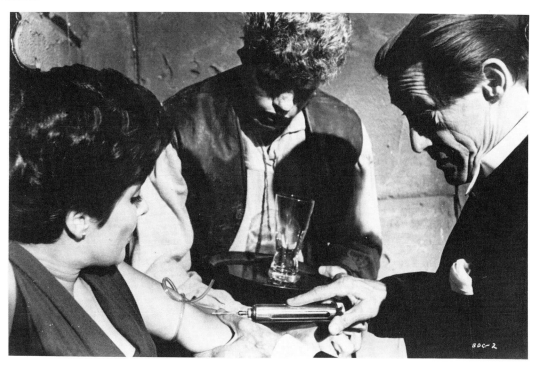

CHAPTER SIX

The 1970's

THE MAN WHO CAME FROM UMMO
1970; Eichberg Film (Italy/Spain/W. Germany) (Color); Producer: Jaime Prades; Directors: Tulio Demicheli & Hugo Fregonese; Screenwriter: Jacinto Molina.

The second film in the Paul Naschy/Wolfman series that began with MARK OF THE WOLFMAN (1968). This horror film is established as a true Dracula film with a twist. Actor Michael Rennie plays a scientist from the distant planet of Ummo. As the alien scientist, Rennie arrives on planet Earth with immediate intentions of conquering the world followed by the conquest of the universe. To do this, he enlists the aide of history's four most infamous and feared monsters: Count Dracula, the Wolfman, the Frankenstein Monster and the Mummy. The alien's mad plot is halted by secret agent Craig Hill, and so is this ridiculous Paul Naschy horror "epic." THE MAN WHO CAME FROM UMMO is undoubtedly the worst entry in the Spanish-made series. Because of budget restrictions, Naschy played both the werewolf Waldemar Daninsky and the Frankenstein Monster. Poor Michael Rennie, who died the following year, was talked into acting in this

dubbed mess. The producers probably hoaxed the aging actor into this vapid film project by convincing him that his role would be similar to and reminiscent of his classic portrayal of the alien Klaatu in the science fiction masterpiece THE DAY THE EARTH STOOD STILL (1951). Of course, we know better.

THE MAN WHO CAME FROM UMMO was released in Great Britain as DRACULA VS. FRANKENSTEIN, which is misleading since neither Dracula nor the Frankenstein Monster engage each other in battle. The film is also known as ASSIGNMENT TERROR in America.

CURSE OF THE VAMPIRES
1970; Hemisphere (U.S./Philippines) (Color); Producer: Amalia Muhlach; Director: Gerardo de Leon; Screenwriters: Ben Feleo & Pierre L. Salas.

Released on a double bill with Hemisphere's BEAST OF BLOOD (1970), CURSE OF THE VAMPIRES, also known as CREATURES OF EVIL, is a weak sequel to THE BLOOD DRINKERS, which was not really a great film to begin with.

Facing page: Udo Keir as Count Dracula in BLOOD FOR DRACULA (1973 - 1974), also known as ANDY WARHOL'S DRACULA.

CURSE OF THE VAMPIRES takes place at the turn of the century. Amelia Fuentes and Eddie Garcia play brother and sister. They return to their father's hacienda in a small island town in the Philippines to discover that their father is both sick and tormented. They also learn that their mother, whom they had supposed dead, is being held prisoner by their father in the basement of their mansion because she is a vampire. A real bloodsucking creature of the night!

Eddie tries to visit his mother one evening. Naturally, she attacks him, turning him into a vampire too. He goes to his sweetheart and turns her into a vampire. Now there are three vampires to stake instead of one. Eventually, the father goes after his wife and drives a wooden stake through her heart, relieving her of her misery. As a result of this heinous act, Eddie kills his father, but Amelia's father-in-law "to-be" tries to kill Eddie and his vampirized girlfriend (the latter happens to be his own daughter) by driving a wooden stake through their hearts.

Ads for CURSE OF THE VAMPIRES claimed that this picture was filmed in *"The real tombs of horror!"*- whatever that means?

THE NIGHT OF THE WALPURGIS
1970; Plata Films/Ellman Enterprises (Spain/W. Germany) (Color); Producer: Plata Films; Director: Leon Klimovsky; Screenwriters: Jacinto Molina & Hans Munkell.

Spanish actor Paul Naschy had just completed two werewolf films (NIGHT OF THE WOLFMAN and THE FURY OF THE WOLFMAN) and was cast to star in this new werewolf epic for director Leon Klimovsky. Although the film was originally released in France as THE CLAWS OF DRACULA, the film was actually based upon the historic figure of Countess Elizabeth Bathory, who was also known to many as Countess Dracula from time to time.

The character of Waldemar Daninsky is revived by a doctor who removes the silver bullet that

Eddie Garcia is approached by his vampire mother in CURSE OF THE VAMPIRES (1970).

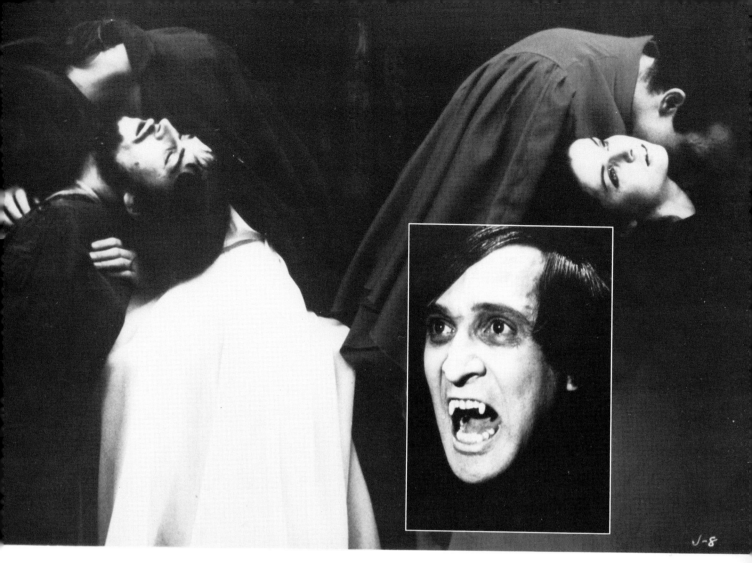

originally destroyed him in a previous "epic." Now restored to life, Waldemar and two young female students search for the tomb of Countess Wandesa de Nadasdy, a dreadful vampiress who once maintained her youthful beauty by consuming the blood of virgin girls. Naturally, they locate the vampire's tomb and she is revived by human blood. Countess Wandesa immediately vampirizes one of the students (there's nothing subtle about this film), who in turn makes advances towards her friend until Waldemar impales her with a stake. Now the Countess attacks the other young girl with plans of sacrificing her to Satan, resulting in the fierce battle between monsters that the American title suggests. The werewolf is destroyed when the young girl stabs him through the heart with a silver cross. Needless to say, the vampire countess is destroyed somewhere in all of this mayhem.

THE NIGHT OF THE WALPURGIS was a big success in Spain, launching a series of horror films similar in content. The film was released in the United States as THE WEREWOLF VS. THE VAMPIRE WOMAN during the mid 1970's, but has not since been seen.

JONATHAN
1970; Iouna Films/New Yorker (W. Germany) (Color); Producer: Iouna Films; Director & Screenwriter: Hans W. Geissendorfer.

Adolf Hitler meets Dracula in this cross between NOSFERATU (1979) and SCHINDLER'S LIST (1994). This once highly controversial and prestigious color vampire/Nazi film was made in West Germany. JONATHAN is a direct adaptation of Bram Stoker's *Dracula* in dialogue. However, the film is more of a political picture rather than one about vampirism in which the Dracula figure is compared to Germany's own real monster: Adolf Hitler.

The story depicts the relationship between the vampire and the town he dominates as a grim lesson

Fascist vampires spread their evil in JONATHAN (1970).
Insert: A closeup of the ringleader of the fascist vampires in JONATHAN.

83

in fascism. The European town is under the rule of a mysterious cloaked figure who is also the head of a very powerful cult of vampires. The vampire feeds on the local peasants while listening to classical music much in the same way Adolf Hitler massacred the Jews void of any conscious. The villagers decide that they have suffered long enough under the evil domination of the vampires and dispatch a heroic young man named Jonathan (Jurgen Jung), the film's version of Jonathan Harker, to the dreaded castle to destroy them. He manages to succeed, driving the Dracula figure and his vampiric minions into the sea to drown.

Hans W. Geissendorfer's often slow but fascinating direction has been compared to the filmmaking styles of both F.W. Murnau and Roman Polanski, and the film has been praised by critics and film historians for its unusual allegorical style. Unfortunately, JONATHAN is a film that is very rarely seen in America. In fact, during its initial release, American distributors were invited to screenings for their reactions and opinions. The film was received with great enthusiasm, but potential distributors found it too slow and lacking for contemporary moviegoers, who were spoiled with the numerous, fast-paced Hammer vampire films and many of those ungodly, awfully-dubbed Mexican and Spanish monster "epics." After a couple years of rejection by distributors, producers decided to add additional scenes of violence and sex, thus hindering the film's mood and style as well as its original impact. Reviews of the edited version were, for the most part, favorable; however, these were the kind of reviews that would turn-away the average, run-of-the-mill horror movie fan and devotee. The result was a limited release in the United States in which JONATHAN would quickly disappear.

It is often seldom that we are given a subtle horror film that will earn an Oscar nomination. History speaks for itself, and there is nothing subtle about the award-winning horror films THE EXORCIST, ALIEN, AN AMERICAN WEREWOLF IN LONDON, SILENCE OF THE LAMBS and BRAM STOKER'S DRACULA. However, had the independent and "artsy" JONATHAN been released in its original format during the right time, the film could have become Oscar material. Still, despite its flaws, JONATHAN is regarded as a contemporary classic. Chances are we will never be given the opportunity to view the film in its original, unedited format.

The film was released in France as THE LAST COMBAT AGAINST THE VAMPIRES.

COUNT DRACULA
1970; World (Spain/Italy/W. Germany/Great Britain) (Color); Producer: Harry Alan Towers; Director: Jesus Franco; Screenwriters: Jesus Franco, Harry Alan Towers, August Finochi, Milo G. Cuccia & Dietmar Behnke.

In 1970, Spain announced an ambitious color production based on Bram Stoker's novel. The film was to be given an impressive budget, to be directed by Terence Fisher and to star horror superstar Vincent Price as Professor Van Helsing. Producer Harry A. Towers eventually cast Herbert Lom as Van Helsing and the film's direction was assigned to Jesus Franco, the director of Italian and Spanish-made low-grade horror films. The changes resulted in what is an adequate film, but had Towers allotted the film a higher budget, positioned Terence Fisher in the director's chair and cast Price as Van Helsing, the final film would most probably would

Christopher Lee as Count Dracula in Jesus Franco's COUNT DRACULA (1970).

84

have been one of the more memorable film adaptations of Bram Stoker's novel.

One of the film's two major assets is that the role of Count Dracula is played by Christopher Lee. Lee's Count is portrayed as an older and heavily mustached vampire the way Bram Stoker had originally described the character in his novel. In fact, with this film, Lee was the first actor to portray the character correctly on screen. In an interview, Lee had admitted that he was tired of playing the role of Count Dracula Hammer style. Instead, Lee wanted a more faithful script that went by the book, and the script of this film was the closest adaptation of the book at that time, which is the film's second asset.

The premise follows the Stoker novel relatively close, with Jonathan Harker arriving at Castle Dracula to be confronted by an older nobleman. With each intake of human blood, the vampire becomes younger in appearance. The film introduces the familiar characters of Van Helsing, Lucy and Mina, and concludes with a final showdown between Count Dracula and Jonathan Harker in which the vampire is burned to ashes.

Despite the low budget and the often disappointing and tedious direction of Franco, the film does offer a serious and quite impressive enactment of the novel, with relatively commendable performances by both Lee and Herbert Lom as Dracula and Van Helsing.

COUNT YORGA-VAMPIRE
1970; AIP (Color); Producer: Michael Macready; Director & Screenwriter: Robert Kelljan.

COUNT YORGA - VAMPIRE was one of the most successful low-budget vampire movies ever made. Ironically, the film was originally intended to be another sexploitation vampire movie. Wisely, producer Michael Macready elevated this film into a PG-rated hit, which spawned a sequel and made a horror star out of its principal actor, Robert Quarry.

Robert Quarry's performance as Count Yorga is perhaps one of the closest movie vampire characterizations to be patterned after the image of Count Dracula. Quarry's vampire, like Christopher Lee's Count Dracula, is both agile and physical, leaving very little room for subtlety or romance. For example, in one of the film's more memorable moments, Yorga races towards a victim and literally rips his throat to shreds with his fangs. The brutal scene was filmed in

slow motion for a more dramatic effect.

Yorga is a polished gentleman on the surface. But beneath the surface lies a savage animal, with superhuman strength; a genuinely devious and cunning bloodsucker. Count Yorga was originally intended to be part of AIP's new image of horror figures during the early 1970's that also included Vincent Price's THE ABOMINABLE DR. PHIBES (1970) and William Marshall's BLACULA (1972). For this reason, director Bob Kelljan wanted to make a strong impression with this new dynamic character, who was both handsome and charming at front face, and quite wise to modern America. Yorga was the first impressionable modern-day movie vampire, and because of this, the film became a big hit, much more so than both Hammer's DRACULA A.D. (1971) and THE SATANIC RITES OF DRACULA (1973), two failed attempts at transporting Chris Lee's Dracula into a modern setting.

The film is set against modern-day Los Angeles, as Count Yorga and his vampire harem attempt to vampirize a group of youngsters. Unbelievably, the vampire meets his death when he receives a wooden broomstick through the heart by the film's hero.

The success of COUNT YORGA- VAMPIRE prompted AIP to immediately launch a sequel entitled THE RETURN OF COUNT YORGA (1971), which reunited Robert Quarry with the title role.

THE VAMPIRE LOVERS
1970; Hammer Films/AIP (Great Britain) (Color); Producer: Harry Fine & Michael Style; Director: Roy Ward Baker; Screenwriter: Tudor Gates, from an adaptation by Harry Fine, Tudor Gates and Michael Style of the novel Carmilla by Sheridan le Fanu; Camera: Moray Grant.

With its Dracula series running out of steam, Hammer needed new material and an opportunity for some greater sensual and erotic vampire films to boost box office returns. Adapting Sheridan le Fanu's sensual vampire tale Carmilla to the screen seemed the right thing for Hammer to realize their goal of producing the screen's most sensual vampire movie. Thus Hammer produced THE VAMPIRE LOVERS, a slow moving but very vicious film loaded with nudity, lesbian sex, blood, violence and shock all under the careful direction of Roy Ward Baker.

Horror actress Ingrid Pitt portrays an erotic female vampire named Countess Mircalla Karnstein.

In the film, she literally sets her *"bite"* on the beautiful breasts of Madeline Smith (yes guys, this is one of those many Hammer *"tits and teeth"* films!). Peter Cushing also stars in the film as ruthless witch finder and vampire-killer named General Von Spielsdorf, who protects his daughter Laura (played by Pippa Steele) from the clutches of Countess Karnstein by literally beheading the vampire in a chapel.

Unfortunately, much of the sexual and graphic content of this film was cut by American sensors, thus resulting in a very confusing script and loss of atmosphere. Hammer director Roy Ward Baker, who would later go on to direct several superior horror films, attempts to spruce up the Gothic le Fanu tale with modern feminist issues as lesbianism, but he fails, and his attempt to deliver graphic violence also spoils what is an otherwise tasteful tale of vampirism. Even with all of its graphic color, THE VAMPIRE LOVERS stands pale next to the more splendid and superior adaptations VAMPYR (1932) and BLOOD AND ROSES (1960). Nevertheless, Baker's film is still good old-fashion Hammer-style entertainment at its best.

THE VAMPIRE LOVERS spawned two sequels: LUST FOR A VAMPIRE (1971) and TWINS OF EVIL (1972).

THE HOUSE THAT DRIPPED BLOOD
1970; Amicus/Cinerama (Great Britain) (Color); Producers: Max J. Rosenberg & Milton Subotsky; Director: Peter Duffell; Screenwriter: Robert Bloch; Camera: Ray Parslow.

This marvelous anthology film from Great Britain offers an interesting short segment on the vampire legend. The segment, entitled *The Cloak*, stars Jon Pertwee as Paul Henderson, an aging horror film actor who is given a mysterious black cloak for his next film: CURSE OF THE BLOODSUCKERS. Whenever Henderson wears the cloak, he transforms into a two-fanged bloodsucker who puts the *"bite"* on his leading lady Carla (Ingrid Pitt). We later learn that Carla was actually a vampire all along. Apparently she wanted Henderson to become one of the undead in admiration of all his numerous vampire films.

This segment was directed as a spoof by Peter Duffell and written by Robert Bloch, the creator of Alfred Hitchcock's PSYCHO (1960).

THE HOUSE THAT DRIPPED BLOOD also offers a variety of different segments that star Delhom

Elliott, Peter Cushing and Christopher Lee in brief but lasting roles. The film is one of the better anthology horror movies to come out of Great Britain.

SCARS OF DRACULA
1970; Hammer Films/EMI (Great Britain) (Color); Producer: Aida Young; Director: Roy Ward Baker; Screenwriter: John Elder (Anthony Hinds); Camera: Moray Grant.

By this point in the Hammer-Dracula series, originality had taken a back seat to a tired formula that once entertained and thrilled moviegoers. By the release of SCARS OF DRACULA, this same formula managed to disappoint fans of the long-lasting series.

SCARS OF DRACULA is both a good film when its good and a bad film when its bad. Sound confusing? In other words, the film succeeds in some aspects while in other areas, it flops. For example, in SCARS OF DRACULA, actor Christopher Lee is given more footage and dialogue than in any of the other Dracula films from Hammer. His welcomed voice echoes loudly, personifying the strong character that he is meant to portray. Fans of Chris Lee were pleased by this, and the film benefits greatly from the actor's bumped up presence and his omnipotent voice. With SCARS OF DRACULA, Hammer had invested more into the character of Count Dracula as an attempt to reinstate the Count as the central character of the film; something that had been missing since HORROR OF DRACULA (1958).

The film also tries to recreate many of the old characteristics of the Universal films by using a mob of angry torch-bearing villagers and oversized vampire bats. There is also a well-mounted scene in which Lee scales the side of a building, paying homage to Bram Stoker's original novel.

Hammer released SCARS OF DRACULA on a double-bill with HORROR OF FRANKENSTEIN (1970), a film that also tried to recreate many of the familiar characteristics and fond memories of the old Universal films. At the time, Hammer was trying to achieve financial success by returning to the basics. Returning to the basics, though, did not fare well for Hammer.

SCARS OF DRACULA did not fare well at the box office, at least not as well as both DRACULA HAS RISEN FROM THE GRAVE and TASTE THE BLOOD OF DRACULA. Nor did it do as well as AIP's COUNT YORGA - VAMPIRE. There are

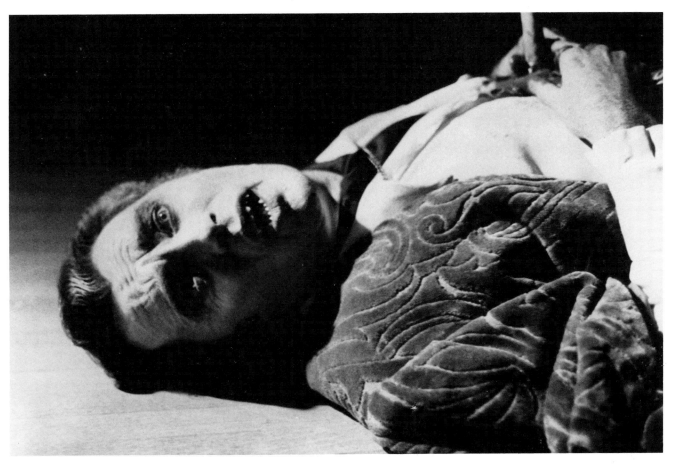

Robert Quarry is staked in COUNT YORGA - VAMPIRE (1970).

Peter Cushing holds the head of vampire Ingrid Pitt in THE VAMPIRE LOVERS (1970).

several reasons that contribute to this, the most obvious being the low production values of the new film. The film was produced on a shoe-string budget Dracula's castle seems to have been hastily constructed on an obvious sound-stage, and the special effects were just awful (especially the bat effects). Hammer's return to the basics also proved fatal, since moviegoers had graduated to more sophisticated horrors of the time (PLANET OF THE APES, ROSEMARY'S BABY, NIGHT OF THE LIVING DEAD). The timing was all wrong. With SCARS OF DRACULA, the Hammer-Dracula series had reached a major turning point, one which would change the series and the vampire movie genre forever.

The plot of SCARS OF DRACULA is quite simple. In this film, Dracula is revived when a loyal vampire bat splatters blood over his remains. Once revived, the vampire takes out his revenge on unsuspecting travelers and on the inhabitants of a nearby village. When Christopher Matthews becomes the victim of both Count Dracula (Lee) and his beautiful vampirized mistress Tania (Anoushka Hempel), his brother (played by Dennis Waterman)

and his girlfriend (Jenny Hanley) arrive at Castle Dracula in search of Matthews. Of course, Dracula cannot resist his sanguinary intentions, even after feeling remorse for himself because of his own undead condition.

As the Count tries to turn Waterman's girlfriend into a vampire during the film's climax, the vampire engages in a fierce battle with the hero. Waterman drives a metal pike into Dracula's side. But the Count yanks the pike out of his own body. Dracula prepares to fire the pike back at his nemesis when suddenly, a bolt of lightning strikes the metal rod and fries Count Dracula to ashes (one wonders if Dracula's destruction by a lightning bolt from the heavens actually offers a hidden meaning? Was this God's way of ridding the world of the vampire's dreaded evil forever)?

Dennis Watermann is atacked by Dracula's misstress (Anoushka Hempel) in this savage scene from Hammer's SCARS OF DRACULA (1970).

HOUSE OF DARK SHADOWS
1970; MGM (Color); Producer & Director: Dan Curtis; Screenwriters: Sam Hall & Gordon Russell from the TV series *Dark Shadows*; **Camera: Arthur J. Ornitz.**

Anyone who is a fan of horror movies is bound to be familiar with *Dark Shadows* the famous and highly popular television series that aired on television from 1966 to 1971 with nearly one thousand episodes (many of which are now available on video cassette). The daytime soap opera gave life to America's most beloved vampire, Barnabas Collins (played with great dedication by actor Jonathan Frid).

In the Gothic TV soap, Barnabas is released after one hundred and seventy-five years of imprisonment in a coffin by the lecherous Willie Loomis (played by John Karlen). Prior to the memorable moment in television history when Barnabas was introduced, the soap was just another rudimentary New England-style

family drama that was quickly declining in its afternoon ratings. Once the supernatural elements were added and Barnabas appeared on the scene, the ratings shot through the roof and the rest, as they say, was history.

HOUSE OF DARK SHADOWS actually sums up the vampire elements of the television soap within a framework of ninety-seven minutes, meaning the film moves rapidly in pace, but the excitement is grand, and the vampire elements are handled very well by the film's director.

The story begins when Barnabas arrives on the scene, after being inadvertently released from his resting place, a sealed coffin in an icy cemetery mausoleum. The film goes straight for the throat, with good performances, strong atmosphere, impressive sets and an exciting new horror movie figure for the BIG screen - Barnabas Collins! Barnabas was Dracula's replacement, a strong monstrous presence that lasted

Nancy Barrett returns from the dead as a vampire in HOUSE OF DARK SHADOWS (1970).
Insert: Jonathan Frid as Barnabas Collins in HOUSE OF DARK SHADOWS.

89

from the late 1960's until the early 1970's. In fact, one could say that Barnabas was the Jason and Freddy Kruger of the early 1970's! In short, Barnabas was the hottest new monster in town, and what a phenomenal sensation he created! Even today, with the original television show back in syndication, fan clubs sprouting all over the world, new video releases, books and even a major network remake with actor Ben Cross as the master vampire, *Dark Shadows* continues to fascinate and entertain thousands, literally millions of horror fans across the world.

The story begins with Barnabas's (Jonathan Frid) resurrection from the undead. Soon, the vampire is claiming the lives of his family members, in particular his cousin Carolyn Stoddard (played by Nancy Barrett), who he turns into a savage female vixen.

In one of the film's superbly staged scenes, Carolyn is cornered by the police and violently staked to death (who said policemen are non-believers)? But Barnabas keeps moving and by the end of the film, nearly half the cast members have been transformed into creatures of the night.

There is one particularly fascinating scene in which Barnabas physically reverts to his true age of 175 years old when an experiment to cure his ailment, conducted by doctor Grayson Hall, goes hay-wires. The make-up used for this scene, designed by Dick Smith, is quite good, considering the time period the film was made, but very similar to Dustin Hoffman's make-up in LITTLE BIG MAN (Smith used the same make-up on both films). The same make-up was also used in the impressive vampire film THE HUNGER, in which vampire David Bowie was made-up to look 150 years old.

Barnabas's death is perhaps one of the most vivid stakings to be recorded on film. As he prepares to vampirize the film's heroine (Kathryn Leigh Scott), actor John Karlen, who plays Willie Loomis - the vampire's servant, drives a wooden arrow through the vampire's back and heart during the film's climax.

Jonathan Frid is brilliant as the centuries old vampire, and it is a shame that the film's creator and director Dan Curtis did not press MGM to produce a sequel in which Barnabas returns to life to claim revenge on the surviving family members of Collinswood. Still, fans had to wait nearly twenty years before Barnabas returned to the screen, that is, the TV screen.

HOUSE OF DARK SHADOWS was and still is an exciting and refreshing new vampire effort. During its original release, the film was listed as one of the

top ten money-making films made in 1970. Today the film holds up rather well (that is, if you are a *Dark Shadows* fan).

The sequel, NIGHT OF DARK SHADOWS (1972), has nothing to do with vampires or Barnabas Collins, unfortunately.

LESBIAN VAMPIRES
Telecine & Fenix 1970; Telecine & Fenix (Spain/ Germany) (Color); Director: Jesus Franco.

Also known as THE STRANGE ADVENTURE OF JONATHAN HARKER and as THE SIGN OF THE VAMPIRE, LESBIAN VAMPIRES is just another mindless and rather silly Spanish/German co-production directed by Jesus Franco.

This film stars Dennis Price (SCARS OF DRACULA) and Susan Korda. The film is based on the novel *Dracula's Guest* by Bram Stoker and tells of how a young girl who dreams she is being seductively menaced by a lesbian vampire.

Vampirized devil worshippers claim another victim in BLOOD SUCKERS (1970 - 1971).

Just as a note of reference, Universal's DRACULA'S DAUGHTER (1936) is also based on the same Bram Stoker novel; the 1936 film is a much better film.

BLOOD SUCKERS

1970/1971; Titan International- Chevron (Great Britain) (Color); Producer: Graham Harris; Director: Robert Hartford Davies; Screenwriter: Julian More, based on the novel *Doctors Wear Scarlet* by Simon Raven.

In this *"clever and refreshingly original"* film, as it was falsely advertised, vampirism is depicted as a perversion of sexual preference rather than the traditional supernatural curse we have all become familiar with.

In the film, actor Patrick Macnee is seduced into vampirism and devil worshipping by a beautiful Greek woman (played by Imogen Hassal) whose husband (Patrick Mower) has also fallen into the cult.

Actors Peter Cushing, Edward Woodward and Patrick Macnee are wasted in this film which explores the theory that some men only achieve orgasm by sucking the blood of others. The film was so bad that even the director removed his name from the credits.

BLOODSUCKERS is also known as INCENSE FOR THE DAMNED and VAMPIRE SACRIFICE. Not to be confused with the 1966 film BLOODSUCKERS, in which a crazed scientist raises blood-sucking trees.

GUESS WHAT HAPPENED TO COUNT DRACULA?

1970; Merrick International (Color); Producer: Leo Rivers; Director & Screenwriter: Laurence Merrick, who also served as the film's Executive Producer.

This low-budget comedy spoof stars Des Robert as Count Dracula disguised as Count Adrian, who, in the film, must adapt to the contemporary ways of 1970 without loosing the traditional ways of his home land of Transylvania. Occasionally, Dracula sports around in the traditional black cape and tuxedo we have all come to recognize, but since the film takes place in modern-day California, the vampire must avoid attracting attention to himself, so he finds himself wearing a turtleneck sweater and a double-breasted suit from time to time.

In modern America, the "inconspicuous" vampire goes after the hippie-inhabited sunset strip, zeroing in on a beautiful young girl named Angelica (Claudia Barron). According to the legend established in this film, if Dracula sucks her blood three times, she will become a vampire. Surprisingly, Count Dracula wins, but before doing so, he must fight the film's hero (John Landon) and challenge another supreme vampire named Imp (Frank Donato).

GUESS WHAT HAPPENED TO DRACULA was actually thrown together by filmmaker Laurence Merrick in record breaking time to beat AIP's COUNT YORGA - VAMPIRE into release, which it did. However, the film did poorly at the box office and was given a very short theatrical life.

DRACULA VS. DR. FRANKENSTEIN
1971; Fenix & Comtoir (Spain/France) (Color); Director: Jesus Franco.

Not to be confused with the low budget independent film DRACULA VS. FRANKENSTEIN (1972) from Al Adamson or the Paul Naschy film THE MAN WHO CAME FROM UMMO (1970), which was also released as DRACULA VS. FRANKENSTEIN, this film is totally different; it's a Jesus Franco movie!

Yes, once again, J. Franco delivers another of his numerous Dracula epics, this one being one of his worst. In this rather obscure picture, Count Dracula (Howard Vernon) and Lady Dracula (Britt Nichols) return to their castle in the Carpathian mountains to initiate a new wave of vampirism. Combatting the vampires are both Dr. Frankenstein (played by Dennis Price, a Hammer horror star) and his assistant Morpho (Luis Barboo). Together, they create a monster which will destroy Dracula. Then there is Dr. Seward (Alberto Dalbes), who, like Grayson Hall in HOUSE OF DARK SHADOWS, has hopes of finding a cure for the Count's vampiric condition.

This low budget effort was released in France as DRACULA, PRISONER OF DOCTOR FRANKENSTEIN. The film is also known as DRACULA AGAINST FRANKENSTEIN, THEY'RE COMING TO GET YOU, THE SCREAMING DEAD and, last, but not least, as REVENGE OF DRACULA!

The sequel, also made by Franco, is entitled THE EROTIC EXPERIENCES OF DR. FRANKENSTEIN (1971). Just a few of the films Franco also directed are: ATTACK OF THE ROBOTS (1962), THE AWFUL DR. ORLOFF (1962), BARBED WIRE DOLLS (1975), THE CASTLE OF FU MANCHU (1968), JACK THE RIPPER (1976), NIGHT OF THE BLOOD MONSTER (1970), SUCCUBUS (1968) and COUNT DRACULA (1970) with Christopher Lee.

DRACULA A.D. - 1972
1971; Hammer Films (Great Britain) (Color); Producer: Josephine Douglas; Director: Alan Gibson; Screenwriter: Don Houghton; Camera: Richard Bush.

By the beginning of the new decade, the popularity level of the Hammer/Chris Lee Dracula series began

Count Dracula meets his first death in the exciting opening scene from DRACULA A.D. - 1972 (1971).

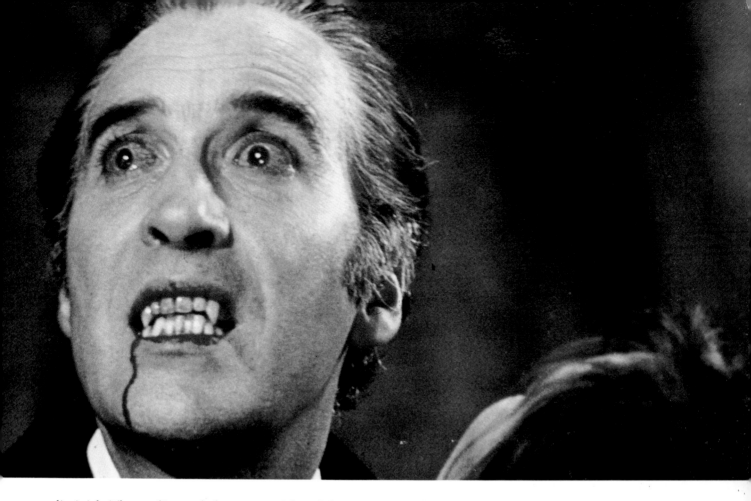

to diminish. The studio needed new material, and they needed it quickly. Fans of the series expected a fresh new Dracula film every year. More important, loyal Chris Lee fans expected each new Dracula film to top the last. Furthermore, with the disappointing SCARS OF DRACULA still fresh in the minds of moviegoers, Hammer knew it was time for a face lift.

Following the box office failure of SCARS OF DRACULA, Hammer decided to shift the Gothic character of Count Dracula to modern-day London. There were several reasons that brought upon the idea to shift the setting to modern times. The first was the success of an American film called COUNT YORGA - VAMPIRE, which depicted an ancient vampire cast against the modern setting of Los Angeles. Secondly, Hammer had simply exhausted every possible scenario for its vampire king in a Gothic setting, or at least they thought they had. In retrospect, we see that Hammer had an unlimited amount of doors unopened that could have kept the Count out of a modern setting. But this is easier said than done, especially when one reminisces on what "could have been." Finally, Hammer received pressure from its American distributor and co-producer to alter the film's setting.

The idea of Dracula in a modern setting just did not work. With the exception of the opening segment, DRACULA A.D. was a total waste, and the film failed miserably at the box office. Hammer's last attempt to give new life to the Dracula myth was a disaster. Needless to say, the film and the series' principal actor, Christopher Lee, was very unhappy with the project, which he publicly stated during an interview. Lee felt that the film was utterly absurd. Despite the film's absurdities and regardless of the weak script, Lee's Dracula maintained the dignity the actor always injected into the character.

DRACULA A.D. starts off very promising with a dramatic scene during which we witness a fierce battle between Count Dracula (Christopher Lee) and Professor Van Helsing (Peter Cushing) on a runaway stagecoach bound to Castle Dracula. They never make it to the castle as the battle is momentarily halted when the runaway coach collides into a large tree. Both the vampire and the vampire-killer are tossed off the carriage. Suddenly, Dracula emerges from behind the coach impaled through the heart with a wooden spoke broken off of a wheel. Franticly, the vampire tries to remove the shaft from his chest before Van Helsing can regain consciousness, but it is too late. The Professor awakens in time just before Dracula can

Christopher Lee, as Dracula, relishes the taste of human blood after a century of "death" in DRACULA A.D. - 1972 (1971).

remove the lethal spoke. Van Helsing rams the wooden spoke deeper into the savage vampire's heart, sending him into the hereafter once more.

The film then shifts from its Gothic setting to modern-day London, England, and from this point onward, the film takes on a new mood not worthy of its Gothic predecessors. The screenplay written by Don Houghton keeps the vampire within the ruins of a desecrated church throughout the remaining film, which is both good and bad; good because the centuries-old vampire is intact among the Gothic setting and bad because his interaction with modern civilization is very limited. But then again, had Dracula been allowed to roam the streets of London, the film most probably would have taken a turn towards comedy. The basic idea behind keeping Dracula confined to the church was to avoid occurrences that could be translated as comical.

Count Dracula's resurrection in this film is very similar to his revival in TASTE THE BLOOD OF DRACULA. This time actor Christopher Neame plays Dracula's disciple, Johnny Alucard (clever), who revives the vampire after a century and a half of sleep. Peter Cushing plays the descendant of the original Van Helsing, who was responsible for destroying the vampire during the more dramatic opening sequence of this film. Now resurrected from the world of the undead, Dracula is out for revenge against his enemies by going after their descendants and turning their lives into a nightmare.

In their attempt to modernize the Count's escapades to appeal to modern-day moviegoers, Hammer produced what is perhaps the series most dated and uninspired outing, where as the previous Gothic entries in the series are considered to be timeless horror classics of the modern cinema.

BLOODTHIRSTY EYES
1971; Toho International (Japan) (Color); Director: Michio Yammamoto.

Released in America as THE LAKE OF DRACULA, BLOODTHIRSTY EYES, despite its Oriental origin (Toho), is a well-mounted modern Gothic horror film with extremely satisfying photography. In many ways, the film imitates the style and mood of the Hammer Dracula films, depicting the vampire as a more supernatural and dynamic figure rather than a creepy old creature whose movements are restricted by its age and undead condition.

The film opens with a little girl chasing her dog through a cave. She passes a lake under a red sky and comes upon a castle hidden in the woods. There she encounters an old man, a pale young girl and a mysterious young gentleman with golden eyes.

The film resumes years later. The girl is now an adult. She now considers the entire experience to have been nothing more than a childhood nightmare, but this is not so. A pale-faced Oriental vampire arrives in her town and places several mortals under his spell, including the woman's sister. Soon her sister unexpectedly dies and re-awakens in the morgue. Shortly thereafter, other town-folk begin to die from a mysterious plague only to suddenly reawaken from death.

It is later discovered by the film's hero through a series of letters that the vampire is actually the descendant of Count Dracula himself. Many years ago, Dracula impregnated an Oriental woman, who gave birth to a boy born with golden eyes and a savage bloodthirsty nature. Are the heroine's dreams of a young boy with golden eyes just a dream?

It is now apparent that the vampire is alive and well and claiming victims galore. During the climax, the hero and the vampire engage in a battle over the film's heroine, staged within the old Gothic castle that once belonged to Dracula. The fiendish vampire is eventually destroyed in a scene inspired by Hammer's DRACULA HAS RISEN FROM THE GRAVE (1968) during which the vampire inadvertently trips backward over a banister and falls onto a wooden stake that penetrates his heart.

BLOODTHIRSTY EYES is one of those rare vampire films that actually works well in its modern setting. Unfortunately, many vampire fans will never get to see what is one of the genre's better vampire offerings from the early 1970's.

In addition to being known as THE LAKE OF DRACULA, BLOODTHIRSTY EYES is also known as DRACULA'S LUST FOR BLOOD. A sequel was made in 1975 entitled THE EVIL OF DRACULA, directed by Michio Yammamoto. Very little is known about this sequel.

THE RETURN OF COUNT YORGA
1971; AIP (Color); Producer: Michael Macready; Director: Bob Kelljan; Screenwriters: Bob Kelljan & Yvonne Wilder.

COUNT YORGA - VAMPIRE proved to be

very successful at the box office, inspiring a slew of other modern-day vampire movies which included DRACULA A.D., HOUSE OF DARK SHADOWS, GUESS WHAT HAPPENED TO DRACULA, BLACULA and THE SATANIC RITES OF DRACULA, to name only a few.

The original "*Yorga*" film was such a big success that producer Michael Macready rushed this hastily-made sequel out in record-breaking time.

Directed again by Kelljan, THE RETURN OF COUNT YORGA reunites actor Robert Quarry with the role of Count Yorga, a very "toothy" vampire who suddenly and miraculously reappears on the scene at a masquerade party after having been destroyed during the climax of the first film. As with many of these low-budget efforts written and directed hastily for commercial interests rather than for its artistic style, THE RETURN OF COUNT YORGA offers its share of flaws, one of which is the vampire's sudden appearance. Yorga's resurrection is never explained.

Once again Yorga spreads terror among the youth of California, this time in San Francisco, with the aide of his vampirized female harem. The vampires' central source of nourishment comes from a nearby orphanage, their new, easily accessible feeding ground.

Eventually, Yorga, the master vampire is destroyed, this time with a silver-tipped dagger by second-time hero Roger Perry. But, still, the vampires win again!

THE RETURN OF COUNT YORGA is studded with surprise performers, such as the late, great George Macready, father of this film's producer. Macready also had a small part in the original "*Yorga*" film. Even actress Mariette Hartley is on hand; she plays the vampire's victim.

Quarry went on to star opposite Vincent Price and Peter Cushing in both DR. PHIBES RISES AGAIN in MADHOUSE, while Kelljan went on to direct SCREAM BLACULA, SCREAM, a sequel to BLACULA.

Another "*Yorga*" sequel was announced, but instead, Quarry went on to play another cinematic vampire in THE DEATHMASTER (1972), also for AIP.

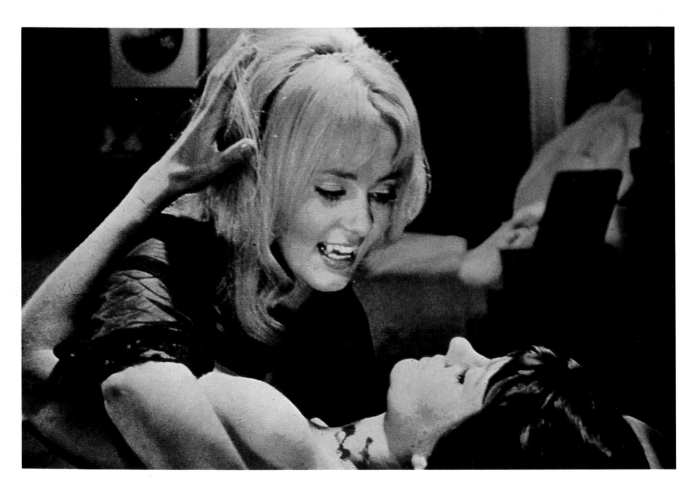

As the vampire Mircalla, Yutte Stensgaard drains the blood of her female lover in Hammer's graphic vampire film LUST FOR A VAMPIRE (1971).

Bloodthirsty vampire Count Mitterhouse (Robert Tayman)
bares his fangs in Hammer's VAMPIRE CIRCUS (1971).

Ingrid Pitt as Countess Elizabeth Bathory shows her true
colors in COUNTESS DRACULA (1971).

LUST FOR A VAMPIRE

1971; Hammer Films (Great Britain) (Color); Producer: Harry Fine; Director: Jimmy Sangster; Screenplay: Tudor Gates from characters created by Sheridan le Fanu; Camera: David Muir.

Originally, this film was intended to star Peter Cushing under Terence Fisher's direction. However, Cushing bowed out to star in another film and Fisher was unavailable due to previous commitments. Instead, Jimmy Sangster took on the film's direction. As a result the final film is a below average Hammer vampire vehicle and an inconsistent and unnecessary sequel to Hammer's THE VAMPIRE LOVERS (1970). In addition, the film has no relation whatsoever to the Sheridan le Fanu novel and was obviously produced with only box office returns in mind. Hammer's apathy in adapting a story faithful to the original film source is discouraging, but then again, let us remember that this is a sequel to a film and should not be judged along the same merits of its original. A sequel does not necessarily have to offer the same basic premise as its original. In fact, a good sequel can actually captivate its audience with fresh new characters and events, as this film tries but fails so miserably at doing.

Replacing Ingrid Pitt as Mircalla is Yutte Stensgaard, who is unconvincing as the vampire figure. Actor Ralph Bates is equally poor in the role originally intended for Cushing. The weak premise, written by Tudor Gates, has Mircalla revived by Count Karnstein (played by Mike Raven). She is enrolled into an all girl's school near the castle where she seduces equally beautiful young virgins with lesbian sex and then turns them into female "bloodsuckers." She even destroys the man who loves her. During the film's climax, Mircalla is impaled by a burning rafter and sentenced to eternal death forever.

LUST FOR A VAMPIRE was Hammer's attempt to put sex back into the genre, and using the word LUST in the title was a good start. The film uses generous amounts of blood and unnecessary violence to achieve it's mood and does not hold up nearly as well as the original film. Finally, Bates, who is usually a adequate horror actor, is unfortunately wasted in this film.

In order to get an R-rating, this feeble exploitation film had to be cut.

COUNTESS DRACULA

1971; Hammer Films (Great Britain) (Color); Producer: Alexander Paal; Director: Peter Sasdy; Screenwriter: Jeremy Paul; Camera: Ken Talbot.

Fans of horror and vampire movies were not pleased with this flat and sadistic story about a Hungarian countess who bathed in the blood of virgin girls.

In the film, which has nothing to do with Dracula, Ingrid Pitt (the sexy female vampire of VAMPIRE LOVERS and THE HOUSE THAT DRIPPED BLOOD) portrays the legendary Hungarian Countess Elizabeth Bathory. As legend has it, Countess Bathory would bath herself in the blood of young virgin girls to restore her youthful appearance; thus she was given the nickname Countess Dracula. Nigel Green plays a police captain who turns a blind eye to the numerous nude corpses that continue to turn up in the nearby village.

Peter Sasdy's version of the story of Countess Elizabeth Bathory is an excellent, well-mounted dramatic piece, however, the film is unavoidably boring to the connoisseur of horror movies and totally void of Hammer's usual graphic violence and action. If anything, COUNTESS DRACULA is more of a curiosity piece.

BLACULA

1971; AIP (Color); Producer: Joseph T. Naar; Director: William Crain; Screenwriters: Joan Torres & Raymond Koenig & William Marshall (uncredited); Camera: John Stevens.

Dracula makes but a brief appearance in this independent film that concerns itself primarily with Prince Mamuwalde (played superbly by William Marshall). The African prince becomes the title character when he is bitten by Count Dracula himself. Though the character of Dracula is only given a brief moment, actor Charles Macaulay delivers an incredible and lasting characterization that is both memorable and promising. Macaulay delivers one highly dramatic performance as the infamous vampire, a characterization that would have given Hammer a run for its money had AIP pursued the Count's further adventures with this actor in the lead.

In any event, BLACULA, despite its commercial title, intelligently succeeds in combining the familiar Dracula legend with the creation of a new vampire terror. The subplot about slavery issues was added to the script by William Marshall, who insisted that this film should deliver a message about African slavery and current bigotry issues that exist in contemporary America against African Americans.

In 1815, the Prince and his wife Luva (Vonette McGee) journey to Castle Dracula to influence the Count to place an embargo on the slave trade. Their plans are thwarted when the bigoted Count Dracula (Macaulay) places a curse on the Prince and seals him in a coffin for one hundred and fifty years. As history has it, Dracula is eventually destroyed for being the ruthless and savage tyrant that he is, but the Prince lives on, sealed in Dracula's coffin for a century and a half, until one day, two gay interior decorators unseal the coffin and release the brutal vampire onto modern society.

The Negro vampire plagues the city of modern-day Los Angeles until he happens across a beautiful reincarnation of his long-dead Princess Luva (also played by McGee). But poor Blacula looses his refound Princess at the mercy of vampire hunters, destroying his only reason to live. As the vampire hunters close in on him, Blacula both voluntarily and courageously exposes himself to the sun's lethal rays, which reduce him to dust forever- so we think?

BLACULA is a quite impressive but dated vampire film that fans will still enjoy and appreciate. With the exception of the opening modern-day scenes involving the two gay interior decorators, the film is taken quite seriously by its director.

This film is part of a series of American-made black exploitation films made during the early 1970's, but BLACULA is perhaps the best of these vehicles and worth taking a look at. BLACULA is "sequeled" by SCREAM BLACULA, SCREAM, an inferior effort that lacks the same punch that this original effort delivers. There is also another "black" vampire

movie made in 1973 entitled GANJA AND HESS, and of course, let us not forget BLACKENSTEIN!

VAMPIRE CIRCUS
1971; Hammer Films/Rank (Great Britain) (Color); Producer: Wilbur Stark; Director: Robert Young; Screenwriter: Judson Kinberg from a story by George Baxt and Wilbur Stark; Camera: Moray Grant.

Originally playing on a double-bill with Hammer's COUNTESS DRACULA, VAMPIRE CIRCUS is one of Hammer's more exciting and original vampire efforts from the 1970's.

The film features a new vampire named Count Mitterhouse (Robert Tayman), who has fangs the size of a King Cobra! The vampire terrorizes the Serbian countryside, draining the blood of innocent children. The villagers eventually storm the vampire's castle and drive a wooden stake through the savage beast's heart. But several months later, strange things begin to occur when Mitterhouse's cousin Emil (played by Anthony Corlan) arrives into town. Emil leads a circus of freaks and oddities and it is he who revives his vampiric cousin to plague the countryside once more.

VAMPIRE CIRCUS is definitely Hammer's goriest vampire film, next to LUST FOR A VAMPIRE. The premise is a bit unusual, bit it works

William Marshall as the negro vampire Prince Mamuwalde perishes at the mercy of the sun in BLACULA (1971).

very well and still manages to hold up rather well by today's standards.

Director Robert Young filmed many erotic, sensual and violent scenes that were unfortunately edited by American censors, which is unfortunate.

Fans of Hammer films, Hammer vampire films in particular, will not want to miss this one! Highly recommended.

VAMPIRE MEN OF THE LOST PLANET
1971; Independent-International (Philippines/U.S.) (Color); Producer & Director: Al Adamson; Screenwriter: Sue McNair; Camera: Vilmos Zsigmond.

Actor John Carradine strikes again with another *"Academy Award-winning"* performance, this time around in this low budget Al Adamson-produced and directed vehicle. Adamson was also responsible for BLOOD OF DRACULA'S CASTLE (1969), BLOOD OF GHASTLY HORROR (1971) and DRACULA VS. FRANKENSTEIN (1972), to name only a few of the many horror exploitation films made by this filmmaker.

In the film, a scientist (Carradine) traces an epidemic of vampire attacks on Earth to a strange planet with the aide of stock footage from other low budget films. We eventually discover that vampirism, as we know it, originated in outer space. John Carradine leads an expedition into space to investigate the source of vampirism (at least in the American version of this film).

This atrocity includes footage from a B&W Filipino movie featuring snake men and unconvincing vampire women with incredibly long fangs. Adamson hired Carradine, Vicki Volante and Robert Dix to film new American footage around the horrible stock footage. Adamson even paid narrator Theodore Gottlieb to help make sense of things. Is it possible that writer Susan McNair saw PLANET OF THE VAMPIRES before writing this film?

In any event, the plot crams eighty-five minutes of neck bites, spear stabbings, cannibalism and crawfish monsters with cheap sets, poor photography and utterly horrendous performances. This bomb of a film is also known as HORROR OF THE BLOOD MONSTERS, HORROR CREATURES OF A PREHISTORIC PLANET, CREATURES OF THE PREHISTORIC PLANET and SPACE MISSION OF THE LOST PLANET.

THE VELVET VAMPIRE
1971; New World (Color); Producer: Charles S. Swartz; Director: Stephanie Rothman; Screenwriters: Maurice Jules, Charles S. Swartz & Stephanie Rothman.

Lesbianism in vampire movies is nothing new to cinema. Traces of such sensual sexuality can be found in vampire films that date back as early as the 1930's with films as Carl Dreyer's VAMPYR and even the Universal film DRACULA'S DAUGHTER. Roger Vadim did it in 1960 with his film BLOOD AND ROSES and Hammer did it with THE VAMPIRE LOVERS, LUST FOR A VAMPIRE and TWINS OF EVIL. And of course, we cannot forget DAUGHTERS OF DARKNESS.

In THE VELVET VAMPIRE, the female vampire of this film (played by Celeste Yarnell) has no quarrels about drinking male blood, however, it is quite obvious that she prefers women for sex. It is the nature of her sexuality.

This laughable film directed by Stephanie Rothman, features actress Yarnell as a very striking Diane Le Fanu (in homage to writer Sheridan le Fanu), a relative of the Karnsteins, who invites a young married couple (Sherry Miles and Michael Blodgett) stranded in the Mojave desert into her desert home. Little do they know, their hostess is a vampire with plans of seducing and then killing each of them. Hippies, armed with crosses and holy water save the day.

The bisexual elements are soft-core and the transfer of the vampire legend is handled stylishly by the film's director.

Adverts for THE VELVET VAMPIRE promised *"Climax after climax of terror and desire!"* The film was re-released under the ludicrous title, CEMETERY GIRLS.

LET'S SCARE JESSICA TO DEATH
1971; Paramount (Color); Producers: Charles B. Moss & William Badalto; Director: John Hancock; Screenwriters: Norman Jonas & Ralph Rose; Camera: Bob Baldwin.

Produced on a low budget but made very effectively, LET'S SCARE JESSICA TO DEATH has got to be one of the more subtle tales of vampirism produced during its era.

Zohra Lampert plays a young woman recovering from a breakdown in a quiet village where she is beset by a Victorian vampire girl (played by Gretchen Corbett), who drowned in a near-by lake.

LET'S SCARE JESSICA TO DEATH, with its subtle sensitivity and uneasy supernaturalistic events, is a very scary but shamefully underrated film.

Hancock would go on to work in various genre films, including a job to re-direct the film WOLFEN and a brief job on the film JAWS 2 (Hancock was contracted to direct JAWS 2, but fired when he tried to steer away from Steven Spielberg's roller-coaster formula and duplicate the stylish lyricism of JESSICA).

THE VAMPIRE HAPPENING
1971; Acquila Films (W. Germany) (Color); Producer: Pier A. Caminneci; Director: Freddie Francis; Screenwriter: August Rieger; Camera: Gerard Vandenberg.

Obviously inspired by Roman Polanski's FEARLESS VAMPIRE KILLERS, this cute German-made vampire film is flawed only by its awful English dubbing. Still, some of the jokes remain in tact despite the translation.

The film takes place in Transylvania 1971, where Dracula still reigns supreme. In the role of the infamous Count is actor Ferdy Mayne (the vampire of FEARLESS VAMPIRE KILLERS), who does not make his lavish entrance on his "bat-copter" until the last quarter of this film. In the dubbed version, Mayne's voice comes across as a Bela Lugosi imitation, and as a result, the film projects itself as being too campy for its own good. But then again, THE VAMPIRE HAPPENING is a comedy, straight from its very beginning to its final moments.

In one scene, there is a radio broadcast from Radio Transylvania that delivers the following announcement: "........*A late bulletin. The blood bank is low. Will all donors report to the clinic of Dr. Frankenstein. Our music continues with 'Full Moon and Empty Days'!*" This is the type of humor to expect from this film; just plain old-fashion, borderline-pornographic fun, loaded with an enormous amount of beautiful topless female vampires, sensual sex scenes, and a generous amount of blood. It's all very sleazy in a 1970'ish kind of way.

This film, loaded with sex-starved monks, busty female vampires, sex orgies and mysterious plot twists, is worth a good laugh. In all honesty though, only fans of vampire and horror films will appreciate the its humor.

CASE OF THE FULL MOON MURDERS
1971; Newport (Color); Producer & Director: Sean Cunningham; Screenwriters: Bud Talbot & Jerry Hayling.

Here's one for horror trivia buffs, an early film produced and directed by the maker of FRIDAY THE 13TH, THE LAST HOUSE ON THE LEFT and A STRANGER IS WATCHING. Not many people know about this picture from Mr. Cunningham.

The story is told in a Dragnet-style and is a parody of sexploitation films in which investigators track down a vampire girl who kills her victims through oral sex. Ouch!

Originally, this feature was released as a hard-core sex "nuddie" with an X-Rating, but later re-released with an R-Rating.

DAUGHTERS OF DARKNESS
1971; Gemini (Belgium/France/Italy/W. Germany) (Color); Producers: Alan Guilleaume & Paul Collett; Director: Harry Kumel; Screenwriters: Harry Kumel & Pierre Drouot, based on the novel *Countess Dracula* by Michael Perry; Camera: Eddy Van der Enden.

Considered to be a visually beautiful and highly erotic vampire movie by film critics, DAUGHTERS OF DARKNESS is undoubtedly one of the best of its kind to deal with lesbianism and the legend of Countess Elisabeth Bathory. It is a class act production, a piece of cinematic art that, on an occasion, a vampire film will rise to. So few films, especially horror films, can rise above the clutter of commercial vehicles that litter the genre to reach the artistic level of excellence that this film has succeeded in reaching.

Filmed in Belgium by director Harry Kumel, DAUGHTERS OF DARKNESS is based on the novel *Countess Dracula* by Michael Parry. The film tells how Countess Elisabeth Bathory (Delphine Seyrig) has managed to survive into the 1970's as an undead vampire, with her lover/companion Ilona (Andrea Rau). Together, the two "vamps" check into a luxurious, seaside European hotel where a handsome sadist named Stefan (played by John Karlen) and his newlywed wife Valerie (Daniele Ouimet) have also just arrived.

Elisabeth's character is one who must have control over her lover. Stefan, an animal quite similar in nature to Elisabeth, also desires control over his wife, but the poor man has other problems far deeper than being the dominant lover. One night at the hotel, after several encounters with the vampires, Stefan beats and degrades his wife Valerie, who races off in pain and disgust to a nearby train station to escape her husband forever. Elisabeth follows in hot pursuit and warns that Stefan's only interest is to gain complete and utter control over her. Of course, as the viewer looking in, we also know that Elisabeth has ill motives, as she desires the same control as does Stefan; only with her, the vampire's manipulation goes far deeper into the soul than that of the mortal man. To achieve her goal, which is to win the mortal women's soul, Elisabeth orchestrates a plan to turn Valerie against Stefan by working her wicked and evil way into Valerie's good graces. Meanwhile, while Elisabeth is working out her own movie, Ilona is implementing part two of Elisabeth's sinister plan to win Valerie over from her husband's clutches. Ilona enters Stefan's room and seduces the handsome young stud into having sex. However, an accident occurs that leaves Ilona dead at the hands of Stefan. Just then, Elisabeth returns to the hotel with Valerie as part of her devious plan to reveal Stefan's infidelity, but instead, the two women encounter the dead body of Ilona. Naturally, Elisabeth is mortified. They then make Stefan bury the corpse on the beach and the next day they kill him by slashing his wrist and slowly draining his blood.

In an attempt to flee the crime scene, Elisabeth and Valerie take off in a car and engage in a frantic speed race to beat the rising sun, during which the two women loose control of the car and crash. Elisabeth is hurled into a tree branch that impales her chest, thus ending her bloody reign of terror forever.

DAUGHTERS OF DARKNESS, though confusing in its meaning, attempts to deliver the profound message that relationships, whether heterosexual or homosexual, whether human or vampire, are basically always about control. There is no love. Love is but a meaningless novelty that wears off. What is left is one who either controls or is controlled.

CAPTAIN KRONOS: VAMPIRE HUNTER

1972; Hammer Films/ Paramount (Great Britain) (Color); Producers: Albert Fennell & Brian Clemens; Director & Screenwriter: Brian Clemens; Camera: Ian Wilson.

Imagine a Nineteenth Century swashbuckler who specializes in slaying vampires! In this color film written and directed by Brian Clemens, Captain Kronos (Horst Janson) is such a swashbuckler who sword fights a vampire lord whose identity remains unknown until the film's climax. Together with his hunchback assistant Professor Grost (John Carson), they battle vampires galore, regardless of what form they come in. But these vampires are not your usual species. Instead, they only drink blood as an appetizer to the main course, which is their victim's youth. These vampires cannot be killed or repelled by crosses, bullets, running water, garlic or wooden stakes. In fact, they can even walk around in the daylight. For this film, Clemens, who wrote the original story, made it so that the original folklore is completely twisted around, making it virtually impossible to destroy these creatures, thus creating a fresh new sense of menace and horror to wet our appetites for original material. Eventually, though, Kronos defeats the vampire by impaling him with a sword driven straight through the heart. Together, the vampire and his mistress (Wanda Ventham) age into

withered corpses after being slain.

What makes CAPTAIN KRONOS: VAMPIRE KILLER fresh and original is that it pokes fun at the traditional cliches established by earlier vampire movies, primarily the straight-laced Hammer/Dracula films. The film provides a larger-than-life hero cast against a middle European backdrop of swashbuckling heroics and dynamic adventure, making this film the freshest and most entertaining vampire movie since Roman Polanski's THE FEARLESS VAMPIRE KILLERS.

A sequel was announced by Hammer, but the film never made it pass the post-production stages. Today we have BUFFY- THE VAMPIRE SLAYER (1992), which is nothing more than a glorified *Ninja Turtle-ish*" version of this classic Hammer film.

THE DEATHMASTER
1972; AIP/RF Productions (Color); Producer: Fred Sadoff; Director: Ray Danton; Screenwriter: R.L. Grove.

Originally announced as KHORDA, this film stars actor Robert Quarry (of COUNT YORGA fame) as a fully-fanged, long-haired hippie vampire who is washed onto the California coast to become a guru for many young hippies. The low budget feature was Quarry's last vampire film and a box office failure for AIP.

Originally, THE DEATHMASTER was intended to be the third "Yorga" film from AIP. In fact, elements from the initial screen treatment found its way into this film, which is why this film offers many similarities to the "Yorga" films. Like both COUNT YORGA-VAMPIRE and THE RETURN OF COUNT YORGA, Quarry's vampire in THE DEATHMASTER terrorizes modern California. However, by this point, the theme of a Gothic-style vampire in a modern setting had become tired completely over-exhausted.

VIRGINS AND VAMPIRES
1972; Box Office International (France) (Color); Producer: Sam Selsky; Director: Jean Rollin.

The 1970's is well known for its many sexploitation vampire films. VIRGINS AND VAMPIRES is another such film, the fourth in a series that included THE VAMPIRE'S RAPE, THE NAKED VAMPIRE and THE VAMPIRE'S

Robert Quarry as the guru-hippie vampire perishes in AIP's low-budget vampire film THE DEATHMASTER (1972).

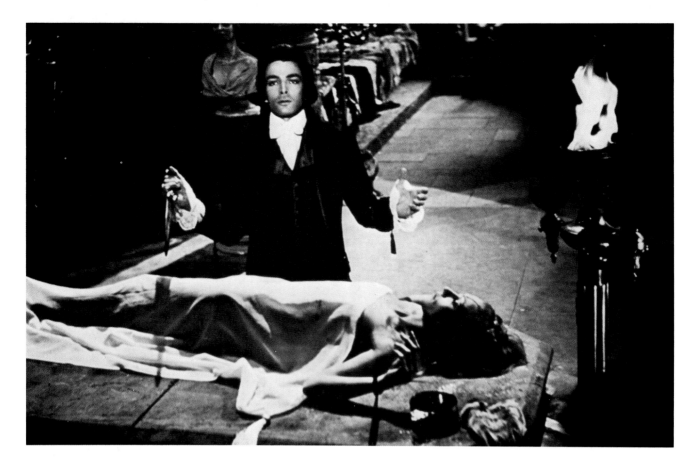

THRILL.

In this X-rated sex feature, two virgin girls are held captive by the vampire king in his castle. One scene shows the vampire as a bat biting the girls between their legs! Ouch!

THE GREAT LOVE OF COUNT DRACULA
1972; Janus/Cinema Shares (Spain) (Color); Producer: F. Laura Polop; Director: Javier Aguirre; Screenwriters: Jacinto Molina & Javier Aguirre.

Actor Paul Naschy returned to the Spanish horror cinema to star as Count Dracula himself.

In this film, co-written by Naschy (as Jacinto Molina), Count Dracula disguises himself as Dr. Wendell to run a nursing home, where he finds his source of nourishment. Dracula makes the fatal mistake of falling in love with a mortal woman (his great love). The Count actually becomes emotionally involved, and rather than endangering her life with his uncontrollable desire for human blood as well as turning her into one of the "undead," the vampire drives a wooden stake through his own heart.

Naschy's portrayal of a sympathetic vampire- a saddened victim of his own curse which forces him to kill, is a fascinating variation on the traditional Dracula theme. For once, Dracula dies a hero and not as a villain. Still, the film is very basic and tame for Spanish horror.

THE GREAT LOVE OF COUNT DRACULA is also known as both COUNT DRACULA'S GREAT LOVE and VAMPIRE PLAYGIRLS.

TWINS OF EVIL
1972; Hammer Films/Universal (Great Britain) (Color); Producer: Harry Fine & Michael Style; Director: John Hugh; Screenwriter: Tudor Gates; Camera: Dick Bush.

In his third and final installment to Hammer's "Carmilla" series, screenwriter Tudor Gates effectively combines the Sheridan le Fanu tale with tales of witch hunting and burning-at-the-stake, changing what could have been another dull and boring rehashing of the le Fanu story into a rather interesting picture.

Mircalla (now played by Katya Keith) is inadvertently revived by the newest of the Karnstein descendants, the decadent and wicked Count Karnstein (Damien

Count Karnstein (Damien Thomas) attempts to sacrifice a female victim in an attempt to summon Satan in Hammer's TWINS OF EVIL (1972).

103

Thomas), in his attempt to summon Satan. Identical twins Maria and Frieda Gelhourn (Madeline and Mary Collinson) are the first to fall prey to the vampire, but their uncle, Gustav Weil (played by Peter Cushing), leader of a witch-hunting group called the Brotherhood, arrives on the scene in time to decapitate Mircalla and to drive a wooden stake through her heart. Weil is destroyed when Count Karnstein hacks him to bits with an axe.

TWINS OF EVIL offers strong atmosphere, good sets and some great camera work by Dick Bush. It is quite evident that Hammer executives invested more into this production, more so than with its two predecessors- VAMPIRE LOVERS and LUST FOR A VAMPIRE. Cushing is exceptionally great, repeating his role from VAMPIRE LOVERS, and Damien Thomas is convincing as the demon worshiper-turned-vampire.

GRAVE OF THE VAMPIRE
1972; Pyramid (Color); Producer: Daniel Cady; Director: John Hayes; Screenwriters: John Patrick Hayes & David Chase.
GRAVE OF THE VAMPIRE is a bit of an unusual and grim vampire tale in which a woman is raped by Count Dracula (Michael Pataki, who would later star in DRACULA'S DOG) in an open grave. She later has a baby who drinks her blood out of a bottle. The mother eventually dies and the baby grows up to become actor William Smith.

Now as an adult vampire, Smith sets out to kill his father, who is now teaching at a college (can you believe?). Of course, there is romance in this film, as Smith falls in love with a neighbor who wants to become one of the undead along with him. The vampire, reluctant to make her a creature of the night, must restrain his urges.

The film is also known as SEED OF TERROR.

THE FEMALE BUTCHER
1972; Film ventures (Italy/Spain) (Color); Producer: Jose Maria Gonzalez Sinde; Director: Jorge Grau; Screenwriters: Juan Tabar & Sandro Contenenza.
Suspiciously made immediately following the release of Hammer's COUNTESS DRACULA, THE FEMALE BUTCHER tells how the evil Countess Elizabeth Bathory (played by Lucia Bose) butchered 610 nubile virgins in her time.

This rather obscure offering is also known as BLOOD CEREMONY and THE LEGEND OF BLOOD CASTLE.

THE DAUGHTER OF DRACULA
1972; Comptoir (Spain/France/Portuguese) (Color); Director & Screenwriter: Jesus Franco.
Director Jesus Franco strikes again with this Spanish, French, Portuguese co-production.
DAUGHTERS OF DARKNESS is another variation of the highly popular "Carmilla" legend in which actress Britt Nichols portrays the modern-day vampire while actor Howard Vernon plays Count Karnstein. The film offers good atmospheric photography and is actually less tedious than both BLOOD AND ROSES (1960) and TERROR IN THE CRYPT (1970), two superior efforts from different filmmakers.

VOODOO HEARTBEAT
1972; Compass/TWI (Color); Producer: Ray Molina; Director & Screenwriter: Charles Nizet.
Horrible, horrible film in which producer Ray Molina stars as a man who periodically transforms into a crazed bloodsucker with fangs.
In the film, which attempts to colorize those highly melodramatic "B" films from the 1950's in which humans were turned into biologically created

Michael Pataki as Count Dracula in GRAVE OF THE VAMPIRE (1972).

monsters - films such as I WAS A TEENAGE WEREWOLF and THE HIDEOUS SUN DEMON, to name only a few, Molina's pseudo-vampire runs around in broad daylight with two silly-looking elongated snake-like fangs protruding from his mouth. Molina is turned into a vampire when he consumes what appears to be a serum of eternal youth.

This unintentionally funny film should be shown on the next edition of *Mystery Science Theater 2000* where it will find some kind of appreciation through laughter.

THE SCREAMING DEAD
1972; Fenix (Spain) (Color); Director: Jesus Franco.

By now, it should be very obvious that Jesus Franco was Spain's leading horror filmmaker. Franco has made more horror films than Terence Fisher and George Romero combined. Franco has made nearly 160 films to date, his next, supposedly entitled JUNGLE OF FEAR, is an adventure film with horror elements.

THE SCREAMING DEAD is yet another Spanish-made Dracula epic in which Dr. Seward drives a silver spike into Dracula's heart during the opening reel. The fiend turns into a large bat and dies.

Several years later, Dr. Frankenstein revives the vampire by splattering the blood of an innocent girl on his ashes. The mad scientist has plans of enslaving the vampire (played by Howard Vernon of DAUGHTER OF DRACULA and SUCCUBUS). The green-faced Count Dracula begins draining the blood of locals until a vengeful gypsy woman sends a werewolf to kill the fiend. As guessed, the film ends in a nasty free-for-all battle, Franco-style. THE SCREAMING DEAD, like many other Spanish and Mexican made vampire films, is also known as DRACULA VS. FRANKENSTEIN.

DRACULA:
THE BLOODLINE CONTINUES
1972; Profilmes (Spain) (Color); Director: Leon Klimovsky.

This film is yet another bizarre variation on Stoker's Dracula figure. In this Spanish-made film, an aging Count Dracula (played by Narciso Ibanez Menta) hopes to insure a suitably vigorous heir to his ghoulish dynasty, so he invites his pregnant niece to his castle and exchanges her evening wine with fresh blood to give the unborn a taste of life among the undead.

We later discover during this confusing film that the Dracula family has stooped to incest to keep the bloodline alive. Therefore, the unborn baby is the new hope for keeping the Dracula legacy alive.

Totally repulsed, the woman (Tina Saenz) kills her own child and stakes the entire family to death (who's the real monster here?). In a struggle with one of Dracula's servants, she inadvertently trips over her supposedly dead child. The mother falls, knocks herself unconscious and begins to bleed. Next we see the child sucking on her blood! Apparently, the blood consumed by the vampire is enough to sustain the dying child.

Although the Lazarus Kaplan script sets the film in a contemporary setting, DRACULA: THE BLOODLINE CONTINUES offers pleasing Gothic atmosphere, stylish dream sequences, and an abundance of sex, nudity and gore. The film is better known as THE SAGA OF THE DRACULAS.

SCREAM BLACULA, SCREAM
1972; AIP (Color); Producer: Joseph T. Naar; Director: Bob Kelljan; Screenwriters: Joan Torres, Raymond Koenig & Maurice Jules.

SCREAM BLACULA, SCREAM is not the first film to combine voodoo and witchcraft with

Ray Molina as the blood crazed vampire of VOODOO HEARTBEAT (1972).

vampirism. The film is a very poor sequel to a relatively good vampire film (BLACULA), combining vampirism and voodooism.

The film tells how a high priest (Richard Lawson) performs a voodoo ritual that inadvertently revives Prince Mamuwalde (Blacula- played again by William Marshall, who really had very little to do with the writing of this film). Now fully restored to life, Blacula and a lot of new vampires must go up against a voodoo priestess (played by Pamela Grier). The vampire is eventually destroyed when a wooden stake is driven through a voodoo doll replica of himself.

SCREAM BLACULA SCREAM was far from being as successful as the original film, and it is hard to believe that the guys who made the highly profitable "Count Yorga" films were also involved with this film. Actor William Marshall once accounted the film's failure to its weak and confusing script.

THE BODY BENEATH
1972; Nova International (Color); Producer/ Director & Screenwriter: Andy Milligan

Originally filmed in the graveyards of England in 16mm by schlock-master filmmaker Andy Milligan, this awful low budget fiasco tells how a modern-day vampire, who has managed to survive for many years by consuming the blood of innocent victims, preys upon a poor British family. In the film, the vampire eventually comes across Dracula's Carfax Abbey.

The commercial failure of THE BODY BENEATH was obviously connected to its extremely low production values. A print of this film is available on a VHS format. Prior to this film, Milligan produced, directed and wrote for Nova International a low budget (of course) effort entitled GURU, THE MAD MONK (1971) in which a female vampiress and her guru torture prisoners on the island of Mortavia, which was actually the island of Manhattan.

DEATHDREAM
1972; Europix (Canada) (Color); Producer & Director: Bob Clark; Screenwriter: Alan Ormsby.

From the makers of CHILDREN SHOULDN'T PLAY WITH DEAD THINGS (Ormsby wrote and Clark produced and directed), comes this rather obscure reworking of THE MONKEY'S PAW, featuring the make-up of Tom Savini, one of the

genre's leading make-up technicians today.

Richard Backus plays a soldier who dies in Vietnam. His mother misses him dearly and wishes her son back to life. Backus returns, but as a bloodthirsty corpse who uses a syringe to obtain nourishment.

DRACULA VS. FRANKENSTEIN
1972; Independent-International (Color); Producer & Director: Al Adamson; Screenwriters: William Pugsley & Samuel M. Sherman.

This atrocity is Al Adamson's most famous horror film; a cult classic that only die-hard fans of horror movies will appreciate, especially aficionados of the independent, low budget sector. Here you have the mad scientist, Dracula, The Frankenstein Monster, the grotesque axe killer and the dwarf midget all wrapped into one picture that will embarrass the pants off of anyone.

Originally planned for production under the title BLOOD OF FRANKENSTEIN, this mundane low budget horror film eventually delivers the inevitable and highly publicized confrontation between the screen's most infamous monsters- Count Dracula and the Frankenstein Monster, which is more than many films can claim, especially all those Mexican and Spanish-made monster movies that misleadingly sported the title: *Dracula Vs. Frankenstein*!

During production, the film underwent numerous and spontaneous changes. Neither the cast nor the filmmakers themselves had any idea as to where this film was heading in terms of its script. The fact that they would actually end up with a confrontation between the two principal monsters was never even considered until halfway through the making of this film (Ah, the novelty of producing low budget independent films). Apparently, the original plot was simply going nowhere and producer Al Adamson came up with the idea of staging a confrontation between the two monsters to actually beef up interest in this otherwise dull film. I remember viewing this movie for the very first time at the local drive-in. Without the "hint" of the title to give the film's climatic confrontation away, a first-time viewer as myself would have never guessed that such a monstrous battle would have actually occurred during the climax. The battle between Dracula (played by Zandor Vorkov) and the hideous Frankenstein Monster (played by John Bloom) is by far the film's

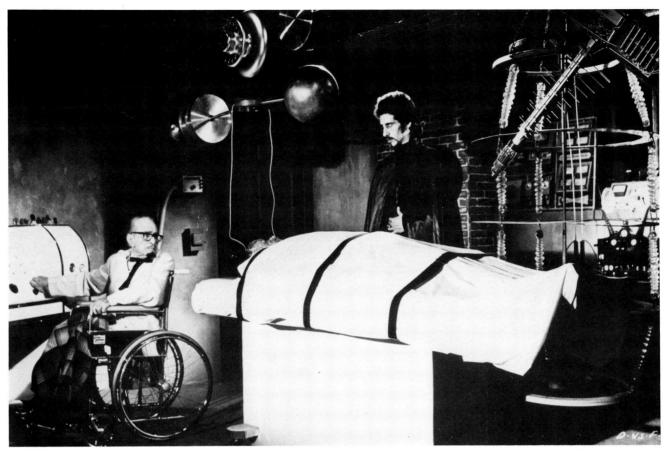

Count Dracula (Zandor Vorkov) and Dr. Frankenstein (J. Carrol Naish) attempt to revive the Frankenstein monster in DRACULA VS. FRANKENSTEIN (1972).

only high point, but it too, is quite laughable today. The entire plot is totally ludicrous, and the performances are unintentionally funny.

Count Dracula wishes to revive the dormant Frankenstein Monster. To do this, he takes the monster's body to an amusement park's demented operator, Dr. Durea (played by J. Carrol Naish), who is actually descendant of the infamous Dr. Frankenstein. Of course, Dracula knows this. Under Dracula's instructions, the scientist devises a serum from the stolen blood of young sexy females axed to death and then decapitated by Durea's servants Groton and Grabo (played by Lon Chaney, Jr. and Angelo Rossito). The serum enables the doctor to revive the monster to its full force. Dracula also has hopes that the serum will enable him to endure the sunlight.

Total mayhem follows as the police begin to close

in on the murderers. Dr. Durea is beheaded in his own Chamber of Horrors, and Groton is shot to death by the police as they attempt to escape. In all the confusion, Dracula uses the Frankenstein Monster to abduct his love interest (played by Regina Carrol) and together they escape to a nearby chapel where the vampire's coffin is secretly hidden. Once there, the vampire begins a ritual that will make the heroine a creature of the night like himself. However, the Frankenstein Monster has also fallen in love with the young girl, and when the monster realizes that the helpless young girl is about to perish at the touch of the vampire's fangs, the Frankenstein Monster attacks Dracula, and a fierce battle between the two monsters ensues. Dracula literally rips the infamous Frankenstein Monster to pieces, leaving him as severed body parts throughout the wooded countryside. Suddenly Dracula realizes that the battle has taken him into the morning hours. Frantically, the vampire races through the woods to his coffin, but the sun reduces him into a rotted corpse just as he comes upon his coffin located just outside the church.

It is a shame to see actors Lon Chaney, Jr. and J. Carroll Naish reduced to such pitiful roles. Naish was forced to act in a wheel chair; the actor died before the film could be released. The ridiculous make-up effects for both Dracula and the rotted Frankenstein Monster are not passable, and really, this entire amateurish production, with its many exploitation devices, meaningless dialogue and pitiful performances, is as bad a film as it is good- meaning, if anything, DRACULA VS. FRANKENSTEIN is good entertainment worthy of a laugh.

THE NIGHT STALKER
1972; TV/Dan Curtis Productions (Color); Producer: Dan Curtis; Director: John Moxley; Screenwriter: Richard Matheson from a story by Jeff Rice.

Producer Dan Curtis made television history way back in 1972 when he brought to life Barnabas Collins in *Dark Shadows*. He also made history with this television feature pilot THE NIGHT STALKER. The film made history when over seventy-five million viewers tuned in the night this film premiered on television.

Actor Darren McGavin plays investigative reporter Carl Kolchack, who follows a series of vampire-related murders in modern-day Las Vegas. Naturally, the police do not believe Kolchack's theory of vampirism, so he sets off on his own to locate the vampire's lair. Actor Barry Atwater plays the very menacing and cunning vampire Janos Skorzeny. In the film, Kolchack does manage to drive a wooden stake through the vicious beast's heart, but not until some very hair-raising moments that are unusually good for a made-for-television film.

The follow-up pilot film to THE NIGHT STALKER is THE NIGHT STRANGLER (1973), also made for television. In this film Kolchack battles a centuries-old alchemist (played by Richard Anderson) who strangles women and drains their blood. The sequel is also directed by Dan Curtis.

THE NORLISS TAPES
1973; TV/NBC (Color); Producer & Director: Dan Curtis; Screenwriter: William F. Nolan.

While Dan Curtis was trying to launch *The Night*

Darren McGavin wards off vampire Barry Atwater in Dan Curtis' television film THE NIGHTSTALKER (1972).

Count Dracula (Christopher Lee) falls to the mercy of a wooden stake during the cunclusion of THE SATANIC RITES OF DRACULA (1973).

Stalker as a series at ABC with his two feature pilots THE NIGHT STALKER and THE NIGHT STRANGLER, the producer also tried to launch a similar series over at NBC with this pilot film, which has since been long forgotten and invisible. As history has it, ABC agreed to launch the highly successful series *The Night Stalker*, which lasted one glorious season of twenty episodes in 1974, with sixty minute episodes such as "*The Werewolf*," "*The Ripper*," and "*The Vampire*" televised weekly; the latter episode was a sequel to the original movie pilot THE NIGHT STALKER, in which a female victim of the Las Vegas vampire emerges. In any event, as a result of the successful *Night Stalker* series, *The Norliss Tapes* pilot and series project went neglected.

THE NORLISS TAPES pilot film tells how an investigator named Norliss (played by Roy Thinnes) investigates rumors of an undead man who turns out to be a vampire.

THE SATANIC RITES OF DRACULA
1973; Hammer Films/Warner (Great Britain) (Color); Producer: Roy Skeggs; Director: Alan Gibson; Screenplay: Don Houghton; Camera: Brian Probyn.

Hammer began production on this film before the box-office results were in from their previous commercial failure DRACULA A.D. (1971). The studio was stuck with yet another awful Dracula outing set in modern-day London, and Warner Brothers decided not to release the film in America (their excuse was that the film was too violent). In 1979, an American distributor named Dynamite issued the film under the ridiculous title DRACULA AND HIS VAMPIRE BRIDES. The poor American marketing of this film is unfortunate because THE SATANIC RITES OF DRACULA is actually a much better film than DRACULA A.D., offering a far more interesting and original premise. To enjoy this film, one must accept it for what it really is and avoid comparing it to its more straight-laced and Gothic predecessors.

The Don Houghton screenplay depicts Count Dracula (Christopher Lee) as a larger than life Howard Hughes-like figurehead obsessed with destroying the world by some form of black plague created by a virus that only he possesses (which would virtually leave him without any victims! Who wrote this film?). Dracula assumes the guise of business tycoon D.D. Denham, an oil man who never grants interviews.

Peter Cushing returns to the role of Professor Van Helsing, who leads a crusade against the evil vampire until he is able to drive a wooden stake through his heart, again, after a fight in a burning house and cat and mouse chase around a thorn bush.

Though Christopher Lee received top billing, he is only seen briefly, and he only delivers a couple lines of dialogue.

THE SATANIC RITES OF DRACULA marked the end of the long Hammer-Dracula series that began in 1958 with HORROR OF DRACULA. In retrospect, THE SATANIC RITES OF DRACULA would not have received such a bad reception at theaters had DRACULA A.D. not failed miserably at the box office and had the film not given fans such a bad taste that lingered all those years.

THE LEGEND OF THE SEVEN GOLDEN VAMPIRES

1973-1974; Hammer/Run Run Shaw Brothers (Great Britain/Hong Kong) (Color); Producer: Don Houghton; Director: Roy Ward Baker; Screenwriter: Don Houghton; Camera: John Wilcox.

Immediately after the release of THE SATANIC RITES OF DRACULA, Hammer began production on another Dracula film intended to star both Christopher Lee and Peter Cushing. However, Lee was not very pleased with the direction his immortal character had taken, especially after the box office failures of both DRACULA A.D. and THE SATANIC RITES OF DRACULA, therefore he decided to bow out from the project, which was a shame since this film managed to maintain more of a Gothic atmosphere over the two previous films.

Hammer proceeded with production despite Lee's decision, replacing the actor with John Forbes Robertson as Dracula. The film was a co-production between Hammer and the Shaw Brothers of Hong Kong, since Warner decided not to be involved in the Dracula series after the poor box office returns generated from DRACULA A.D. One of the stipulations in the agreement between Hammer and the Shaw Brothers was that there be some kind of martial arts footage and subplot. The result was *Count Dracula Meets Kung Fu*!

The film takes place in the Orient where the legendary Seven Golden Vampires ride across the screen mounted on their demonic horses armed with swords, evil spirits and an army of mindless zombies; all of which fall under the command of one person, Count Dracula! In the film, Dracula has now taken on the physical identity of an Oriental Warlord, and under his new disguise, he deceives the people of the Orient. Meanwhile, Professor Van Helsing (Cushing) ventures to the Far East to investigate rumors of Satanic worshipping and confronts his life-long nemesis. Once again, the two foes engage in another battle, during which Dracula reveals his true physical identity to the professor.

Had Hammer invested more into this film, the outcome could have actually been more exciting.

DRACULA

1973; TV/Dan Curtis Productions (Color); Producer & Director: Dan Curtis; Screenwriter: Richard Matheson.

In this follow-up to the Dan Curtis TV movie FRANKENSTEIN, Academy-Award winning actor Jack Palance is superb but unattractive and unappealing as the very sympathetic Count Dracula in this Dan Curtis production made originally for theatrical release in Europe. The film was actually released in theaters in Europe first before airing on American television.

The film, loosely based on Bram Stoker's novel by screenwriter Richard Matheson, tells of Jonathan Harker's (Simon Ward) journey to Castle Dracula and Dracula's journey to England to claim the reincarnation of a woman (Fiona Lewis) he once loved hundreds of years ago.

The script was the first to cleverly combine the true legend of Vlad Tepes (the real life warrior who Count Dracula was originally based upon) and the Stoker novel. Matheson has eliminated many of the familiar characters featured in the Stoker novel and replaced them with new characters. However, one character that remained is Professor Van Helsing (played in this film by Nigel Davenport). In this version, Dracula is destroyed by the sun's rays in a dramatic confrontation with Van Helsing.

Although the film is considered quite talky, DRACULA received very good ratings when aired on television and is perhaps one of producer Dan Curtis' more interesting films. The premiere of DRACULA on American television was delayed by a Nixon speech announcing the resignation of Vice President Agnew. Shame on him! Didn't anyone tell Nixon that Jack Palance's DRACULA was airing that night?

GANJA AND HESS
1973; Kelly-Jordan Enterprises (Color); Producer: Chiz Schultz; Director & Screenwriter: Bill Gunn.

"......*The Devil wanted their souls! She wanted their bodies and more.....!*" read advertisements for this rather obscure, little known black exploitation horror film.

Actor Duane Jones, of NIGHT OF THE LIVING DEAD fame, returns to the genre to star as a modern vampire with visions of his native Africa. Marlene Clark becomes Jone's bride, and even director Bill Gunn has a small part in the film as a victim of the vampire.

This odd and confusing-at-times film is both "artsy" and exploitative, but interesting. One version substitutes soul music for the original haunting African music that accompanied the original print.

Also released as DOUBLE POSSESSION and BLOOD COUPLE.

CRYPT OF THE LIVING DEAD
1973; Coat Industries; (Color); Producer & Screenwriter: Lou Shaw; Director: Ray Danton.

From the director of THE DEATHMASTER and PSYCHIC KILLER, comes this rather dismal low budget effort poorly written by Lou Shaw.

The film takes place on Vampire Island where a vampire from the 13th Century is revived by an

In this scene from THE LEGEND OF THE SEVEN GOLDEN VAMPIRES (1973 - 1974), Dracula (John Forbes Robertson) takes on the identity of an oriental warlord.

Jack Palance as Count Dracula takes his bride (Fiona Lewis) in DRACULA (1973).

American engineer.

CRYPT OF THE LIVING DEAD is undoubtedly a poor excuse for a horror film. In fact, the film is so bad that it makes THE DEATHMASTER look like a classic. With Mark Damon.

THE DEVIL'S WEDDING NIGHT
1973; Dimension/AIP (Italy) (Color); Producer: Ralph Zucker; Director: Paul Solvay; Screenwriters: Ralph Zucker & Alan M. Harris.

When producer Ralph Zucker set out to make this horror film, he decided to make it appealing to everyone by making reference to just about every type of horror possible. For example, the film makes reference to the infamous Karnsteins of Sheridan le Fanu's *Carmilla*, a trip to Castle Dracula, a mysterious countess that resembles Countess Elizabeth Bathory,

a cult of Satanists- you get the point! One really never knows what type of film they are watching when under the hypnotic spell of this awful film.

Originally planned under the title COUNTESS DRACULA, THE DEVIL'S WEDDING NIGHT is Italy's answer to COUNTESS DRACULA, with actress Sara Bay in the role of Countess de Vries, who is really Countess Dracula. Bay also starred in the low budget film LADY FRANKENSTEIN (1971).

In the film actor Mark Damon portrays twin brothers Franz and Karl. Karl traces an ancient ring to Castle Karnstein in Transylvania. The ring is a long lost treasure and the most powerful amulet on Earth, the possessor of which could control the world. Karl wishes to keep such powers out of the wrong hands. His brother, on the other hand, wishes to obtain the ring; he wishes to control mankind. Franz's journey eventually leads him to Castle Dracula, where he becomes possessed by the spirit of Dracula himself. Meanwhile Karl journeys to Castle Dracula in search of his brother and instead he finds a Countess (Bathory?) named de Vries, who has a shiny set of white fangs and the prize ring of the Nibelungen. In order to gain possession of the ring, Karl is forced to battle with the Countess's vampirized bodyguard, a bald-headed fiend with fangs. Karl pins the brute against a wall with a silver spear and kills him. Next, he does away with his twin brother and takes his place in a Black Mass held by the evil Countess, who still has the ring in her possession. Eventually, the Countess is destroyed when Karl cuts off her ring hand. But there's a very confusing twist that leaves the viewer wondering, "*What*?"

SON OF DRACULA
1973; Apple Films/Cinemation (Great Britain) (Color); Producer: Ringo Starr; Director: Freddie Francis; Screenwriter: Jay Fairbanks.

Producer Ringo Starr of *Beetles* fame plays Merlin the Magician, while Harry Nilsson portrays Count Down, son of Count Dracula. Count Down is a musician who plays with a rock band in the basement of Castle Dracula.

The plot involves the offspring's discontent with replacing his father as an Overlord Of The Netherworld along with such famous monsters as the Wolfman, the Mummy, the Frankenstein Monster and other famous monsters. Dennis Price plays Professor Van Helsing.

Freddie Francis also directed the horror films THE EVIL OF FRANKENSTEIN (1964), DRACULA HAS RISEN FROM THE GRAVE (1968), and THE LEGEND OF THE WEREWOLF (1974).

BLOOD FOR DRACULA
1973-1974; Bryanston (Italy/France) (Color); Producer: Andrew Braunsberg; Director & Screenwriter: Paul Morrissey; Camera: Luigi Kuveiller.

First there was ANDY WARHOL'S FRANKENSTEIN followed by ANDY WARHOL'S DRACULA (a.k.a. BLOOD FOR DRACULA), then there was ANDY WARHOL'S BAD. Or was Warhol's FRANKENSTEIN before DRACULA? In any event, you will either like this gory and graphic film adaptation of Bram Stoker's novel from the "*Campbell Soup Man*" .....or you will hate it!

Directed by Paul Morrissey for the late Andy Warhol's underground film company, BLOOD FOR DRACULA stars actor Udo Keir as Count Dracula. The Paul Morrissey script introduces the concept that

Dracula can only stomach the blood of virgins, male or female.

Dracula is dying from a lack of virgin blood, simply because there aren't enough virgins in Transylvania. The Count decides to flee his country for Italy, the land of purity and Catholicism. The nobleman takes up residence in a wealthy businessman's house. Immediately, the wheel-chair bound vampire puts the bite on his host's first daughter, but he soon discovers that she is not a virgin when he vomits up her contaminated blood. Next, Dracula sets his sights on the other three daughters, but one step ahead of him is the gardener (played by Jo Dallesandro), a libidinous soul whose only interest is to make sure Dracula dies! As Dracula chases the last pure daughter, the gardener manages to screw her in time to save her soul. Now, the gardener pursues Dracula with an axe, hacking him to bits as blood spews everywhere. Finally, in one last attempt to destroy Count Dracula, the gardener impales what is left of the vampire with a wooden stake.

Although BLOOD FOR DRACULA is a mostly graphic and gory, especially the climax in which Dracula's arms and legs are hacked off by the film's hero, the film manages to poke fun at the many serious and straight-laced Hammer films with Christopher Lee. Some critics felt that the film was not "spoofy" enough, while others felt it was too graphic. Nevertheless, BLOOD FOR DRACULA delivers such spoofing and blood with a sense of elegance and style.

The film was released originally at the Atlantic International Film Festival in 3-D. BLOOD FOR DRACULA originally received an X-rating; this original uncut version is currently available on video by Video Gems.

EROTIKILL
1973; Eurocine Films; (Spain) (Color); Producer, director & Screenwriter: Jesus Franco.

Jesus Franco actually stars in this unusual vampire film which he also produced and directed (under the fictitious name of J.P. Johnson).

In the film he plays an investigative reporter tracing a string of vampire-like killings (he's no Carl Kolchack!). Lina Romay, Franco's wife and the film's lead actress, plays the lead vampire as a sex goddess. She kills off her victims in a combination of traditional throat-ripping and nontraditional and erotic deep-throating that porno fans will appreciate.

The film is poorly dubbed in English and offers Franco's usual style of meaningless graphic violence. EROTIKILL is also known as THE BARE-BREASTED COUNTESS.

THE HORRIBLE SEXY VAMPIRE
1973; Paragon (Spain) (Color); Producer: Edmondo Amanti; Director: Jose Luis Madrid.

Undoubtedly the worst exploitation film, horror film and vampire film ever made in which Waldemar Wohlfahrt portrays the reincarnation of a baron vampire from the 14th Century.

From the same company that released the dismal John Carradine film, BLOOD OF DRACULA'S CASTLE.

VAMPIRA
1973; AIP (Great Britain) (Color); Producer: Jack H. Wiener; Director: Clive Donner; Screenwriter: Jeremy Lloyd.

This comedy/horror spoof stars the late David Niven as the screen's most ultra-suave Count Dracula, complete with fangs, mustache and a widow's peak.

Dracula's castle is now a tourist trap. When the aging Count revives Vampira (played by Teresa Graves), his mistress of the dark, with a blood transfusion, she turns black! Dracula's countess, becomes upset when she learns that the dirty old man is involved with lovely young women (*Playboy*

bunnies). In the end, Niven's Dracula also turns black!

Unfairly compared to Mel Brook's YOUNG FRANKENSTEIN, VAMPIRA, or OLD DRACULA as it is also known, is not a bad film, though a bit on the silly side. Niven makes an interesting Dracula, but the comedy trappings are no different than DRACULA - THE DIRTY OLD MAN (1970), the latter an inferior production.

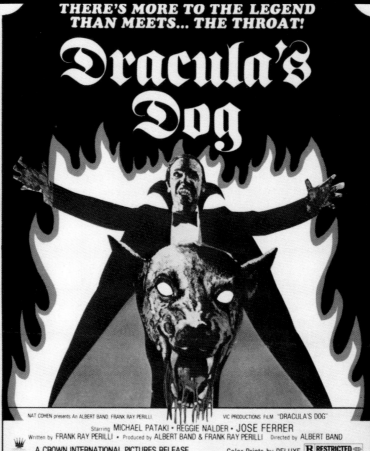

THERE'S MORE TO THE LEGEND THAN MEETS... THE THROAT!

Dracula's Dog

NAT COHEN presents An ALBERT BAND, FRANK RAY PERILLI VIC PRODUCTIONS FILM "DRACULA'S DOG"
Starring MICHAEL PATAKI • REGGIE NALDER • JOSE FERRER
Written by FRANK RAY PERILLI • Produced by ALBERT BAND & FRANK RAY PERILLI Directed by ALBERT BAND
A CROWN INTERNATIONAL PICTURES RELEASE   Color Prints by DELUXE   [R] RESTRICTED

THE BLOOD SPLATTERED BRIDE
1974; Europix (Spain) (Color); producer: Antonio Perez Olea; Director & Screenwriter: Vincent Aranda.

Another film based on the sensual vampire tale *Carmilla* by Sheridan le Fanu, only this version focuses more on the lesbian aspects of the story, more so than the Hammer films.

Director Vincent Aranda delivers a confusing script muttered with bizarre scenes that often make no sense whatsoever.

Why anyone would waste their time with this senseless poor man's version of *Carmilla* is unimaginable, especially when there are so many better versions of the same novel available. THE BLOOD SPLATTERED BRIDE is ideal viewing for fans of the totally obscure.

NIGHT OF THE SORCERERS
1974; Avco-Embassy (Spain); Director: Armando Ossorio.

This horribly dubbed film is the macabre tale of murder, violence, rape and unquenchable lusts set deep in the jungles of the Congo, where beautiful young women are sacrificed to the vampire leopard women.

The vampire species here are very savage and lethal. Unfortunately, the film itself is twice as lethal, complete with a poor script and horrible acting. Of course, the film was produced on a minuscule budget. In other words, NIGHT OF THE SORCERERS is not one of the better vampire films made during the 1970's. Be warned and steer away from this mess.

BLOOD
1974; Bryanston (Color); Producer: Walter Kent; Director & Screenwriter: Andy Milligan.

Director Andy Milligan, who directed the obscure horror film THE BODY BENEATH (1972), delivers this gritty, neo-porno vampire "epic" in which the Wolfman's son and Dracula's daughter fall in love and decide to settle down somewhere in Staten Island. Once there, they begin growing carnivorous plants. BLOOD is actually a poor excuse for a vampire film and is totally unwatchable.

Next to H.G. Lewis, Milligan is regarded as the legendary schlock merchant and the foremost producer of obscure splatter movies. This should give you an indication as to the nature of this film. BLOOD was Milligan's final film.

TENDER DRACULA
1974; AIP (Color); Director: Alain Robbe-Grillett.

In an all-time first and last, actor Peter Cushing traveled to France to star as Count Dracula himself in this light-hearted comedy-horror film. It is ironic that Cushing portrays the infamous vampire here since most of his film career in vampire movies was devoted to playing Dracula's nemesis Professor Van Helsing.

In this film directed by Alain Robbe-Grillett, Cushing portrays an aging horror actor who wants so much to desert the genre for a more versatile career. His role was patterned after horror actors Lon Chaney, Jr., Bela Lugosi and Christopher Lee, all of which desired to desert the horror movie genre at one point during their career to avoid becoming typecast.

In real life, Cushing never really objected to starring in numerous horror films unlike his colleagues.

The film was never issued in America, at least not to this writer's knowledge and is also known as CONFESSIONS OF A BLOODSUCKER.

VAMPYRES, DAUGHTERS OF DRACULA
1975; Cambist (Great Britain) (Color); Producer: Brian Smedley-Aston; Director: Joseph Larraz; Screenwriter: D. Daubeney.

Fangless, bisexual vampires? *Playboy* said about this film, "....*More sex appeal per puncture than any Dracula outing on record!*" While *Variety* said, ".....*Suspense! Sex! Mayhem! Unusually erotic!*" Boy were they right.

This light porn flick revolves around Anulka and Marianne Morris, two fangless, bisexual vampires who lure men and women to their castle for erotic bisexual sex orgies that turn bloodier with each orgasm. Each sex victim is left bloodless! ....As you will become after watching this horrid erotic vampire flick - "Bloodless!"

DRACULA'S DOG
1975; Crown International (Color); Producers: Charles Band & Frank Ray Perilli; Director: Albert Band; Screenwriter: Frank Ray Perilli, based on the character created by Bram Stoker.

Did Count Dracula finally go to the dogs? Just when you thought that Hollywood had made the shabbiest Dracula epic, Crown International comes along and releases this low budget fiasco from director Albert Band.

The film stars Michael Pataki as a descendant of Count Dracula and the last of the Dracula family line. Pataki plays Michael Drake (or, Drak-e-la?).

The film begins in Transylvania where Dracula's dog Zoltan (no joke!) is accidentally revived. He, in turn, removes the wooden stake from the heart of Veidt Smit (played by Reggie Nalder, who also played Barlow the vampire in SALEM'S LOT), Count Dracula's manservant of many years gone by. Together, fully revived, Smit and Zoltan travel to Los Angeles to serve the last of the Draculas, Michael Drake! Once in Los Angeles, the vampire duo are hunted down by Inspector Branco (Jose Ferrer), the film's Van Helsing-type. Together, Drake and the inspector chase the vampirized doggie and his companion throughout Los Angeles to put an end to the curse of the undead.

DRACULA'S DOG, despite it comical title, takes itself serious, however, there are moments that are unavoidably funny. With a different title, a bigger budget, and a better script, DRACULA'S DOG could have been a better film.

DEAFULA
1975; Signscope (B&W); Producer: Gary Holstrom; Director & Screenwriter: Peter Wechsberg.

And you thought the title DRACULA'S DOG was awful, here's one for you: DEAFULA - the world's first film to feature sign language, and, of course, it features a vampire! And no, Marlee Matlin does not star in this feature.

This very low budget feature includes a classical-looking vampire figure, a hunchback servant with tin-can hands and a very limited sound track for the hearing audience. Chances are, though, many of you will not be given the opportunity to view this obscure, hard-to-find feature.

SPERMULA
1975; PPFC (France) (Color); Producer: Bernard Lenteric; Director & Screenwriter: Charles Matton.

A film that by no means should be taken seriously, as with films like DEAFULA, GAYRACULA, DRACULA SUCKS, and DOES DRACULA REALLY SUCK.

Beautiful females from outer space live in a plush castle. These babes from space are vampires, who live on sperm instead of blood!

This atmospheric blend of horror and erotic sex scenes stars Udo Keir and, in this author's opinion, is much better than setting through KILLER KLOWNS FROM OUTER SPACE.

LEMORA- THE LADY DRACULA
1975; Blackburn/Media Cinema (Color); Producer: Robert Fern; Director: Richard Blackburn; Screenwriters: Richard Blackburn & Robert Fern.

This film is also known as LEMORA - A CHILD'S TALE OF THE SUPERNATURAL and features actress Cheryl Smith as Lila Lee, a young girl and church singer who leaves her repressive community in search of her long-lost gangster father. In her travels through Georgia, Lila encounters Lemora (Leslie Gilb), an elegant, sexy vampire who seduces her with drink, dancing, raw meat and lesbian sex, vampire style, of course. Lemora's followers are mostly little children, so Lila falls right in as the perfect new victim.

Screenwriter and director Richard Blackburn, who also plays a preacher in this film, later co-wrote the popular film EATING RAOUL. Blackburn tries very hard to establish an artistic mood, using the vampire as a mode of female liberation. But because of its low budget and the lack of a more experienced director at the helm, LEMORA has many flaws.

LEMORA- LADY DRACULA, although an obscure film to most, is regarded as a cult classic by diehard fans.

MARY MARY, BLOODY MARY
1975; Summit/Translor (Mexico) (Color); Producer: Proa Films; Director: Juan Lopez Moctezuma; Screenwriter: Malcolm Marmostein.

From the director of DR. TARR'S TORTURE DUNGEON comes this equally horrid, vapid, inept production which vampire movie fans should really avoid.

Former model and ex-Mrs. DeLorean Christina Ferrare is featured in this film as a sexy lesbian vampire/artist named Mary, of course, whose victims are dying to quench her thirst for blood. The lesbian vampire stabs her lovers in the neck and drinks their blood; oh, Mary, bloody Mary! Soon Mary's insatiable desire for blood threatens those she loves and cares about. John Carradine plays her father, who, together with the Mexican authorities, tries to come between her and her next victim's throat. Mary eventually kills her lesbian lover in a bloody bathtub scene, but not until she has destroyed half the town. Next, the viewer is subjected to ridiculous plot twists during which we later discover that Carradine is actually the vampire responsible for most of the murders. Or is he? By the film's last quarter, the murderer, we learn, isn't Carradine. Instead, Carradine left the set of this atrocity and was replaced by some unconvincing double in a fashion that Ed Wood used to make PLAN 9 FROM OUTER SPACE.

MARTIN

1975-1977; Braddock/Libra (Color); Producer: Richard Rubinstein; Director & Screenwriter: George A. Romero; Camera: Michael Gornick.

Writer/director George A. Romero is the true talent behind the film MARTIN. It is his best work so far, though it is not the big commercial success that his *"Living Dead"* films have become.

The film deals with the mentally ill, primarily Martin (played by John Amplas), who believes he has inherited the family curse of vampirism. The teenage boy, who believes himself to be eighty-four years old, attacks women in their sleep by drugging them first and then slitting their arms with razors, to finally drain their blood with syringes. Yes, Martin goes the full nine yards and drinks their blood.

The clever script has Martin believing that he is actually a vampire, but we, the viewers, know that he is suffering from his feelings of sexual inadequacy and from a severe repressiveness of his emotions. The story also offers clever hallucinations in which Martin envisages his vampiric behavior as some kind of evil romanticism; these black and white scenes are inserted into this otherwise color film, adding a surreal dimension to what is really a straight-forward case of psychotic behavior. Romero also inserts an interesting touch to the film in which Martin becomes a regular caller on an all night phone-in radio show to talk about his problems. Clever!

Unlike Romero's other films (DAWN OF THE DEAD, CREEPSHOW and DAY OF THE DEAD), MARTIN does not overflow with an abundance of blood and gore, even when Martin is wrongly staked through the heart by his elderly cousin.

MARTIN is the most thorough re-examination of the vampire figure to this date, and the film is bound to become a cult classic that is certainly worth a look at.

RABID

1976; Cinepix/New World (Canada) (Color); Producer: John Dunning; Director & Screenwriter: David Cronenberg; Camera: Rene Verzier.

Like George Romero's MARTIN, David Cronenberg's RABID is an interesting departure to the traditional vampire theme. Cronenberg's first treatment of this film was called *Mosquito* because the film's main character only required very little blood to survive, unlike a regular vampire, who must replenish most of its blood within a twenty four hour cycle.

In the film, a woman (played by ex-porno star Marilyn Chambers) becomes the victim of a new technique in plastic surgery. Chambers is severely injured in a motorcycle accident and during a major plastic surgery operation, she receives an experimental graft of skin. As a result of the accident, she has also lost much of her intestine, therefore the morphologically neutral skin develops into a digestive organ. This side effect creates a retractable syringe-like growth in her arm pit. At first, Chamber's new projection sucks the blood of her sleeping partners, taking very little blood each time to survive, like a mosquito. Soon she feels compelled to attack people with her syringe for human blood in order to stay alive. Her victims develop a rabies-like disease which causes a form of homicidal mania that spreads rapidly throughout Montreal, where most of the movie was filmed.

John Amplas in Georgio Romero's psychological vampire thriller MARTIN (1975).

RABID moves at a very fast pace and is often predictable, but depicts its story in a more elaborate fashion than Cronenberg's earlier film SHIVERS (1976). The film is also known simply as RAGE.

BLOOD RELATIONS
1977; Netherland Films (France/Dutch) (Color); Director: Wim Linder.

Not to be confused with the 1987 film BLOOD RELATIONS, directed by Graeme Campbell, this rather obscure offering is yet another unusual and offbeat vampire film.

In this restrained vampire film, a young nurse discovers that Dr. Steiger (Maxim Hamel) is stealing blood plasma because he is a vampire. Steiger belongs to a cult of vampires who also require the same type of feeding patterns. Claiming to be a vampire too, she infiltrates the cult, but her plans ultimately fail.

BLOOD RELATIONS is directed by Wim Linder in a fashion similar to Roman Polanski's ROSEMARY'S BABY (1968), wherein the viewer is frightened mostly by paranoia and uncertainty. The film, like most horror films, questions the truisms we live by day to day.

DEAD OF NIGHT
1977; TV/Dan Curtis Productions (Color); Producer & Director: Dan Curtis; Screenwriter: Richard Matheson.

DEAD OF NIGHT was the second pilot for the TV series *Dead of Night*, also produced by Dan Curtis, however, this feature is inferior to the first, TRILOGY OF TERROR (1975) with Karen Black.

The first segment of this anthology film is entitled *No Such Thing As A Vampire* and stars Horst Buchholz and Patrick Macnee in a tale about a vampire's lair in a small village. The story-line follows the basic premise set forth by Stephen King's *Jerusalem's Lot*, which later became another made-for-TV vampire movie, SALEM'S LOT.

The other two stories in this quickly-made, undoubtedly forgotten film stars Ed Begley, Ann Doran and Christian Hart.

DRACULA: FATHER AND SON
1977; Quarter Films (France) (Color); Producer: Alain Poire; Director: Edouard Molinaro; Screenwriters: Edouard Molinaro, Jean-Marie Poire & Alain Godard.

Count Dracula (Frank Langella) battles the forces of goodness in John Badham's eight million dollar extravaganza DRACULA (1979).

A bloodthirsty vampire attacks another victim in David Cronenberg's interesting vampire film RABID (1976),

Quite obviously the inspiration for the vampire comedy LOVE AT FIRST BITE (1979), which was an extremely successful American-made spoof on the Dracula legend, DRACULA: FATHER AND SON was not, at least in America. The reason is quite obvious. The film is perhaps the worst dubbed foreign film in movie history. The American distributors chopped the film to bits, adding jokes and gags that were not even funny. Poor Christopher Lee, who plays the father in this otherwise wonderful film. After refusing to play the vampire king all those years, he finally gives in and look what happens! It's no wonder why the actor gave up.

Actor Christopher Lee is considered to be one of the great movie Draculas, and I might add, with some very good films to his credit, including Hammer's HORROR OF DRACULA (1958), DRACULA-PRINCE OF DARKNESS (1964) and DRACULA HAS RISEN FROM THE GRAVE (1968). In fact, no other actor has portrayed the King of Vampires more than Lee. Eight times to be exact. Usually, however, Lee's characterizations of the master vampire have always been straight forward.

In this spoof on the Dracula legend, Lee plays the title role for laughs. Old Dracula wants his son (Bernard Menez) to take over as the Lord of the Vampires. The trouble is, young Dracula would rather be a florist before becoming some supreme monster like his father.

The film mixes blood with laughs, and, despite the bad dubbing, it is good to see Lee as Dracula after a four year absence from the role. DRACULA: FATHER AND SON was Lee's last performance as Dracula to date.

NIGHTMARE IN BLOOD
1978; PFE (Color); Producers & Screenwriters: John Stanley & Kenn Davis; Director: John Stanley.

John Stanley's low-budget, rarely seen comedy spoof about a horror film actor who turns out to be a real-life vampire at a horror film convention.

Actor Kerwin Matthews makes a cameo appearance in this rather obscure independent.

DRACULA

1979; Universal Pictures (Color); Producer: Walter Mirisch; Director: John Badham; Screenwriter: W. D. Richter from the novel *Dracula* by Bram Stoker; Camera: Gilbert Taylor.

John Badham's frightfully theatrical DRACULA has received so much criticism since its 1979 release. Many film historians have questioned the film's authenticity as a real horror film as opposed to it being a flamboyant parody of the Dracula legend. Others feel that Frank Langella's Dracula is too vocal and theatrical and less menacing. In short, aficionados and critics have criticized the film from its actor (Langella) to its screen treatment.

The film was released simultaneously with two other vampire movies that same year: NOSFERATU- THE VAMPIRE (1979) and LOVE AT FIRST BITE (1979). Werner Herzog's NOSFERATU- THE VAMPIRE is a tale of pure, straight-forward horror, while Stan Dragoti's LOVE AT FIRST BITE makes no pretense about being a camp parody on the Dracula legend. Both Herzog and Dragoti's films work well within their own frameworks, however, Badham's DRACULA seems to steer an uneasy course between the two films, at times theatrically frightening, while at other times a bit camp. One thing is certain, the film takes its characters serious, especially the character of Dracula. At the time the film was made, however, it would appear that Universal would have preferred to label its film as a supernatural romance story rather than a horror film. But then why did they entitle the film DRACULA- a title that very clearly in itself suggests horror? Regardless of what others call or would like to call this film, DRACULA is a horror film, from its very beginning to its very end. In

addition, DRACULA is quite good, too.

Dracula is portrayed by the handsome Frank Langella as a suave, Valentino-like hero with burning, hypnotic eyes, slick black hair, pretty facial features and a deep and trance-inducing voice. In the film he sweeps actress Kate Nelligan off her feet with all the decadence his character can possibly muster. Unlike many aficionados, this author feels that Langella is superb at portraying the vampire as a tragic figure and he should be commended for his bravo performance, since it is all too seldom that we see a screen actor inject this tragic, broken-hearted characteristic into the infamous and immortal character of Count Dracula. Bela Lugosi tried, but failed, and Christopher Lee's vampire was too brutal to be romantic and tragic, although Lee's Dracula came close to capturing that personality once in SCARS OF DRACULA. Aficionados of the horror cinema argue that Langella's vampire is no match against the mysterious aura of Bela Lugosi's Count Dracula, nor does the actor deliver the combination of suaveness and menace that Christopher Lee's Dracula quite clearly possessed in the Hammer films. I, too, agree in this respect. However, the actor has created a tragic and menacing figure of his own, obviously patterned after his successful Broadway characterization of the vampire. Oddly enough, Langella's theatrical performance works on film too. In summary, Langella's Dracula is frightfully articulate and precise, an incarnation of pure evil, packaged and delivered in a pretty wrapping.

In DRACULA there are moments of great horror that critics seem to overlook. For example, there is a scene in which the Count scales down the side of a wall head first (taken directly from Bram Stoker's novel and overlooked by both Universal's 1931 version

Reggie Nalder as the evil bloodsucker, Barlow, in SALEM'S LOT (1979).

and Hammer's 1958 version). There is also a scene in which Professor Van Helsing (played by the late legendary actor Lord Laurence Olivier) confronts his vampirized daughter Lucy. The foul, pasty-faced creature of the night attacks her own father as she chants to him in Dutch; her eyes ablaze like two balls of fire.

The film also offers other thrilling moments and clever additions to the vampire folklore. In one scene, a white horse is purposely led into a nearby cemetery to sniff out the grave of the vampire. In a highly imaginative scene, the horse digs up the vampire's grave with its hoofs.

Like always, Dracula can transform into a bat or even a wolf, via the tricky special effects of Roy Arbogast.

Badham's DRACULA, at one point the biggest budgeted vampire movie of all time, is first rate, with superb special effects and a sweeping music score by John Williams that is near brilliant. The sometimes Victorian-while other-times-Edwardian sets are quite lavish, especially the creepy Carfax Abbey. What a shame that Badham does not make great use of these interior sets.

Many connoisseurs of horror and vampire movies would agree that DRACULA lacks fangs and blood; an obvious disappointment to fans who expected more. It is quite possible that Badham was trying to upstage the legend, and deliver it with more sophistication and less exploitation, and in this respect, the filmmaker succeeds. As a last note, one should avoid comparing this film with Francis Ford Coppola's 1992 version of Stoker's novel, which is an entirely different picture altogether and more of an elaborate horror film, produced at five times the cost that Universal allotted for this picture.

SALEM'S LOT
1979; TV/Warner (Color); Producer: Richard Kobritz; Director: Tobe Hooper; Screenwriter: Paul Monash from the novel by Stephen King.

Tobe Hooper's SALEM'S LOT, based on Stephen King's novel *Jerusalem's Lot*, in its original format, is far too long for its own good. The four-hour long film was originally made as a two-part television mini-series, therefore half of the original film is flat and void of the thrills we would expect from a Stephen King story or a Tobe *"Texas Chainsaw Massacre"* Hooper film. In addition, because of its made-for-

television format, the film does not present too many disturbing and scary moments, as it attempts to avoid any television taboos. In this respect, SALEM'S LOT is much milder in content than both King's IT and THE STAND, two made-for-television horror thrillers made nearly twelve to fourteen years apart. However, this is not to say that SALEM'S LOT does not offer any good, old-fashion scary moments.

SALEM'S LOT takes its central vampire figure very serious, keeping the monster virtually unseen through three quarters of the film, which is actually a blessing since the Paul Monash script misleadingly elevates the viewer's expectations of Barlow, the ringleader and procurer of the vampire village (by three quarters of the film, most of the town of Jerusalem's Lot is predictably transformed into undead creatures by the unseen vampire leader). Barlow is depicted as a cunning, centuries-old creature. But when the time arrives for Barlow to make his grand appearance, viewers, primarily fans of this fare, are greatly disappointed. The inarticulate Barlow makes his first meaningless appearance as he crashes through a kitchen window to attack a family and local priest. It is obvious that this meaningless scene was just thrown in to spice up this otherwise lengthy and boring flick. Furthermore, it appears as if Barlow was a last minute decision created out of haste and patterned after the vampire of NOSFERATU - THE VAMPIRE (1979).

In addition to the film's lengthy running time and the disappointing central vampire figure, the film is muddled with numerous other flaws. For example, the vampire sequences are indeed a bit cliche and thus ineffective, and then there is David Soul's colorless performance as the film's hero. Who cast this film?

There are, however, some gruesome moments of shock and suspense. For example, there is a scene when a vampirized James Mason (Barlow's right-hand man and the film's real villain) literally throws actor Ed Flanders against a wall of piercing antlers. This rather gruesome scene was filmed in a fashion reminiscent of the attack scene on Martin Balsam in Alfred Hitchcock's PSYCHO. There is also a scene when a vampirized boy floats outside his brother's window, lurking for blood. Unfortunately, these rather abrupt images of horror quickly fade away into oblivion as another meaningless sequence follows.

SALEM'S LOT is not the tedious disaster that other King film adaptations have turned into. In fact, considering the constraints of network television of 1979, the film is more respectable than devastating.

The strongest element of the film is indeed James Mason's Richard Straker character, delivering clever dialogue with a nasal sneer, as the actor often did in his later films. Mason is more the cunning and subtle villain that Barlow should have been, while Barlow, the vampire, is nothing more than a cheap devise used to spice-up a film which did not require a central vampire. In short, the producers and the screenwriter(s) should have paid much more attention towards Barlow.

SALEM'S LOT was released on American television as a new, more rapidly pace two-hour film, followed by yet another release on cable TV that offered stronger scenes that were later added. This bloodier version is currently available on video.

SALEM'S LOT is also known as BLOOD THIRST. Sequel: A RETURN TO SALEM'S LOT (1987).

THIRST
1979; New Line Cinema (Australia) (Color); Producer: Anthony I. Ginnane; Director: Rod Hardy; Screenwriter: John Pinkney.

The premise of this stylish and classy shocker revolves around a vampire cult that tries to brainwash actress Chantal Contouri, who plays the descendant of a distinguished vampire family (the Draculas, perhaps?), into becoming the leader of their cult. David Hemmings is the ringleader of these blood-drinkers, who normally obtain their nourishment under cover by hitting blood banks and hospitals instead of the traditional neck-biting way. The international community of vampires known as the Hyma Brotherhood meet annually in a health farm. There, they drug humans and milk them for blood as part of a spiritual ritual.

THIRST, which is a cross between THE BELIEVERS and BLOOD TIES, is highly recommended as alternative viewing to the traditional vampire film.

VAMPIRE
1979; TV/ABC (Color); Producer: Gregory Hoblit; Director: E. W. Swackhammer; Screenwriters: Steve Bocho & Michael Kozell.

VAMPIRE was ABC's answer to Universal's DRACULA (1979) with Frank Langella, without the eight million dollar budget, obviously. But don't be

Chantal Contouri finds herself at the mercy of an unholy vampire cult in THIRST (1979).

fooled, because this made-for-television movie is quite fascinating considering its origin.

The film intelligently presents all the standard trappings of a Gothic vampire film set in foggy modern-day San Francisco. The cast is superb, as actors Jason Miller (of THE EXORCIST) and E.G. Marshall stalk the vampire through the city streets. Richard Lynch, who normally portrays movie villains, appears quite comfortable as the central vampire figure. The vampire in this film is over eight hundred years old. Lynch's blonde vampire is ruthless, very cunning and purposely reminiscent of David Peel's Baron Meinster in Hammer Films' BRIDES OF DRACULA (1960). Marshall is equally great as the film's Van Helsing-type, and Jessica Walter (PLAY MISTY FOR ME) is cast as the film's heroine.

ABC never followed this semi-successful television film with a sequel or series.

NOCTURNA

1979; Compass International (Color); Producer: Vernon Becker; Director & Screenwriter: Harry Tampa Hurwitz.

NOCTURNA plays the Dracula legend for laughs. Aging John Carradine and Yvonne DeCarlo (the latter goes by the name of *"Jugulia"* in this film) play Count and Countess Dracula. Their lovely granddaughter (played by the ex-belly dancer and star of HOODLUMS, Nai Bonet) is taken in by disco dancing and stripping and falls in love with a mortal man in New York (played by Tony Hamilton). In a movie first, She is turned into a mortal like him.

Bonet's acting is poor, but both Carradine and DeCarlo are great as old flames in this comedy spoof.

MAMA DRACULA

1979-1980; Valisa Films (France/Belgium) (Color); Producer & Director: Boris Szulzinger; Screenwriters: Pierre Sterckx, Marc-Henri Wajnberg & Boris Szulzinger (English dialogue by Tony Hendra); Camera: Willy Kurant.

This often crude but comical film is a parody on the Countess Elizabeth Bathory sub-genre in which the Countess, or Mama Dracula, stays young by drinking the blood of young virgins. Mama has two sons, Vlad and Lad. Lad is too shy to bite and the other is a gay dress designer. But Mama Dracula (played by Academy-award winning actress Louise Fletcher) runs a boutique to attract victims, and she is not too shy to put the bite on her own clients! Unlike centuries ago when she could just order out, she must now rely on her boutique and her two bumbling twins to attract the attention of young virtuous women, primarily actress Maria Schneider.

English dialogue was added by Tony Hendra for a very limited American release to capitalize on the success of LOVE AT FIRST BITE and the Dracula movie craze of that year. MAMA DRACULA was not released on video until 1986.

NOSFERATU - THE VAMPYRE

1979; Gaumont/Fox (Germany) (Color); Producer, Director & Screenwriter: Werner Herzog from the 1922 film *Nosferatu*; Camera: Jorg Schmidt-Reitwein.

The German version of this film is entitled NOSFERATU, THE PHANTOM OF THE

Richard Lynch as a centuries old vampire in VAMPIRE (1979), a made for television film.

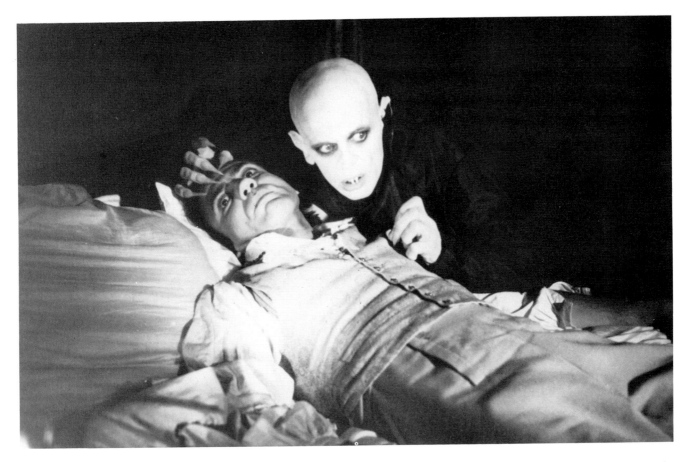

Klaus Kinski as the creepy and hideous Count Dracula in Werner Herzog's NOSFERATU - THE VAMPYRE (1979).

NIGHT. Originally, producer, director and writer Werner Herzog filmed two versions of this film; one in German and the other in English. The English version was a request by the film's financier 20th Century Fox. But, when Herzog/Gaumont delivered both versions, Fox very wisely decided to import the German version with subtitles. The English-speaking version was actually too comical to issue in America, since neither Herzog nor the film's cast spoke any English.

Intellectually directed by Werner Herzog, this color remake of the silent 1922 classic is both slow-moving and elegant for a modern-day vampire movie. Actor Klaus Kinski is accurately made-up to look like Max Schreck's Count Orlock. Kinski is brilliant as the growling, groveling vampire; a creature powerless in resisting its own bloodthirsty craving. Unlike Frank Langella's Dracula, there are no admirable qualities in this vampire. Kinski's Dracula is a fiend so horribly and unthinkably foul, driven only by forces beyond his power. The actor's remarkable portrayal of Dracula reflects a careful study of the rat-like Count Orlock of the 1922 silent version. Kinski is brilliant. In addition, actress Isabelle Adjani gives a stylish performance as Lucy Harker, who sacrifices her own life to destroy the vampire by way of the early morning sunlight, much like the climax of the original silent film.

In his colorful remake, Herzog adds a clever new twist-ending to the film: Jonathan Harker, who has also become one of Dracula's infected, rides off maniacally to carry out Dracula's doom to the rest of the world. The director delivers a message of doom and gloom, which is the mood that the film takes on from its very beginning.

NOSFERATU - THE VAMPYRE is a story of permeating evil, cast against an impressive backdrop of rotting decadence, atmospherically photographed by Jorg Schmidt-Reitwein and directed in an attractive and subtle style by Herzog. NOSFERATU - THE VAMPYRE, far removed from the normal Hollywood-style commercial vehicle, is a *true* contemporary horror film that takes itself seriously, much more so than John Badham's DRACULA (1979). This is a film for the connoisseur of fine quality filmmaking. NOSFERATU - THE VAMPIRE is undeniably one of the better contemporary horror films ever made.

VAMPIRE HOOKERS
1979; Capricorn Three (Philippines) (Color); Producer: Robert E. Waters; Director: Cirio H. Santiago; Screenwriter: Howard Cohen.

It's hard to keep a good horror film actor down, such as the case with the late John Carradine, who returns one final time as the vampire king in this film! Yes, good old John Carradine, now 73 years old, returns to the screen as Count Dracula in this erotic horror flick straight after his role in NOCTURNA!

Dracula dispatches three of his sultriest succubi to prowl the night for human blood. The three vampires lure several innocent men to the graveyard to meet their doom.

The film was produced under the title THE SENSUOUS VAMPIRES, and was released in America by Saturn International under its original production title.

DRACULA SUCKS
1979; M.H.E. (Color); Director: Philip Marshak

Director Philip Marshak presents porno star James Gillis as Count Dracula in this soft porn version of the infamous legend. The opening dialogue is almost a word for word remake of Tod Browning's DRACULA (1931), only with added sex and horrible jokes.

Actor Reggie Nalder, who starred in both DRACULA'S DOG and SALEM'S LOT, is also on hand in this fiasco. Bram Stoker must have been turning in his grave when this film was being made.

LOVE AT FIRST BITE
1979; AIP (Color); Producer: Joel Freeman; Director: Stan Dragoti; Screenwriter: Robert Kaufman; Camera: Edward Rosson.

American International Pictures began during the 1950's with low budget programmers and sleazy horror films, and later went on to produce and release good box office money-makers like THE LAND THAT TIME FORGOT, EMPIRE OF THE ANTS, THE AMITYVILLE HORROR and LOVE AT FIRST BITE, a spoof on the Dracula legend and AIP's biggest money-making genre film.

"AIP made this film?" The answer is "Yes," and it's actually funny! The film hilariously pokes fun at the legend, from the very beginning to the very end. Comedian George Hamilton gives freshness to the character of Count Dracula. Hamilton's flamboyant characterization of the vampire king actually outshines Frank Langella's theatrical performance in Universal's big budget 1979 version. In fact, LOVE AT FIRST BITE did better box office than DRACULA, which is ironic, since AIP specifically made this film to capitalize on the success on the straight-laced Universal film. It is actually nice to see how LOVE AT FIRST BITE pokes fun at the Langella film.

In the film, the Transylvanian vampire (Hamilton) decides to move away from his boring motherland to Twentieth century New York! Apparently, the Count wants to take a bite out of the big apple! Once there, he and his servant Renfield (played by Arte Johnson) disrupt a funeral in a Harlem chapel, raid a local blood bank for food and disco dance up a storm with model Susan St. James.

Hamilton cunningly romances St. James with his hypnotic charm, while her former husband (played by Richard Benjamin), who is a relative of the infamous Professor Van Helsing, tries to rid the Big Apple of this bloodsucking menace and save St. James from the vampire's clutches. Dracula actually wins and transforms his bride into one of the undead, and we, the viewers, are all very happy for them. For once, Dracula is the hero, so-to-speak.

The script's one liners are often good, and Hamilton is great as Dracula with a heavy Lugosi accent. Director Stan Dragoti paces this film much better than Mel Brooks' parody on the Frankenstein legend, YOUNG FRANKENSTEIN (1974).

AIP's OLD DRACULA (1973), though quite good, cannot hold a candle to LOVE AT FIRST BITE, a funnier, better-written spoof that never really lets up.

AIP announced a sequel entitled LOVE AT SECOND BITE, but the film unfortunately never materialized. It would have been nice to see what happened to our lucky lovers of the night! Sequels, anyone?

Another scene of Klaus Kinski as the groveling Count Dracula in NOSTERATU - THE VAMPYRE (1979).

George Hamilton plays Count Dracula in LOVE AT FIRST BITE (1979). Above, he seduces Susan St. James while below, he and Arte Johnson are forced to leave Transylvania by a lynch mob of angry villagers.

CHAPTER SEVEN

The 1980's

A POLISH VAMPIRE IN BURBANK
1980; Simitar Entertainment (Color); Producer, Director & Screenwriter: Mark Pirro.

This independently produced vampire film is not exactly considered to be a mainstream production. In fact, most vampire film buffs probably never even heard of this rather obscure comedy (thank your lucky stars if you haven't seen this film).

According to this film, Dracula has two siblings, a daughter and a son. The Count is very happy with his daughter, who walks the streets of Burbank at his side collecting blood for his feeble son, who sleeps all day and stays indoors all night watching repeats of *The Three Stooges* on television. The son even sleeps with a Frankenstein Monster doll in his coffin, which he cuddles while he sleeps (sounds like *The Munsters'* Eddie Munster)?

Dracula feels that his full-grown vampire son wastes his nights doing nothing while he should be out attacking young ladies and biting necks. Tired of bringing home his son's nourishment in a plastic bag with a straw, the mighty Count Dracula (whose not so mighty in this film) pushes his son out of the nest to seek fresh, warm human blood on his own. "*Why,*

when I was a young vampire, I sucked more blood than a California landlord," proclaims Dracula!

The result of Dracula's anger has poor junior roaming the streets with his Carpathian sister sucking the blood out of Burbank!

A POLISH VAMPIRE IN BURBANK, though an impoverished title, offers enough tacky and really funny moments to qualify the film for selection on the next episode of *Mystery Science Theater 2000*!

THE CRAVING
1980; Dalmata Films (Spain) (Color); Producer: Dalmata Films; Director & Screenwriter: Jack (Jacinto) Molina.

Paul Naschy returns as an older Waldemar Daninsky, Spain's werewolf at large. In this film written and directed by Jacinto Molina (Naschy), Waldemar and his sidekick Countess Bathory (Silvia Aguilar) are executed for witchcraft. Once again, the film shifts to modern times, and grave-robbers yank the ever so valuable silver dagger from Waldemar's chest, and soon the werewolf is back on

Russell Clark transforms into a bloodthirsty vampire in FRIGHT NIGHT II (1988).

the prowl. But what of Countess Bathory?

Meanwhile, a young female student of the occult locates the tomb of the countess. The student strings up one of her three friends over the casket of the Countess and with a dagger, she cuts an incision that allows the human blood to drench Bathory's casket in a scene straight out of DRACULA - PRINCE OF DARKNESS. Suddenly, the coffin's lid miraculously rises into the air, and from within emerges the vampire, fully restored and very hungry. In return for being released from the world of limbo, Countess Bathory bites the young girl in the neck and turns her into a vampire, giving the gift of immortality to the young female student. By this point in the film, it seems like forever has come and gone before the vampire is revived. But the wait is worth it, for the vampire's resurrection is the best scene this film has to offer.

Now fully revived, Bathory begins to vampirize young virgins while Waldemar chomps down on the locals in werewolf form, of course. The killings are displayed graphically in blood-dripping color, and it is the vampire killings that are the juiciest, for all those splatter fans in the house. For example, in one scene, the newly vampirized student prepares to sink her fangs into another friend (boy, with friends like these?). Just as she reaches over to give the fatal bite, her friend pulls out a crucifix and places it on her forehead, branding the holy symbol onto her skin (we've seen this timeless scene before). Just when the viewer is fooled into thinking that the powers of goodness have prevailed against the evil vampire, the vampirized student unexpectedly leaps onto her friend and savagely rips her throat apart with her fangs as blood splatters everywhere (the scene was cut in America).

There is also another scene in which the nude vampire takes a shower in the dripping blood from one of her strung-up and slashed victims. Talk about splatter?

Another fine quality of this otherwise horrid foreign import is the screenwriter's attempt to pay homage to Sheridan le Fanu's *Carmilla*. In the film, Countess Bathory pays another young female student sensual midnight visits, during which the vampire drains a little blood each time. Although the lesbian aspects of these scenes are virtually unexplored by the director, the thought of such erotic behavior is planted in the viewer's mind by the powers of suggestion. We are never really given the opportunity to see the two female engaged in any type of sexual behavior, at least not in the American version.

Finally, the showdown of showdowns occurs. In his human form, Waldemar drives a wooden stake through one of the vampires' hearts. But before he can finish the job, he falls victim to his dreaded curse and transforms into a werewolf. In a fierce battle between werewolf and vampires, Waldemar kills yet another vampire. But Countess Bathory still lives. The Countess rises from her grave and tries to control the werewolf by way of her hypnotic supernatural powers, but to no avail. Waldemar savagely ends the vampire's reign of terror by ripping her throat apart in yet another gory scene. He too is destroyed when his own lover jabs him with a silver crucifix.

In addition to being a serious horror film, THE CRAVING tries to be funny at times, but the humor is very much overshadowed by the graphic content of the film. Most of the attempts at comic relief fail. Ironically, the one scene that stands out as being funny is unintentionally so as a result of bad dubbing and editing. Once the villagers realize that there is a vampire loose, they try to come up with a solution. One man suggests, "....*the town folk are terrorized. Many die bloodless, because vampires have appeared, rising from their tombs. The authorities don't know what to do, and panic is spreading among the people. There's only one solution if you ask me. Garlic! A lot of garlic. Garlic up to your ass!*"

There are several other unintentionally funny sequences throughout this film, primarily as a result of bad editing. In fact, the main problem with THE CRAVING, as with so many other foreign horror films, is the poor editing and dubbing, which is unfortunate, since the film cleverly combines the Gothic atmosphere and trappings of the previous Paul Naschy epics with 1980's-style splatter.

THE CRAVING is also known as RETURN OF THE WOLFMAN.

DRACULA'S LAST RITES
1980; Cannon (Color); Producer: Kelly Van Horn; Director & Screenwriter: Domonic Paris.

Appropriately, the vampire of this film is the local town mortician. Lucard, the vampire, is surrounded by darkness and coffins all day and night. He works with the sheriff and local doctor, who bring him accident victims that turn into food. Yes, Lucard sucks them dry and then drives a wooden stake through their hearts to avoid competition. Being a coroner has its perks, for the vampire covers up any wounds from the nasty stakings before burial. However poor Lucard screws up when he accidentally allows one victim, an old lady, to slip by without a staking before burial.

This low budget fiasco tries to invent new vampire folklore, but falls flat on every level. Even the bald vampire is unimpressive.

This film was also released as LAST RITES.

I DESIRE
1982; TV (Color); Director: John Llewellyn Moxley.

This highly underrated and little seen vampire tale is also known these days as DESIRE, THE VAMPIRE. The film is a bizarre tale about a Los Angeles prostitute who turns out to be a female vampire who does her victims in while doing the dirty deed.

Actor David Naughton (of AN AMERICAN WEREWOLF IN LONDON) plays a coroner's aide who suspects a glorified, high-paid prostitute (played seductively by Barbara Stock) of being a vampire. There are several confrontations between the two foes, the final of which is staged in the vampire's elaborate penthouse apartment-lair.

The average film, directed by John Llewellyn Moxley, is mostly all bark and very little bite, but the contemporary setting holds up rather well. Moxley, who also directed THE NIGHT STALKER (1972) for Dan Curtis, does an excellent job at capturing the mood of the seedy, big city night-life, which serves as the backdrop for this cross between VAMPIRE HOOKERS and THE HUNGER.

THE HUNGER
1983; MGM/UA (Color); Producer: Richard A. Shepherd; Director: Tony Scott; Screenwriters: Ivan Davis & Michael Thomas from the novel by Witley Strieber; Camera: Stephen Goldblatt & Tom Mangravite.

The Sultry Catherine Deneuve delivers a riveting and sensuous performance as a beautiful and virtually ageless vampire whose lovers briefly share her immortality before suddenly growing old and withering away.

THE HUNGER, like JONATHAN, MARTIN,

Vampire Catherine Deneuve comforts dying lover David Bowie in the visually sumptuous film, THE HUNGER (1983).

BLOOD RELATIONS, BLOOD TIES and THIRST, is one of those unusual modern-day vampire offerings that defies tradition. Here, the "vampire" is the last of a dying breed who live forever. Like most vampires, they need blood for nourishment, but they also require blood to maintain their youthful appearance. These vampires are not affected by running water or sunlight, and they quite clearly cast reflections in mirrors.

Deneuve's vampire, Miriam Baylock, leads an otherwise normal life, living in a Manhattan apartment. At night, she picks up her victims in a trendy disco nightclub. She also shares her life and her nocturnal feeding habits with David Bowie, who plays John Baylock, who, up until now, has remained young-looking for many years. But suddenly, Bowie begins to degenerate into the centuries-old vampire that he really is (via the spectacular make-up of Carl Fullerton and Dick Smith).

In one of the film's more notable moments, actor David Bowie changes from youthful beauty into a nearly rotting corpse in just a single afternoon. Bowie tries to get gerontologist Susan Sarandon to stop his aging process before he crumbles away. He ages nearly a hundred years while on hold in her waiting room.

Distressed over his degenerating condition, Bowie begins to suffer from paranoia and then hysteria, as he desperately attacks two youthful females for their blood in order to retain his youthfulness. But all of this proves hopeless in preventing an unavoidable aging cycle that eventually affects each and every one of Deneuve's lovers infected by her venom. In a rather disturbing but effective scene, Deneuve places Bowie's nearly dead body among the remains of her previous lovers in the attic, all of which are sealed in caskets.

THE HUNGER is stylish and very artistic at times, using fluttering doves, shafts of sunlight, erotic lesbian sex, buckets of blood and the transfer of personalities from vampire Deneuve to her woman victim (played by Susan Sarandon) to create a type of nightmarish mood, however confusing it may all seem. The lesbian aspects of the film between Deneuve and Sarandon are sensual and erotic, but not as juicy as DAUGHTERS OF DARKNESS.

THE HUNGER was made by Tony Scott, brother of accomplished filmmaker Ridley Scott and based on the novel by Whitley Strieber. This otherwise visually sumptuous vampire movie suffers only from Scott's background in television commercials and his lack of experience in motion pictures. But this is merely minor and petty stuff. Still, THE HUNGER is undoubtedly one of the better, more artistic offerings the genre of vampire movies has to offer; a film that is destined to become a classic.

THE BLACK ROOM
1983; Lancer Productions (Color); Producer: Aaron C. Butler; Directors: Elly Kenner & Norman Thaddeus Vane; Screenwriter: Norman Thaddeus Vane; Camera: Robert Harmon.

THE BLACK ROOM is a fascinating low budget film in which immortal brother and sister vampires (played by Stephen Knight and Cassandra Gavioa) are too nervous to take blood the traditional way. Instead, they rely on medical transfusions to keep their hereditary anaemia status quo, or so it seems.

The siblings place ads in the personal columns for uninhibited swingers. They rent out a room in their Beverly Hills Mansion to a philandering couple who answers their ad. The husband uses the room to cheat on his wife, while the wife does a little cheating of her own. During all of this meaningless cheating, the two twins find it amusing to photograph their victims having sex through a two-way mirror in the black room. With the help of his sister, the brother drains various visitors of their blood, but eventually, the siblings move in on the original couple and have a real blood feast! So much for transfusions.

While there is a lot of senseless blood spilling in this film and many aspects of the script go unexplained or virtually unexplored, THE BLACK ROOM offers the brilliant photography Robert Harmon, which, in itself, raises this vampire film above mediocrity.

THE TOMB
1985 Trans World Entertainment (Color); Producers: Fred Olen Ray & Ronnie Hadar; Director: Fred Olen Ray; Screenwriters: Kenneth J. Hall & T.L. Lankford from a story by Bram Stoker.

"*The Mummy Meets The Vampire!*" cleverly describes the premise of this film. Fortune hunters desecrate an Egyptian tomb and must pay the price when the Egyptian princess Nefratis (Michelle Bauer) returns to life as an ancient-old vampire.

THE TOMB, under the direction of Fred Olen Ray (director of BIOHAZARD and THE ALIENATOR), offers very generous amounts of blood and gore. There are some great but gory neck biting scenes and dreadful decapitations that are not for the squeamish. In fact, many of the original gory scenes had to be cut to achieve an R-rating before it was released theatrically. THE TOMB is ideal for enthusiasts of splatter.

Fred Olen Ray also made BEVERLY HILLS VAMPIRE in 1989.

ONCE BITTEN
1985; Samuel Goldwyn (Color); Producers: Dimitri Villard, Robby Wald & Frank E. Hildebrand; Director: Howard Storm; Screenwriters: David Hines, Jeffrey Hause & Jonathan Roberts from a story by Dimitri Villard; Camera: Adam Greenberg.

This underrated and funny vampire movie will please fans of actor Jim Carrey, who stars here long before his rise to stardom in the television show *In Living Color* and his film ACE VENTURA: PET DETECTIVE (1994) and THE MASK (1994). Still, Carrey is hilarious, but not as wild as he is today with his comedy antics. He plays the only male virgin in America in the 1980's, and this is exactly what the beautiful and sensual vampire Countess (played by Lauren Hutton) requires to maintain her longevity and youthful appearance. The Countess must have the blood of a virgin male before Halloween night passes, otherwise she will loose her immortality and youthful vigor and beauty. All of the vampire's servants, who are all previous victims of her pre-Halloween bite and once virgins, are dispatched to locate a male virgin, but to no avail. It is the Countess who finds Carrey at a local pick-up bar.

Once Carey becomes Hutton's victim (She bites him in the penis) he quickly begins changing. Soon he's wearing dark sunglasses during the day, ordering raw meat and sleeping in a clothes trunk by day. There is a dream sequence in which Carrey, cloaked in a black cape and baring vampire fangs, puts the bite on his mortal girlfriend, with Lauren Hutton watching close by.

Finally, Carrey's girlfriend manages to have sex with him on Halloween night before Hutton can put the final bite on him. As a result, the Countess reverts to an older woman and cries, *"I'll never find another virgin! Never!"*

The film is loaded with funny lines like the scene in which Hutton's loyal servant says, *"Wake up sleepy head. It's Sunset!"* And her servant Sebastian (played by Clevon Little) is a riot in himself, delivering one witty line after another.

ONCE BITTEN was intentionally made for laughs and targeted toward the same audience as FRIGHT NIGHT, LOVE AT FIRST BITE, VAMP and BUFFY THE VAMPIRE SLAYER.

FRIGHT NIGHT
1985; Columbia (Color); Producer: Herb Jaffe; Screenwriter & Director: Tom Holland; Camera: Jan Kiesser.

Tom Holland's trendy vampire thriller FRIGHT NIGHT was originally intended to do for vampires what Joe Dante's THE HOWLING (1981) did for werewolves. THE HOWLING is by far a more serious horror outing, while FRIGHT NIGHT, unfortunately, is a Count Yorga-ish film illuminated with some jazzy special effects and some horrible but bearable adolescent comedy. Somehow the flat pranks and uninspired funny dialogue are too overwhelming, and as a result, FRIGHT NIGHT is more of a horror comedy that falls somewhere in between John Landis' AN AMERICAN WEREWOLF IN LONDON and Stan Dragoti's LOVE AT FIRST BITE.

Still, despite the flat-at-times comedy and the cliche vampire trappings, FRIGHT NIGHT is a very entertaining modern vehicle, occasionally rising to the level of being "spooky," especially for those viewing the film for the very first time. Although the fright scenes seem to loose their impact with each viewing, the film is indeed superior to its inept sequel.

The beginning of the story resembles the Tom Hank film THE BURBS to a degree. A young boy (played by William Ragsdale) notices activity in the once-abandoned house next door. After a series of shocking events, Ragsdale comes to the conclusion that his new neighbor, Jerry Dandridge (played by Christopher Sarandon) is a horrible, evil vampire. In a desperate attempt to save his girlfriend, his mother, and his neighborhood, the young lad employs movie vampire hunter Christopher Vincent (played brilliantly by veteran actor Roddy McDowall). McDowall, the host of a late-night horror-flick series, reluctantly agrees to help destroy the cunning vampire next door. What follows is a series of predictable encounters between the heroes and the villains, the highlight of which are some flashy and dazzling transformation scenes in which the vampire shape-shifts into a horrendous mechanical vampire bat. But don't get too excited horror fans, because its all for

laughs and cheap shocks. Ken Diaz's special effects are great, but runs a close tie against McDowall's memorable performance as a cowardly vampire killer. McDowall is the film's real star, but credit must also go to Sarandon for delivering one of the screen's most seductive and decadent male bloodsuckers.

FRIGHT NIGHT is, by no means, a classic vampire movie, but the film is quite entertaining despite its comical approach to the legend of movie vampires.

LIFE FORCE

1985; Cannon/Tri-Star (British) (Color); Producer: Menahem Golan & Yoram Globus; Director: Tobe Hooper; Screenwriters: Dan O'Bannon & Don Jakoby from the novel *Space Vampires* by Colin Wilson; Camera: Alan Hume.

Based on the novel *Space Vampires* written by Colin Wilson, and originally planned for filming under the same title, LIFEFORCE starts out as an outer space epic, then becomes a vampire yarn that eventually turns into an end-of-the-world saga reminiscent of Hammer's FIVE MILLION YEARS TO EARTH (1968).

Christopher Sarandon as the bloodthirsty vampire Jerry Dandridge in FRIGHT NIGHT (1985).

In the film, a space probe, originally dispatched from earth to explore outer space and examine Halley's Comet up close, uncovers an alien spacecraft whose occupants carry with them a deadly disease. With just a kiss, the humanoid aliens can actually drain the life force out of a single human body. Their victims are then turned into mindless zombies who must then suck the life force from others to stay "undead." Controlling it all is a beautiful nude space vampiress. When the surviving astronaut returns to earth, he unknowingly brings along the "space vampires" and soon all of London falls under their destructive spell.

The premise of this film is so ridiculous that certain moments are actually unintentionally funny. Tobe Hooper's direction here is clearly a tribute to the many Hammer horror films of the 1960's. Anyone who has an admiration for Hammer films cannot help but notice the very obvious similarities

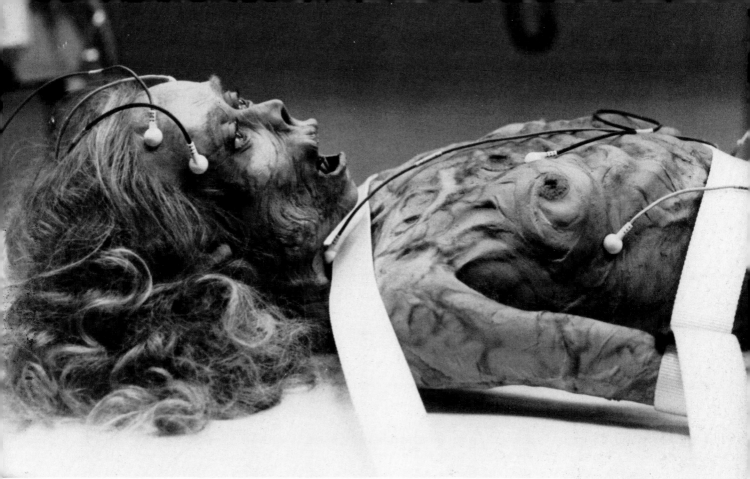

A victim of the alien vampire of LIFE FORCE (1985).

effects are grandiose and worthy of impressive big budget science fiction movies like STAR TREK: THE MOTION PICTURE and ALIEN. But unfortunately, not even the lavish effects can save this film from its otherwise horrid and inept screen adaptation. In a positive note, the ingenious fashion in which the "space vampires" first seduce their victims and then suck their life-force, leaving behind withered corpses, is quite impressive and very cleverly executed by Hooper. LIFE FORCE is a film that fans will either love or hate.

between the climax of LIFE FORCE and the climax of Hammer's FIVE MILLION YEARS TO EARTH (1968), during which London is totally devastated under mass destruction. In both films, the city falls under the control of an evil force or entity. The film also takes-off on George Romero's *"Living Dead"* movies for an added modern-day horror movie appeal.

Originally, producers Golan and Globus set out to make a larger-than-life horror/science fiction movie, however, once most of the film's budget was absorbed by John Dykstra's expensive special effects, the producers ordered that the script, originally drafted by Dan O'Bannon, be redrafted by Don Jakoby. The alterations had to meet the restrictions of the film's limited budget. Therefore, this explains the confusing and hasty climax, obviously filmed in a hurried fashion. The last half of the film appears out of place with the film's first half, of which the special

VAMP

1986; New World (Color); Producer: Donald P. Borchers; Director & Screenwriter: Richard Wenk.

Very much in the same league as FRIGHT NIGHT, VAMP is an equally entertaining tale of modern-day vampirism that intentionally combines adolescent humor with horror. VAMP makes no pretense about being a comedy, and the humor is actually more stomachable and less cliche and predictable than FRIGHT NIGHT.

VAMP stars Grace Jones as Katrina, the sultry leader of a den of vampires who owns the seedy After

Dark Club, naturally located in the most undesirable part of a big city. These vampires dovetail with human society, using a strip joint as their cover to attract lonely men who are hardly likely to be missed. They are the vampires' perfect victims. But when three college kids (led by Chris Makepeace and Robert Rusler) visit the After Dark Club, Katrina puts the bite on Rusler in what is the most sensual and erotic biting scene imaginable. Most of the remaining part of the film has the film's hero (Makepeace) running away from and then chasing after the modern-day vampires to save his vampirized friend (Rusler).

Grace Jones is both brilliant and exotic as the scary vampire leader who was once an Egyptian queen (this part of the film is never explored, but why bother, when the film's running time is a quick ninety-three minutes). In fact, it's hard to think of anyone better for the part of Katrina than Miss Grace!

The film takes place all in one night, and is therefore fast-paced. The vampires are slain by way of fire (ala the climax of THE HOWLING), bow and arrow and even the wooden heel of a shoe pump! Grace's vampire is destroyed by sunlight when Makepeace corners her under the sewer catacombs of the city during the early morning hours. VAMP is a lot of fun!

I MARRIED A VAMPIRE
1986; Prism Entertainment (Color); Producer, Director & Screenwriter: Jay Raskin; Camera: Oren Rudavsky.

I MARRIED A VAMPIRE is yet another silly and mindless spoof on the vampire legend with a bad sound track and dismal editing.

In this film, Rachel Gordon delivers a horrid performance as Viola, a young voluptuous woman who runs away from her small town life style and her parents to the big city (New York). The people there prove to be very cold and her romantic notions of living in such a big city are shattered by its harshness and sleaziness. Her one great savior arrives when she unknowingly marries a vampire named Robespiere (Brendan Hickey). But the twist works well.

Poor Viola, the signs were not clear enough in the beginning: The groom wants a honeymoon in Transylvania and he sleeps in a king-size casket! Someone really needs to tell this woman to wake up! But of course, who can? Anyone watching this film will probably fall to sleep within the first fifteen minutes as a result of utter boredom. In any event,

Vampire Katrina (Grace Jones) performs an erotic dance in VAMP (1986).

the fact that her husband is a vampire only helps her to get along in the big city. Together they share sweet love and happiness as they carry out sweet revenge on the low-life scum of the city.

This vapid film from the creators of TOXIC AVENGER and NUKE 'EM HIGH is told in flashback by actress Gordon. Advertisements for the film read *"Till Death Do Us Part!" "A Vow They Won't Have To Keep!"*

I MARRIED A VAMPIRE is not a very impressive vampire movie, and anyone who admires the genre will steer far away from this bomb.

GRAVEYARD SHIFT

1987; Cinema Ventures (Color); Producer: Michael Bockner; Screenwriter & Director: Gerard Ciccoritti; Camera: Robert Bergman.

Not to be confused with Ralph Singleton's 1990 Stephen King film of the same title, Gerard Ciccoritti's GRAVEYARD SHIFT deals with an undead member of a vampire harem in New York City. Our vampire hero is played by Silvio Oliviero, who, at three hundred and fifty years old, drives an all

night cab as a clever device to obtain human blood.

Each time the vampire prepares to sink his teeth into a fresh neck, he turns gray, but his fangs remain a shimmery white. Plenty blood is spilt in the back seat of his cab. However, this vampire has a heart. He soon becomes undone by his softheartedness when he betrays his coven-like harem of previous victims to settle down with a suicidal lady film director.

The entire film is played out much like a bad dream, and is inferior in many ways to FRIGHT NIGHT, VAMP, THE LOST BOYS and NEAR DARK. The killings carried-out by the vampires are meaningless, with the exception of the opening scene in which the lead vampire puts the bite on a female customer in his cab. An example of one such meaningless killing is a scene that involves a female vampire who dances at a strip joint. She seduces a man into a dark and deserted alley. There, she pulls out a razor, slashes his neck and drinks his blood.

Quite honestly, the film could have been handled much better, but the low budget, bad sound effects, the meaningless dialogue and the poor photography simply ruin the effect. This pretty much sums up GRAVEYARD SHIFT, another silly vampire film that should have never been made.

Three hundred fifty-year-old vampire (Silvio Olivero) takes care of business in GRAVEYARD SHIFT (1987).

Sequel: THE UNDERSTUDY: GRAVEYARD SHIFT II.

NEAR DARK
1987; DEG (Color); Producer: Steven Charles-Jaffe; Director: Kathryn Bigelow; Screenwriters: Eric Red & Kathryn Bigelow;
Camera: Adam Greenberg.

A mosquito lands on a human arm. It injects its receptor into the skin and begins drinking blood. All of this is shown in close-up, magnified hundreds of times for a clear picture. Suddenly, the insect is smacked by a hand, the hand of the film's main character and hero, played by Adrian Pasdar. Blood splatters all over his arm. Next we are shown the quickly setting sun as we listen to the eerie soundtrack by Tangerine Dream.

The opening scene of NEAR DARK only hints at the horror that is soon to follow for Pasdar.

In the film, Lance Henriksen (ALIENS) leads a group of trashy American vampires who drift around the lonely Midwest highways, terrorizing redneck bars and sucking the blood out of cocky cowboys. The vampires are depicted as gypsies who constantly move from one Midwest city to another, hiding by day, eating by night.

The film's premise of how these vampires dovetail with modern-day society begins when a female vampire bites a young man (Adrian Pasdar) on his neck. She fails to "bleed" him (a method in which a victim's blood is completely drained therefore preventing them from transforming into one of the immortal bloodsuckers). As a result of the vampire's venomous bite, Pasdar partially transforms into one of the nocturnal creatures. The boy just does not have it in himself to kill for blood, but bad boy vampire Bill Paxton (ALIENS & PREDATOR II) teaches him how to prey on humans in several grisly sequences that will please the splatter enthusiast.

As in his previous genre films, Paxton delivers his usual slick and comedic lines. In one scene where he's about to bite a redneck victim in a cowboy bar, he comments, *"Boy, I hate when they don't shave!"*

NEAR DARK offers some interesting vampire trappings, such as when Pasdar, who is unable to kill for human blood, sustains himself by feeding off his girlfriend's stolen blood. Original to the vampire tradition is the method in which Pasdar's vampire

A teenage vampire bares his fangs in THE LOST BOYS (1987).

becomes human again after his vampiric blood is drained and his father's blood is transfused into his body. He then becomes the film's savant and destroys the other vampires with the help of the sun's rays.

There are many nice touches in this film, such as when Pasdar introduces his newly found girlfriend to his pet horse. Naturally, animals can sense evil, at least in movies. The horse goes berserk and runs away. The scene is a bit cliche, but adds a familiar touch of traditionalism to this otherwise contemporary non-traditional film.

Another nice touch is their fear of sunlight. These vampires are afraid of the sun, thus the title NEAR DARK! There's always a constant fear over their heads, and director Bigelow makes the viewer quite aware of this handicap.

The grisly tale is well mounted with a great script that lends its traditional vampire legend to a contemporary setting with very little room for comedy antics. The film also features some great special effects, and the music by Tangerine Dream is exceptional and adds to the fast-paced horrific mood.

NEAR DARK is a refreshing variation on the traditional vampire genre that actually works well in its contemporary Midwest setting.

before it, THE LOST BOYS deals with borderline horror and comedy, as a new family moves into a small California town and the oldest son is immediately taken with a local teenage girl who just happens to be a vampire. The coming out of our hero-turned vampire (played by teen idol Jason Patric) is handled in comic fashion, but the moments in which Patric must confront the lead vampire (played by Kiefer Sutherland) and his vampirized rat-pack-clan is played for cheap thrills and hollow melodramatics.

Schumaker teases the viewer with some very stylish scenes and some interesting vampire folklore, as well as a shocking twist ending. Corey Haim plays Jason Patric's brother and the film's teenage savant and Van Helsing type while Jami Gertz plays his teenage love interest, who wants desperately to be freed from Sutherland's evil hold and her own dreadful curse. The performances and dialogue are above average for this type of film and the vampire scenes are quite good.

The fact that THE LOST BOYS was a big box office hit, bigger than all of the modern-day vampire vehicles released around its time (FRIGHT NIGHT, VAMP, NEAR DARK and BUFFY THE VAMPIRE SLAYER), should say something about this film.

THE LOST BOYS
1987; Warner (Color); Producer: Bo Welch; Director: Joel Schumacher; Screenwriters: Janice Fischer, James Jeremias & Jeffrey Boam; Camera: Michael Chapman.

Joel Schumaker's big budget tale of teenage vampires reduces the vampire legend to *"MTV meets the vampires!"* Like FRIGHT NIGHT and VAMP

A RETURN TO SALEM'S LOT
1987; Warner (Color); Producer, Director & Screenwriter: Larry Cohen, based on the characters created by Stephen King.

This film actually works as a dark comedy much like SLEEPWALKERS and NEEDFUL THINGS, for example, but without the adolescent trappings of

A young bloodthirsty drifter from NEAR DARK (1987), begins to decompose after being exposed to the sun.

FRIGHT NIGHT and VAMP. Genre director Larry Cohen uses comedy as an even darker device to relieve the shock effects and horror of this film. The vampires of this community prefer to drink the blood of farm animals, but an old grandma-like vampire who can't give up human blood complains that she has a "*drinking problem!*" Also, there is a scene in which the central vampire figure of this film is impaled on the American flag!

Michael Moriarty and his son return to their home town to find that it is infested with hundreds of vampires and demon-like creatures. The town has literally become a den of evil and corruption since the original film. The film's plot, also written by Cohen, is weakened by acts of senseless violence. The traditional myths about garlic and reflections in mirrors are dispelled with this unimpressive but watchable sequel to SALEM'S LOT (1979).

MONSTER SQUAD
1987; Vestron (Color); Producer: Jonathan A. Zimbert; Director: Fred Dekker; Screenwriters: Shane Black & Fred Dekker.

Universal's most infamous monsters rise from the dusty vaults to take back a magical amulet from a group of kids who call themselves the *Monster Squad*.

The monsters, which include the Frankenstein Monster, the Wolfman and the Creature from The Black Lagoon are led by Count Dracula (played by Duncan Regehr). Dracula wants the powerful amulet in his possession so that he may rule over the world. Naturally, the Monster Squad wins and saves the world from the domination of the evil vampire, his army of "*Famous Monsters*" and his female vampire minions.

The name Alucard is even mentioned as part of the film's many nostalgic jokes cleverly written into

the script by screenwriters Shane Black and Fred Dekker. The fast-paced film directed by Dekker is surprisingly suspenseful at times and visually satisfying with some very atmospheric cinematography that one wishes filmmakers would use in their serious horror films.

Dekker's MONSTER SQUAD pays homage to those many "B" Universal horror films like HOUSE OF FRANKENSTEIN, SON OF DRACULA, THE WOLFMAN and ABBOTT AND COSTELLO MEET FRANKENSTEIN!

VAMPIRE AT MIDNIGHT
1987; New Age (Color); Producers: Jason Williams & Tom Friedman; Director: Greg McClatchy; Screenwriter: Dulany Ross Clements.

Gustav Vintas portrays vampire Doctor Victor Radkof, a new age hypnotherapist who finds himself falling for actress Lesley Miline. Jason Williams plays a police inspector investigating a string of vampire-style murders together with the "good" doctor, who, to his horror, turns out to be the vampire responsible for the murders.

The plot thickens when Wilson competes with the monster for the same woman (Miline) and a climatic battle to the finish ensues.

Director Greg McClatchy stylishly delivers a refreshing new vampire tale with clever plot twists, great special effects and some light gore to satisfy both the vampire and splatter enthusiast. Still, VAMPIRE AT MIDNIGHT is good entertainment, considering its independent, low budget origin.

Duncan Regehr plays Count Dracula in THE MONSTER SQUAD (1987).

NOT OF THIS EARTH

1988; Miracle Pictures (Color); Producers: Jim Wynorski & Mark Hanna; Director: Jim Wynorski; Screenwriters: Jim Wynorski & R. J. Robertson.

This pseudo-remake of the 1958 Roger Corman film actually looks cheaper than the original low budget effort. Arthur Roberts assumes the role of the alien vampire in dark shades who is transporting suitcases of human blood to his hungry planet.

Former porn star Traci Lords plays the nurse who he hires to give him occasional blood transfusions while on earth. To the alien's dismay, Lords catches onto his scam and brings about his downfall.

The original Corman film was played straight, whereas this remake does offer an occasional laugh and snicker, such as the gory scene in which one of the alien vampires goes on a murderous knife stabbing rampage when he is accidentally given the transfused blood of a rabid dog.

NOT OF THIS EARTH is definitely a bomb on every level; the Corman film is superior in its subtleties. The special effects by Alex Rambaldi are also inadequate, but most of this has nothing to do with Rambaldi's talents; rather, the low budget has taken its toll on every level - beginning with the script and finishing with the special effects.

THE REJUVENATOR

1988; SCSV Films/Jewel Productions (Color); Producers: Steven Mackler & Robert Zimmerman; Director: Brian Thomas Jones; Screenwriters: Simon Nuchtern & Brian Thomas Jones.

Released on video as REJUVENATRIX, this Brian Thomas Jones state-of-the-art horror film offers a unique twist to the vampire theme. Writers Simon Nuchtern and Brian Jones have come up with a premise in which a scientist, Dr. Gregory Ashton (played by John MacKay), develops an anti-aging formula from the brain cells of cadavers. He uses old film star Elizabeth Warren (Vivian Lanko) as his guinea pig. We later learn that the effects of the serum are temporary, and larger doses are required to maintain youth and beauty. Soon Warren becomes a hideous monster and finds herself attacking the living, killing them and eating their brains to stay young and beautiful in a fashion much like RETURN OF THE LIVING DEAD.

Jones uses state of the art special effects and enormous amounts of gore to raise the interest and commercial level of this film, but unfortunately, despite the innovative effects, THE REJUVENATOR is just another splatter variation on the vampire legend and a modern rehashing of Edward Dein's THE LEECH WOMAN (1960), Roger Corman's THE WASP WOMAN (1959) and Terence Fisher's THE MAN WHO COULD CHEAT DEATH (1959).

DRACULA'S WIDOW

1988; DEG (Color); Producer: Stephen Traxler; Director: Christopher Coppola; Screenwriters: Kathryn Ann Thomas & Christopher Coppola.

Director Christopher Coppola brings together Dracula's widow with the descendants of both Jonathan Harker and Dr. Van Helsing in this laughable rehashing of the Dracula legend. Actress Sylvia Kristel performs here as Dracula's sultry widow Vanessa.

The premise introduces us to a young Raymond Everett (Lenny Von Dohlen), the owner and operator of a house of horrors wax museum. Raymond has an affection for old vampire movies, and his new exhibit, direct from Romania, is on the Dracula legend. For his new exhibit, Raymond receives six large crates from Romania, one of which carries the body of Dracula's Widow! Immediately upon her revival, she goes on a killing spree, wiping out most of Hollywood at the blink of an eye, turning her victims into hamburger meat. She even turns young Raymond into her Renfield-like slave.

The Van Helsing character in the film is portrayed as a washed-up old man by actor Stefan Schnabel, who, during the last quarter of the film, is also transformed into a bloodsucker! Can you believe, Van Helsing, a vampire?

The violence exhibited in this film is senseless, but fans of gore and splatter will get a kick out of it, while the remaining viewers will simply laugh in disgust. The script's dialogue, co-written by Coppola, is flat and unimaginative. But most disappointing is Kristel's characterization of Dracula's widow, which is flat-out horrible. Her strong Romanian accent is too obvious, to the point that it becomes overwhelming. She's a bitch of a vampire with a very bad attitude and with little-to-no meaningful dialogue nor any humanistic emotions of sympathy or sensuality. The one opportunity to deliver a lasting image as a female vampire in a contemporary film is

Traci Lords gives a blood transfusion to vampire Arthur Roberts in NOT OF THIS EARTH (1988).

totally wasted here. Kristel is definitely no Ingrid Pitt nor is she a Catherine Deneuve. Can't Hollywood deliver a new female vampire character that can hold her own against the likes of Count Dracula and other male master vampires?

DRACULA'S WIDOW is an amateurish attempt by Coppola to update the Dracula legend to modern times. The film simply falls flat on its face, and it's no wonder distributors bowed away from handling its national theatrical distribution. One wonders how a film company (DEG) that turned out such a superior fright film like NEAR DARK can lower their standards and produce and actually release an atrocity like DRACULA'S WIDOW. Actually, DRACULA'S WIDOW was never released in theaters.

FRIGHT NIGHT II
1988; Columbia (Color); Producers: Herb Jaffe & Mort Engelberg; Director: Tommy Lee Wallace; Screenwriters: Tim Metcalfe, Miguel Tejada-Flores & Tommy Lee Wallace based on the characters created by Tom Holland; Camera: Mark Irwin

Roddy McDowall returns to the role of fearless vampire killer Peter Vincent in this sequel to FRIGHT NIGHT (1985). Also returning is actor William Ragsdale, who is again the first to encounter the new clan of bloodsuckers. The film waste no time and goes straight for the throat during the first fifteen minutes.

Columbia hired four writers, including director Tommy Lee Wallace, to come up with this film's cliche premise. The story begins when the seductive and beautiful Regine (Julie Carmen), sister of the vampire Jerry Dandridge who was destroyed by William Ragsdale and McDowell in the first film, moves into a large apartment building next to a college dormitory with her entourage of vampires: a manimal creature (Jonathan Gries), a Renfield-type servant (Russell Clark) who eats moths and a black female vampire on roller skates.

The sultry vampire Regine is totally bent on revenge against those responsible for her brother's death, but Ragsdale calls upon McDowall to aide him in extinguishing the beast by using mirrors to reflect the sunlight.

Unlike the original, the sequel offers much more graphic and violent sequences, from bloody impalements to rotting bodies. The film's most graphic scene occurs when the vampire's manimal-friend is killed and his tummy bursts open as buckets of bugs, maggots and creepy-crawlies emerge. Yuck!

The original film is superior to the sequel in terms of its script and the manner in which it successfully balances horror and comedy, but FRIGHT NIGHT II delivers the massive amount of fangs and blood and flashy special effects that moviegoers have come to expect. Still, the sequel is entertaining and often mesmerizing. The transformation scenes are fabulous and worthy of the very best. What separates the sequel from its predecessor is that it goes more for the throat and less for humor. Fans of vampire movies will enjoy this effort. Hopefully Columbia writers will come up with fresh material for a third film.

DANCE OF THE DAMNED
1988; Virgin/New Classics (Color); Producer: Andy Ruben; Director: Katt Shea Ruben; Screenwriters: Any Ruben & Katt Shea Ruben; Camera: Phedon Papamichael.

The title of this film suggests that if you are a strip-tease dancer in a seedy joint, you will be damned for all eternity and subjected to becoming one of the undead's prey. Sounds pretty confusing? So is the Andy Ruben and Katt Shea Ruben screenplay for this rather dismal, noir-ish vampire film.

A female stripper and exotic dancer named Jodi (played by Starr Andreeff) finds herself contemplating suicide. A vampire (played by Cyril O'Reilly) is stalking the city streets in search of his next victim. In doing so, he passes a strip joint. From the sidewalk, the vampire telepathically sense Jodi's desire to die. He enters and offers her $1,000 to spend the rest of the night with him until dawn as a device to take her home and drink her blood. She all too easily accepts, and soon discovers the lonely creature the vampire really is.

For the first time ever, the vampire, whose name we really never know, finds himself becoming interested in and then falling in love with Jodi. As the vampire explains his condition and his sorrows to Jodi, he finds that he cannot bring himself to killing her, but towards the film's ambiguous conclusion, the vampire tries to kill her when she tries to escape. Jodi no longer wants to know the pain and the pleasures of his other-worldly existence. The conclusion of this film is ambiguous because we never really know whether the vampire dies from exposure to the sun. Apparently director Katt Shea Ruben feels that the answer should remain anonymous.

In an all time movie first, the vampire is given the supernatural capability of seeing and hearing through solid objects. The vampire can also move at a undetectable speed that would make even *The Flash* envious. Finally, this vampire also has the ability of telepathy.

DANCE OF THE DAMNED is certainly not one of the better contemporary vampire movies, but it does offer incredible performances for a low budget horror film. In fact, it is the performances of both O'Reilly and Andreeff that carry this film. Director Ruben does a super job at developing the film's two main characters. He also succeeds in delivering the lonely side of an immortal existence, which few films have managed to do. Naturally, being immortal and handicapped by the sun has its down-side, and Ruben successfully captures this emotion on film. In this respect, the film and its filmmaker's honest attempt to deliver a well-rounded and logical horror tale is well-received, noted and totally respected.

DANCE OF THE DAMNED was remade as TO SLEEP WITH A VAMPIRE in 1992.

BEVERLY HILLS VAMP
1988; Trans World Entertainment (Color); Director: Fred Olen Ray

Although filmmaker Fred Olen Ray's THE TOMB combined trappings from both the mummy and vampire genres, BEVERLY HILLS VAMP remains as his first full-fledged vampire movie.

In the film, genre actress Britt Ekland plays the madame vamp who leads a lair of other sexy female vampires, who are actually prostitutes, against red-hot-blooded males. Eddie Deezen plays the hero, and he and two other aspiring male filmmakers go up against the bloodsuckers.

BEVERLY HILLS VAMP is Ray's vampire version of his previous work CHAINSAW HOOKERS.

VAMPIRE KNIGHTS
1988; Filmtrust (color)

Advertised as "*The vampire comedy of 1988,*" VAMPIRE KNIGHTS is far removed from the praises of its own advertisement. In fact, the film should have been advertised as "*The most ridiculous vampire film of 1988!*"

The title of the film "Vampire Knights" refers to a gang of mortals devoted to extinguishing the vampire race off the face of the earth. The Knights are fully committed to protecting mortals from the savage vampires in this film, who are committed to literally sucking their young male victims dry in the most erotic ways.

The story-line concerns a young man who travels to a small town to visit his friend. There he discovers that the night life is more than he bargained for.

There are inept plot twists, one of which reveals that only one of the Knights is truly mortal.

The film was later mimicked more successfully by BUFFY- THE VAMPIRE SLAYER (1992), another bad vampire movie.

TO DIE FOR
1988; Skouras/Trimark Pictures (Color); Producer: Brian Kumar; Director: Deran Serafian; Screenwriter: Leslie King.

Producer Brian Kumar's loose, post-modern adaptation of Bram Stoker's *Dracula* tells how real estate agent Sydney Walsh (the film's Jonathan Harker and Mina characters all rolled into one) is sent out to Vlad's (Brendan Hughes) new Beverly Hills home. Naturally, Vlad is taken in by her beauty and it is not long before he is putting the move on her.

In addition to Hughes' vampire, actor Steve Bond plays Tom, another bloodsucker and Vlad's archenemy (apparently, Vlad once stole his woman). Amanda Wyss is Lucy, who becomes Vlad's first victim and who later becomes very foul as she descends into vampirism (I believe the technical term is "*vamped*"). Wyss' vampirization is very impressive and should be noted as being one of the few female vampires to leave a lasting impression.

The Leslie King script uses scenes directly from the Bram Stoker novel, one of which shows us how Vlad cuts his chest open to offer his blood to Walsh. For the most part, the vampire trappings are a bit cliche and are often silly, such as the scene when the two vampire foes fight each other during the film's climax. Most of these unintentionally funny sequences result from a weak script and for once, has very little or nothing to do with inadequate funding.

About the only truly interesting aspect of this film is Vlad's destruction, which is very similar to Paul Naschy's death in COUNT DRACULA'S GREAT LOVE. In TO DIE FOR, Vlad commits suicide by walking into the sunlight. As a result, the sun's rays reduce him into a pile of decomposed ashes. Apparently, the vampire of this film felt that his love for Walsh was "*To Die For!*"

A superior sequel was made entitled TO DIE FOR II: SON OF DARKNESS (1991).

LAIR OF THE WHITE WORM
1988; First Fright (Great Britain) (Color); Producer, Director & Screenwriter: Ken Russell, based on the novel by Bram Stoker; Camera: Dick Bush.

Ken Russell's bizarre mix of vampirism and underground horror is truly funny at times, but the film plays more like a bad horror film that was not originally made to be humorous. Russell has stated and confirmed in certain published interviews that he most certainly set out to make a film that was simultaneously horrifying and funny, but in an inseparable fashion; a style that dates back to the days of filmmaker James Whale, who virtually created this style of horror movie with films like FRANKENSTEIN, BRIDE OF FRANKENSTEIN, THE OLD DARK HOUSE and THE INVISIBLE MAN. Russell's LAIR OF THE WHITE WORM is far from being subtle and like some of his other films, LAIR OF THE WHITE WORM is also more on the satirical side, this one based on Bram Stoker's novel about a vampire who worships an ancient snake god.

In the film, Hugh Grant plays the Lord of D'Ampton manor and the descendant of the man who was responsible for destroying the infamous D'Ampton worm. Amanda Donahoe is Lady Sylvia Marsh, the vampire guardian of the worm that has managed to survive in an underground network of caverns. The vampire has been sacrificing virgin women to her snake god for hundreds of years and intends to give Grant's girlfriend (played by Catherine Oxenberg) to the beast.

Although THE LAIR OF THE WHITE WORM is less a vampire film and more of a film about Paganistic sacrifices and Roman mysticism, there are scenes in which Donahoe's vampirism is briefly explored, such as the nasty sequence when she literally bites off the willy of a naked boy and devours his blood. There is also the scene in which she comes across a crucifix and savagely sprouts fangs and spits venom all over he holy symbol.

LAIR OF THE WHITE WORM is a great variation on the vampire legend that should not be missed.

THE WICKED
1989; Hemdale/Cine-Funds/Somerset Film (Australia) (Color); Producers: Jan Tyrrell & James Michael Vernon; Director: Colin Eggleston; Screenwriters: David R. Young & Colin Eggleston; Camera: Garry Wapshott

This Australian horror film is more of a cheap and tacky spoof on both the *"old dark house"* theme and the vampire legend rather than a straight-forward vampire film. Not much really happens during the first half of this "wicked" film, and what occurs during the last half is too confusing for consumption. The viewer is never really sure what the hell is going on.

A group of travelers (Richard Morgan, Brett Climo and Angela Kennedy) in the Outback come across the house of Sir Alfred (played very campy by John Doyle). He's a vampire, and so are the other inhabitants of the manor, all of which sport fangs and drink human blood from the neck of their victims.

Sir Alfred, the central vampire, actually grows to thirty feet tall during the film's climax and chases after the heroes. He can also float in the air! The vampire is finally destroyed while floating in thin air above his victims when suddenly heroine Angela Kennedy throws a rock and hits him causing the maniac to explode. Can you believe this? What will screenwriters think of next?

The dialogue of this film is vapid and the effects are equally horrid. But what is worse is the fact that this film purposely tries to be funny, but fails. The viewer will be happy when this mundane "epic" from down-under has ended. No doubt there will be a sequel.

THE UNDERSTUDY: GRAVEYARD SHIFT II
1989; Cinema Ventures (Color); Producers: Stephen R. Flaks & Arnold H. Bruck; Screenwriter & Director: Gerard Ciccoritti; Camera: Barry Stone.

One wonders how a fairly awful low-budget horror film like GRAVEYARD SHIFT can justify a superior sequel. Apparently producers Stephen Flaks and Arnold Bruck thought they could do it all over again, but only the second time around, do it much better than before. Frankly, they have succeeded, and the result is a fairly good vampire movie with better production values and a smoother script than before.

This time around the central vampire is actually an actor in a vampire movie in the midst of production; sort of like a film within a film. Director Gerard Ciccoritti, who also directed the original, pays homage to Carl Dryer's VAMPYR with hints of lesbian bloodsucking. He also pays homage to Hammer's HORROR OF DRACULA (1958), in which the hero of this film pulls down red drapes to expose the vampire to the sun's lethal rays. As a result, the film delivers familiar trappings and cliche lines and therefore is superior to the more experimental original (most moviegoers prefer familiar material - it's easier to identify with). The script works much smoother and flows easier than the original as a result of the standard trappings.

In the film, the vampire understudy (played by Silvio Oliviero, now with long curly hair), who cast a reflection in a mirror, kills the leading man and promises the leading lady, Carmilla (Wendy Gazelle), an immortal life. So what's new? The premise, also written by Ciccoritti, does not really deliver anything unique or fresh, but the film is still worth a look for those who truly admire vampire films. There is a twist in which the vampire's curse still lives on and a chance that producers Flak and Bruck will exploit the series with yet a third installment.

THE VINEYARD
1989; Northstar Entertainment (Color); Producer: Harry Mok; Directors: William Rice & James Hong; Screenwriters: James Hong, Douglas Condo & James Marlowe.

A closeup of Sylvia Kristel as Dracula's sultry widow in DRACULA'S WIDOW (1988).

A sorcerer and scientist (played by James Hong) lures horrible actors and actresses to his isolated island abode to consume their blood in order to maintain his youthful appearance in this ghastly and often gory R-rated film.

With this film, it does not matter whether the victim's blood is that of a virgin female or male, nor do the traditional vampire trappings apply. There are enough impalements and arrowings to shake a wooden stake at!

THE VINEYARD is a vapid blend of mumbo-jumbo black magic, vampirism and immortality issues combined with walking human zombies-on-the-rampage that will literally turn your stomach. Speaking of turning your stomach- in this film there is a scene when actress Cheryl Lawson actually spits up spiders! What's worse is that the spider scene is the film's highlight.

CARMILLA
1989; Showtime (Color); Producer: Bridget Terry; Director: Gabrielle Beaumont; Screenwriter (Teleplay): Jonathan Furst, based on the story by Sheridan le Fanu; Camera: Ron Vargas.

Sheridan le Fanu's classic horror tale about the beautiful and mysterious vampire Carmilla and her control over a family in a secluded mansion is reset in the American South.

Carmilla is played by Meg Tilly. As a victim of a coach accident, she is taken in by a family and befriended by Maria (Played by Ione Skye). It does not take the vampire long to turn everyone in the household against each other, resulting in some deaths that the local authorities and doctors classify as part of some unknown plague. Roddy McDowall portrays Inspector Amos, who has different ideas. In the film he suggests, "*The plague does not bite!*" It is Inspector Amos who sets a trap to prove Carmilla is a vampire, but he too meets his demise when the vampire shoves a wooden stake through his mouth and head.

Eventually, Carmilla is impaled during a struggle with Maria but this is after we learn that the beautiful young creature was once involved with several other vampires, perhaps the Karnsteins? Maybe even the Draculas?

In accordance with the well-filmed *Carmilla* legend, CARMILLA does offer some good atmospheric photography, as well as the usual lesbian aspects between the vampire and her victim. There is one fabulous but bizarre scene to look out for. In it, Carmilla is shown floating in thin air while biting Maria's neck for blood. The scene is quite effective for this otherwise slow and dull adaptation.

Amazingly, the film, which runs approximately ninety-three minutes, is produced by Shelly Duval. Still, much better is BLOOD AND ROSES made in 1960.

VAMPIRE'S KISS
1989; Hemdale/Magellan Pictures (Color); Producer: Christopher Nowak; Director: Robert Bierman; Screenwriter: Joseph Minion; Camera: Stefan Czapsky.

Like the Julian Sands film BOXING HELENA, VAMPIRE'S KISS is one of those far-off and very bizarre "artsy" movies that seem to make absolutely no sense as to what the hell is going on. VAMPIRE'S KISS is a confusing tale of vampirism and psychotic behavior in which the viewer is never really sure whether Nicholas (MOONSTRUCK) Cage is a so-called creature of the night or nothing more than just a psychopath who, like the demented title character of the George Romero film MARTIN, believes himself to be a vampire.

The film flows ever-so-slow and during its beginning seems very promising and faithful to the genre. Cage plays Peter Loew, a young business executive for a literary agency. Peter is frustrated because he cannot really find himself a steady girlfriend. In the film, he discusses his emotional frustrations to psychiatrist Elizabeth Ashely, who, incidentally, delivers a great performance here.

One night, Cage creates the illusion in his mind that he is visited by a mysterious and sultry vampire named Rachel (Jennifer Beals). In a very impressive scene, Rachel sinks her venomous fangs into Peter's neck. From this point onward the young executive descend into madness as he starts believing that he is actually transforming into a real-life bloodsucker. Peter even goes so far as to buy a pair of plastic Halloween vampire fangs and begins walking the streets of New York in a Max Schreck-type fashion, harassing women at night clubs and loudly screaming out, "*I'm a vampire!*" These scenes are both hilarious and pathetic as we watch the poor lad descend deeper into madness.

It soon becomes evident that Peter is suffering from his own emotional and psychological frustrations and the vampire persona he has adopted for himself is a form of emotional release, which means that Rachel, the sultry vampire, is nothing more than a figment of his imagination. It is later explained that Rachel is the creation of the dark side of Peter's mind that eventually forces him to the point of murder. Even his psychiatrist is a figment of his own imagination, representing the good side of his inner-self. Maria Conchito Alonso plays Alva, Peter's secretary and the true victim of his madness. During Peter's descent into madness, Alva is pushed too far, and it is her brother, who literally believes that Peter is a vampire, that actually drives a wooden stake through Peter's heart during the climax of this ambiguous film. Naturally, a wooden stake driven into anyone's heart, mortal or immortal, will cause death. Peter's fantasy of being a real-life bloodsucker is lived up to his last breathing moments. But was it all a dream? Who the hell knows! And by the film's conclusion, the viewer will most probably find himself asking, *Who the hell cares! Kill the lunatic!*"

VAMPIRE'S KISS is by no means a faithful tale of vampirism, but the pseudo-supernatural elements featured in this film are surprisingly effective enough to keep the viewing guessing right the way through. Cage gives a wonderful performance that even Jack Nicholson would bow to and it is his performance that steals the show.

TRANSYLVANIAN TWIST
1989; MGM (Color); Producer: Roger Corman; Director: Jim Wynorski

In the great style of Mel Brook's YOUNG FRANKENSTEIN, TRANSYLVANIAN TWIST, a Roger Corman production directed by Jim Wynorski, is a spoof on the vampire and horror genres.

In the film, Steve Altman accompanies pop star Teri Copley to her uncle Byron Orlock's castle in Transylvania. Orlock is played by actor Robert Vaughn, in his first and only performance as a bloodsucker. At the castle, Copley inadvertently locates her dead father's book of witchcraft.

The film is abundant in horror jokes and cameos, one of which includes the late Boris Karloff (via clips from his film THE TERROR). Most of the horror and supernatural elements are predictable and played for laughs.

MONSTER SQUAD (1987) is superior if you love *"Famous Monsters"* with a giggle. Wynorski also directed the remake NOT OF THIS EARTH.

Amanda Donahoe as the venomous vampire guardian of Ken Russell's
LAIR OF THE WHITE WORM (1988).

CHAPTER EIGHT

The 1990's

VAMPIRE COP
1990; Panorama Entertainment (Color); Producers: Max & Faye Chesney; Director & Screenwriter: Don Farmer.

Vampirism takes a back seat to this violent and graphic film from the director of such blood feasts as CANNIBAL HOOKERS (1987) and DEMON QUEEN (1986). This Don Farmer vampire tale is full of gushing, bloody gore and unnecessary violence.

The premise, in which the vampire once again dovetails with society, is quite clever. During the daylight hours he sleeps upside down in his apartment, but an night, the central vampire hides behind the badge, infecting local drug dealers, who otherwise would go uncared for and never missed.

Of course, VAMPIRE COP would not be much a vampire movie without the traditional throat chompings, blood drinking and sunlight disintegration scenes we have all come to expect.

I BOUGHT A VAMPIRE MOTORCYCLE
1990; Hobo Films (Great Britain) (Color).

Are you ready for this one about a motorcycle that drinks human blood? What will filmmakers think of next?

A man buys a motorcycle and soon after he discovers that the bike will not take gas. Instead it prefers human blood. Soon, the poor guy begins to find his friends dead, drained of all their blood. For God's sake, the bike will only start at night! Can you believe?

I BOUGHT A VAMPIRE MOTORCYCLE by far the poorest and most inept conception offered by a vampire film. Watching this film is like watching ATTACK OF THE KILLER TOMATOES Parts I & II. Be warned!

RED BLOODED AMERICAN GIRL
1990; Prism (Color); Producer: Nicolas Stiliadas; Director: David Blyth; Screenwriter: Alan Moyle.

The AIDS scare comes around in full circle with this bizarre and campy vampire tale directed by David Blyth. The film is very similar to David Cronenberg's RABID (1976) in that the premise tries to combine

Paul "Pee-Wee Herman" Reubens as the nasty, one-armed vampire Amillyn in
BUFFY - THE VAMPIRE SLAYER (1992).

science with the traditional curse of vampirism.

Actors Christopher Plummer and Andrew Stevens play scientists who dabble in the development of pharmaceuticals. Plummer is working on a new drug that will cure AIDS, only this new and addictive drug is like a virus that actually causes people to desire a taste for human blood. Before you know it, everyone in this film becomes addicted, including Plummer himself, who claims, *"Yes, I'm a blood-user, but I love garlic and hate sleeping in coffins!"*

Heather Thomas plays a clinic volunteer who gets bitten by a bloodlust-infected inmate, and soon she goes on a blood craved rampage, cutting people's toes open and taking claim to the title character of this film.

Hollywood has definitely made better.

THE HOWLING VI: THE FREAKS
1991; Allied/Lane Pringle Productions (Color); Producer: Robert Pringle; Director: Hope Perello; Screenwriter: Kevin Rock based on the series of books *The Howling I, II & III* by Gary Brandner; Camera: Edward Pei.

"Vampire vs. Werewolf, The Ultimate Clash of the Forces of Evil!" ....read the advertisements for this routine contemporary werewolf/vampire film.

THE HOWLING VI, released right under the heels of THE HOWLING parts four and five, revolves mainly around a carnival of sideshow freaks commanded by a vampire named Harker, who is played by British actor Bruce Martyn Payne. The vampire in this film is "mostly" nocturnal, and sports long blonde hair and a nasally, sneering British accent. He is hardly convincing and he is barely tolerable as the film's central menace, but he is nonetheless depicted as a sinister creature of sorts.

Actor Brendan Hughes (TO DIE FOR) plays the film's new werewolf, who is first conceived as the evil monster responsible for slaying the inhabitants of a small American town. In a ridiculous scene, he is captured by the vampire and displayed in his circus of freaks as an oddity of nature's dark side. Naturally, the premise leads to that "ultimate" battle in which the werewolf becomes the hero and slays the vampire by driving a metal spike into his throat. To add excitement to this otherwise dull film, the werewolf dramatically leaps onto a curtain and shreds it with his claws, allowing the sun to burst through the window and onto the vampire. The sun's rays literally roasts the vampire to a pile of black ashes. Of course, vampire film buffs will know that this scene was inspired by the climax of HORROR OF DRACULA. But what is puzzling is how the werewolf, a savage and bloodthirsty beast void of human emotions, thoughts and temperament, can actually think and reason clearly enough to be able to rip some curtains apart in order to allow the sun's rays to enter the room?

THE HOWLING VI is far removed from the original concept created way back in 1981 with the original *Howling* film. Somehow, the series has lost its impact along the way. The novelty of adding a vampire into the series was simply a commercial device to increase video sales. This last film in the series was never released theatrically.

I WAS A TEENAGE VAMPIRE
1990; New World (Color); Producer: Jim McCullough; Director & Screenwriter: Samuel Bradford; Camera: Richard Mann.

I WAS A TEENAGE VAMPIRE is far from being anything like TEEN WOLF or TEEN WOLF II, and quite frankly, most fans will probably enjoy I WAS A TEENAGE WEREWOLF and BLOOD OF DRACULA better than this low budget fiasco.

Young Murphy Gilcrease is the giek and laughing stock of the class. He's totally uncool, until one night he visits Jo-Dan's Motel and local whorehouse. There he becomes the victim of a vampirized prostitute and soon after finds his instant ticket to the cool life as he descends into vampirism.

With his cool leather jacket, dark sunglasses and his super-human strength, he becomes the envy of his entire high school. Bullies shy away from him and delicious blondes find him irresistible. But honestly, the entire film is so bad you'll die from boredom.
Writer-director Samuel Bradford uses cheap corny lines such as when Murphy's mother discovers her son's fangs for the first time and comments, *"I'll have to take you to the orthodontist."* The comedy elements and the vampire trappings are just so bad that they really hinder what is already an non-salvagable film.

Released on video as TEEN VAMP for those who dare to sit through eighty-seven minutes of adolescent vampire mayhem. BUFFY THE VAMPIRE SLAYER is by far superior to this fiasco, which really does not say much for this film.

SUNDOWN: THE VAMPIRES IN RETREAT
1990; Vestron Pictures (Color); Director: Anthony Hickox; Camera: Levie Isaacks.

Stop the press! Vampires who actually walk in the heat of the day's sunlight wearing UV-protection sun glasses, sunblock, sombreros and gloves? Can this be true? It's true, and in this incredibly funny, rarely-seen vampire picture that should not go unseen by admirers of vampire spoofs, the traditional vampire legend is thrown to the dogs.

Three old geezers run an obsolete gas station just outside of a desert town located somewhere in the mid-west. The town is called Purgatory, and its inhabitant are all vampires. Whenever fresh meat pulls up at the gas station, these three old men activate an alarm that rings into the homes of all the vampires. But, normally, these town folk do not attack mortals, since their main source of nourishment is artificially produced. However, an accident occurs that sends off a series of events. One of these old relics, Mort (Played by M. Emmet Walsh) accidentally and literally knocks off the head of an obnoxious, coke-snorting, city-slicking passerby, unaware that he has been seen by a nearby couple camping in the distance. When the couple report the murder, they are put in jail by the sheriff (played by John Hancock) of the small town. Of course, the sheriff is also a bloodsucker.

Meanwhile, Dave Harrison (played by John Metzler) is sent for by the inhabitants of Purgatory under the command of Count Dracula (played by David Carradine), who remains incognito throughout the first half of the film. Harrison is sent for to repair and reactivate a blood synthesizing apparatus that feeds the vampirized town folk. But its not long before Mrs. Harrison (played by Morgan Brittany) is attacked by a stop-motion vampire bat in the likeness of Maxwell Caulfield, who is actually an attractive blonde bloodsucker and a great villain!

Caulfield plays the villainous Shane, who, together with a Pilgrim vampire named Jefferson (played by John Ireland), plots to destroy the blood synthesizer. They both feel that their colony of vampires should revert to the bloodsucking terrors they once were and suck blood the traditional way. Opposing them is Dracula, who is tired of all the blood-shed (Dracula, a good guy?). Tired of all the killings and stakings, Dracula formed the town of Purgatory and sank loads of money into the blood synthesizer device so that all of his victims and his victims' victims-turned-vampires could live happily without having to attack humans for innocent blood.

For the most part, the majority of the inhabitants side with Dracula, but Jefferson vampirizes an entire army of motorcycle hoodlums to help fight against Dracula's opposition. Armed with wooden bullets, the opposers begin shooting the uncooperative vampires, which results in a rowdy western-style free-for-all. The final showdown is between Dracula and Jefferson. In a scene reminiscent to those many Clint Eastwood/ Spaghetti westerns, the two foes face each other in the streets of Purgatory, each armed with pistols loaded with wooden bullets. Dracula, of course, wins. Sounds awful, doesn't it? But SUNDOWN is loaded with fun and unexpected and unlimited entertainment that will make you want more by the film's climax.

This ambitious effort from director Anthony Hickox also stars horror personality Bruce Campbell (from the EVIL DEAD films) as Van Helsing, a descendant of the original professor, who arrives in town to destroy master vampire Carradine. By the way, Carradine's vampire offers an uncanny resemblance to Christopher Lee's Dracula of earlier years - without the cape. Needless to say, Van Helsing is eventually turned into one of the undead. Also, look for actor Brenden Hughes, of TWO DIE FOR II and THE HOWLING VI. The actor has a small bit part as a vampire in this delightful little film that says it's okay to be a bloodsucker in modern America.

ROCKULA
1990; (Color); Director & Screenwriter: Luca Bercovici.

In the tradition of VAMP and FRIGHT NIGHT comes this comedy spoof on the vampire legend that combines vampire trappings with Bo Diddley!

Dean Cameron is a three hundred-year-old vampire who is looking to loose his virginity. Did we also mention that he can play the guitar? Not for the avid fan of vampire movies, but Bo Diddley fans will love this film.

NIGHTLIFE
1990; TV/USA Network (Color); Producer: Robert T. Skodis; Director: Daniel Taplitz; Screenwriters (teleplay): Daniel Taplitz & Anne Beatts from a story by Beatts; Camera: Peter Fernberger.

NIGHTLIFE cleverly and successfully combines comedy with horror, and as a result of such a whimsical combination of genres, is one of the better recent vampire movies to be cast against a contemporary setting. In fact, at times, this made-for-television film is superior to such theatrical features as FRIGHT NIGHT and VAMP.

NIGHTLIFE succeeds as a comedy because the comedy elements are truly funny to begin with, and they are used at the right times throughout the film.

The film is set in Mexico, and the graves of one hundred year old mummies are being unearthed. Uncovering one of the coffins, two Mexican grave-diggers reveal the fresh, non-decomposed body of Angelique (Maryam D'Abo), a beautiful vampire who purposely buried herself alive for one hundred years to hide from her evil and wicked master Vlad (Ben Cross of the new DARK SHADOWS television mini-series). It is uncertain whether Cross's Vlad is actually Dracula. The film leads us to believe that Vlad is possibly the infamous Count Dracula, although this is only hinted at but never verified during the film.

Angelique's discovery is publicized and Vlad is soon in Mexico in search of his great lost love. Meanwhile Angelique falls in love with her doctor, a scientist named David (Keith Szarabajka), who falls in love with Angelique's blood condition (how ironic!). With the help of her doctor, Angelique realizes that she does not have to kill for blood (surprise honey, there are blood banks in the modern world)! But this is no good. According to this film, consuming blood through transfusions is virtually no good to the vampire. The transfusions of regular blood are just like drinking a Bloody Mary cocktail without the vodka! In this film, the vampire must first scare their victims before drinking their blood. By scaring them first, the victim releases a certain chemical into

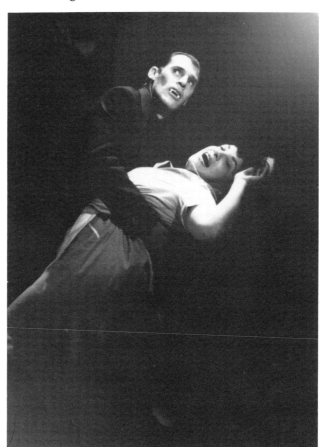

their bloodstream which, when consumed by the vampire, keeps them young and alive.

The climax is staged in a Gothic castle where Vlad is staked in the heart. However, despite Vlad's destruction, director Taplitz closes the film with a hint of a sequel.

In addition to some great atmospheric scenes, the film offers some really funny lines such as, ".....*Give me a lite. A blood lite!*" And "......*Whatever you do, don't ever bury yourself alive!*" Finally, the film ends with the soundtrack of the song, "*I'll put a spell on you!*"

NIGHTLIFE is a refreshing variation on the traditional vampire theme that is highly recommended for fans of vampire spoofs. Surprisingly good for a television production.

TO DIE FOR II: SON OF DARKNESS
1991; Trimark Productions (Color); Producer: Richard Weinman; Director: David F. Price; Screenwriter: Leslie King; Camera: Gregory Lively.

Three years in the footsteps of its original, TO DIE FOR II is a thoroughly enjoyable vampire tale that often surpasses its predecessor on both a technical level and in terms of entertainment.

Returning are actors Steve Bond, Amanda Wyss and Scott Jacoby. The film tells how Count Vlad Tepish, having assumed the identity of Dr. Max Schreck (now played by Michael Praed), runs a hospital near Los Angeles where he dispenses blood plasma to vampires Amanda Wyss and Steve Bond, the latter plays Praed's evil and sadistic brother Tom. Vlad is hardly the bloodthirsty, murdering fiend that his brother would really like him to be. In fact, Vlad

Vampire Ben Cross romances then bites poor Maryam D'Abo in NIGHTLIFE (1990).

is such a "bore," and nothing would please Tom more than to have his brother completely out of the way.

Once Tom learns that Vlad is the father of actress Rosalind Allen's (who plays the character of Nina) infant son Tyler, the evil brother begins to concoct plans that jeopardize both Allen and Tyler's lives.

The film moves at an incredibly fast pace, but it doesn't really matter because the actors here are professional, and you actually find yourself caring about what happens to them.

Returning to his Van Helsing/vampire killer role of Martin is Scott Jacoby, who becomes alarmed when mysterious deaths begin to plague the country-side. At first, the authorities think him to be another crazed psychopath, rambling on about modern-day vampires, but once released from incarceration, Martin seeks the aid of Jane, a benevolent vampire who actually helps him locate the vampires' lair.

Learning of Jane's deceit, Tom handcuffs Jane to a large tree just before sunrise. In one of the film's more splendid moments, Jane agonizingly perishes at the mercy of the sun's rays.

The film concludes with a colossal battle between the two vampire brothers which results in the staking of Tom, the destruction of Cellia (Wyss) and the decapitation of Nina's vampirized brother. Finally, only Vlad remains, and as he is about to convince Nina into becoming an immortal vampire like himself and little Tyler, Martin drives a wooden stake through Vlad's heart. In a scene very reminiscent of Hammer's DRACULA HAS RISEN FROM THE GRAVE, Vlad painfully removes the wooden stake from his heart and commands, ".....*Do you think you are a match for me?*" Just then, in yet another scene to imitate the climax of Hammer's HORROR OF DRACULA, Martin leaps towards the thick drapes that cover the windows, pulls them down, and allows the sunlight to blast into the room. In an elaborately orchestrated special effects scene worthy of the very best vampire movies, the vampire disintegrates right before our eyes.

Is this the end of the road for the "To Die For" films? Probably not. The film leaves us wondering what will happen to poor little Tyler, the infant vampire? I am sure the producers have plans for Tyler in the third film in what could end up being another vampire trilogy like SUBSPECIES.

TO DIE FOR II offers some splendid atmospheric photography, great special effects and some really sensual love scenes between Vlad and the film's heroine, Nina. The gore level is not bad for an independent, but director David Price does not shy away from a little blood here or there. Price focuses more on delivering a good, well-written story and convincing characters as opposed to familiar theatricals. Mark McKenzie's sweeping music score also helps liven things up.

TO DIE FOR II is really a great vampire film worth watching. Fans will not be disappointed.

VAMPYRE

1991; Panorama Entertainment (Color); Producers: Bruce G. Hallenbeck & Antonio Panetta; Director & Screenwriter: Bruce G. Hallenbeck.

VAMPYR pays homage to Carl T. Dreyer's VAMPYR (1932) and many of the Hammer vampire films made during the 1960's. The film becomes mottled by the director's obvious personal fondness of Hammer horror films, and therefore, many of the early aspects of this film that resemble Dreyer's classic, quickly take a back seat to the Hammer-style of thrills and chills. As a result of this combination of styles, Hallenbeck's film becomes a bit unfocused and often baffling in its premise.

VAMPYRE suffers from many weaknesses, beginning with inadequate performances, unconvincing characters, and, most obvious of all, insufficient funding. However, there are a couple instances in which the film appears to have been professionally made, occasionally rising above its obvious and troublesome financial limitations, but for the most part, VAMPYRE fails to achieve the level of technical excellence it strives for.

SUBSPECIES

1991; Full Moon/Paramount (Color); Producer: Ion Ionescu; Director: Ted Nicolau; Screenwriters: Jackson Barr & David Pabian from an original story by Charles Band; Camera: Vlad Paunescu.

This gem of a horror film was produced by Full Moon Entertainment, an independent film company that normally delivers low-budget, inept and commercial efforts that are usually clouded by horrible photography, inadequate special effects, poor stories, and amateur actors. In lieu of these flaws, SUBSPECIES remarkably came as a great surprise, because it defies the norm and rises above the usual mediocre level of these vehicles. SUBSPECIES is not

A female "Subspecies" craves human blood in Ted Nicolau's SUBSPECIES (1991).

just another commercial splatter entry into the vampire movie genre. While the film never reaches the visually stunning and technically superior excellence of Francis Ford Coppola's $40 million epic BRAM STOKER'S DRACULA, released one year later, SUBSPECIES is one of the better, well-mounted contemporary vampire films ever made.

Director Ted Nicolau successfully maintains a Gothic atmosphere cast against a contemporary backdrop. The film's Transylvanian setting and Gothic-style architecture have a lot to do with this film's eerie mood.

The premise revolves around Transylvanian folklore and customs, and opens in a Gothic medieval castle wherein an ancient vampire named King Vladimir (Played by contemporary horror star Angus Scrimm) drinks the blood produced by the precious and legendary bloodstone. According to the folklore, the infamous stone holds the blood of saints and, when consumed, the elixir keeps the vampires from preying on humans for fresh blood.

King Vladimir has two sons, one of which, Radu, is a bad apple. Radu (Anders Hove) is the King's first born son and an incredibly hideous, foul-looking creature of the night. Radu is very much a vampire, with two elongated fangs at the center of his mouth and claws that will slice apart a piece of steel (Radu's

monster make-up was obviously inspired by Count Orlock's image in the 1922 film NOSFERATU). The evil vampire is both articulate and intelligent; a cunning villain that will give even the best of movie Draculas a run for their money!

Radu kills his good-hearted King and father by stabbing him with a sword made of silver. In a scene that would later be mimicked by Coppola's DRACULA, Radu takes the blood-dripped weapon and licks it clean with great delight; his father's blood smears his horrid face.

The story picks up years later, as Radu turns two

young and beautiful American tourists (Laura Tate and Michelle McBridge) and their Transylvanian friend (Irina Movila) into his next victims. The vampire succeeds in transforming both McBridge and Movila into foul vampires, but, as he makes the move on Tate, Radu is stopped in his tracks by his more handsome and kinder-spirited half-brother Stefan (Michael Watson). Stefan is nothing like the monster Radu.

The film ends with a nicely staged battle between the vampirized brothers resulting in the impalement and decapitation of Radu and the ultimate slaying of the vampire girls. Interestingly, Tate offers herself to Stefan, and together they live eternally happy as vampires, so we are led to think.

SUBSPECIES nicely blends together eroticism and horror. In one scene, Radu's shadow is shown creeping through the corridors of a Gothic structure and into the room of a female victim. Slowly, he drains the young girl's blood from her wrist. During his next visit, the perverted creature drains the remaining blood from her breast (a scene that filmmakers can only get away with in an R-rated picture). In yet another effective scene, Radu summons one of his dead but vampirized female victims from her grave. Slowly she crawls her way through the earth and up to the surface to do her master's bidding.

The film is great fun and loaded with familiar vampire trappings and some new folklore. There is also great use of stop-motion photography, in which Radu's severed fingers grow into miniature demonic creatures whose sole existence is to serve unholy their master.

SUBSPECIES, proceeded by two sequels, is undoubtedly one of the more interesting vampire movies to come out of Hollywood in years and should not be missed by fans. Much better than this film is part two, entitled BLOODSTONE: SUBSPECIES II.

CHILDREN OF THE NIGHT
1991; Fangoria Films/Columbia (Color); Producers: Norman & Steven Jacobs; Director: Tony Randel; Screenwriters: Christopher Webster & Nicolas Falacci.

From *Fangoria's* own publishers Norman and Steven Jacobs comes this unusual tale of modern vampirism; and who else other than this team can better tackle such a project?

The film is directed by Tony Randel, who also

directed HELLRAISER, and stars Karen Black and Peter DeLuise. The premise is a refreshing switch from the traditional vampire film, set in the small and rather quiet Midwest town of Allburg. Far beneath the small town church is a secret underground crypt where a master vampire named Czakyr (David Sawyer) resides. To get to the vampire's crypt, you must swim underwater through secret taverns. The town's children are kept underwater in suspended animation, eventually to be fed upon by Czakyr.

Karen Black and Maya McLaughlin play mother and daughter vampires and Peter DeLuise is the visiting teacher sent to free the village from the evil vampire's hold.

This otherwise original effort unfortunately suffers from improper editing and poorly constructed time sequences. The idea of the vampire's lair being subterranean is quite clever. There are even some good atmospheric moments worthy of some of the better vampire films. It is unfortunate that CHILDREN OF THE NIGHT never received theatrical distribution by Columbia. The film is available on video and should not be missed by fans of vampire movies.

PALE BLOOD
1991; (Color); Director: Dachin Hsu.

This very obscure, rarely-seen modern-day vampire tale tells how a serial killer in Los Angeles is leaving his victims bloodless. Director Hsu gives us a bit of uncertainty as to whether this killer is actually a vampire. The film stars George Chakiris and Wings Hauser.

VAMPIRES IN VENICE
1992; (Italy) (Color); Director: Alan Cummings.

Not since NOSFERATU (1979) has actor Klaus Kinski returned to another performance as a vampire in this obscure picture. In fact, Kinski's vampire is performed in a "*Nosferatu*-style" and fashion.

According to the legend set forth by this film, if a vampire falls in love with a virgin who is in love with him, he will be destroyed. Of course, this is exactly what happens when Dracula (Kinski) is released from his death by a gypsy gang in Spain. He returns to Venice, where he supposedly has relatives. There, he falls in love with a virgin, and the rest is very predictable.

VAMPIRES IN VENICE has yet to be made available on video cassette in America.

VAMPIRE HUNTER D
1992; Epic/Sony & CBS (Japan) (Color); Director: Toyoo Ashida.

An imaginative Japanese-made animated feature directed by Toyoo Ashida in which Hero D turns out to be a human vampire composite who hunts down an evil race of vampires led by Count Magnus Lee and his beautiful daughter Anneka. The Count and his daughter are revealed as descendants of the infamous Count Dracula.

The film's climax has Anneka stressing her nobility and choosing to end her family's blood line rather than tolerating the Count's mating with commoners.

Director Ashida animates this feature with gory gusto and brief nudity. Most impressive are the backdrops and action sequences.

This animated feature was originally produced and released in Japan in 1985 as HERO D - VAMPIRE HUNTER and released in the United States in 1992 by Streamline Pictures.

MY GRANDPA IS A VAMPIRE
1992; (Color); Director: David Blyth.

Al "The Munsters" Lewis stars as the title character in this film about a youn gboy and his friend who visit their Grandpa Cooger down in New Zealand. They soon discover that he is a vampire, but his unusual traits do not stop the boys from having fun with the old geezer.

A VAMPIRE IN PARADISE
1992; Auramax (France) (Color); Director & Screenwriter: Abdelkrim Bahoul.

Released in France in July of 1992 and in America in October 1992, this French-made film is an offbeat, cross cultural comedy with a tinge of mysticism. The story, written by Abdelkrim Bahoul, tells of how an escaped lunatic who thinks he is a vampire perches himself cloaked in a cape outside a young girl's window. The man goes by the name of Nosfer Abi (Farid Chopel).

With his ideal sunk-in features and the appropriate cape, Nosfer Abi runs around Paris as a nosferatu, sinking his fangs into innocent people in hopes that he will be killed (Sound familiar? Try Nicholas Cage in VAMPIRE'S KISS). Soon the young French girl (Laure Marsac) perturbs her parents when she begins throwing random fits in Arabic. What follows is offbeat mixture of comedy and supernatural elements as the parents send for an African exorcist.

Like VAMPIRE'S KISS (1989), A VAMPIRE IN PARADISE pokes fun at both sanity and insanity, however, the pseudo-vampire and supernatural elements in this film are used to unite the two youths from different cultures.

BUFFY - THE VAMPIRE SLAYER
1992; Fox (Color); Producers: Kaz Kuzui & Howard Rosenman; Director: Fran Rubel Kuzui; Screenwriter: Joss Whedon; Camera: James Hayman.

Those who loved FRIGHT NIGHT, THE LOST BOYS and VAMP will certainly get a kick out of this horrid vampire flick made for reasons totally unknown. Yes, one wonders why this silly film was ever made. It should have been called I WAS A TEENAGE VAMPIRE KILLER!

In an attempt to alter the vampire legend with a twist, BUFFY THE VAMPIRE SLAYER, as a result, is flat and humorless. The film, produced and directed by Fran Rubel Kuzui, is technically bargain basement material aimed at the diehard fans of *Beverly Hills 90210*. The film's central character is of course Buffy (played by Kristy Swanson), lead cheer leader and voted Miss Popular at Hemery High School in San Fernando Valley. Just as vampires live eternally, so, apparently, do female vampire slayers, who are reincarnated lifetime after lifetime to kill bloodsuckers. A dirty old man in a long overcoat named Merrick (Donald Sutherland) turns up to inform Buffy that she is one of these rare breed. He requests that she accompany him to the graveyard where she passes her first trial as a vampire slayer. Merrick trains Buffy in preparation of combatting actor Rutger Hauer as vampire King Lathos, who is planning a full scale invasion of Los Angeles with the aide of his vampirized thugs. Actor Luke Perry plays Buffy's new found love Pike; together Pike and Buffy go after the vamps! In a ridiculous final climax, the vampires crash a high school dance, but as predicted, Buffy slays the undead creatures of the night.

Bloodthirsty vampires go on a killing frenzy in BUFFY - THE VAMPIRE SLAYER (1992).

Interestingly, the vampire folklore remains pretty much unchanged. Vampires still do not cast mirror reflections, nor can they walk about during the daylight hours. They can, however, float in the air and they are easily destroyed by wooden stakes. And, although it does not really matter much with this film, a vampire cannot enter a dwelling until asked to do so.

The only salvation of this inept film is actor Paul *"Pee Wee Herman"* Reubens, who is totally unrecognizable here as one of the nasty bloodsuckers. As Amillyn, Reubens is complete with long hair, a mustache and beard and two nasty-looking fangs protruding from his mouth! Reuben's character is more satanic than that of Rutger Hauer' uninspired and totally boring lead vampire.

The film waste the talents of both Hauer and Donald Sutherland; the latter seems as if he's reading his lines from cue cards off-screen. Could it be that he was wondering to himself how he got talked into this boring and meaningless production?

In short, Hammer did it better twenty years earlier with CAPTAIN KRONOS: VAMPIRE HUNTER! Finally, one last dig at BUFFY - THE VAMPIRE SLAYER; Joss Whedon's script is flat, relying on Buffy's air-headed clique to constitute the main source of laughs. Swanson is, however, appropriate as the air-headed cheerleader.

Can you believe Fox invested $7 million into this vapid vampire fiasco?

BLOOD TIES
1992; New Horizons (Color); Producer: Gene Corman; Director: Jim McBridge; Screenwriter: Richard Shapiro; Camera: Alfonso Beato.

From the brother of Roger Corman comes this nontraditional but eye-catching modern vampire tale.

The film, originally made for television but released on video instead, is rather simple and a bit on the bloodless side, making it ideal for those who are tired of gore.

In the film, we are introduced to a larger-than-life businessman and industrialist named Eli, who happens to be the ringleader of a rather large family of ancient Carpathian vampires who have assimilated in Long Beach, California. The character of Eli is similar to Robert Loggia's crime boss-turned-vampire in INNOCENT BLOOD, though he is far from being the ruthless creature Loggia portrays.

The film begins when a family in Texas is visited at night by a group of vampire hunters led by Bo Hopkins. They manage to kill the mother and father, but the son escapes wounded to California, where he hooks up with Eli and his Carpathian family of vampires. Following in his tracks are the vampire hunters, who wish to rid the world of these "foul" creatures of the night.

In the film's only bloody scene, the vampires turn hostile and gang up on the vampire-killers during the climax. The bloodsuckers savagely attack them in hordes, ripping their throats apart in a style reminiscent of George Romero's DAY OF THE DEAD. They then consume their enemies' blood and throw the bloody remains into the sea below.

BLOOD TIES works well in its attempt at portraying the vampires as, first, bad guys-turned good guys, and secondly, the vampire-hunters as good guys-turned bad guys by the film's climax. Viewers will feel a sense of happiness when the vampires triumph over the vampire hunters. However, director McBridge fails to fully develop the young boy's "coming out of the coffin." Still, the film is effective for a television production and an interesting variation on the vampire them.

TALE OF A VAMPIRE
1992; Tsuburaya/State Screen International (Japan/Great Britain) (Color); Producer: Simon Johnson; Director: Shimako Sato; Screenwriters: Shimako Sato & Jane Corbett from a story by Sato; Camera: Zubin Mistry.

A vampire's love is timeless, according to the message delivered by the script of this film written by Japanese-born, London-trained director Shimako Sato.

Julian Sands, the star of the two-part horror film series WARLOCK, plays Alex, a centuries-old vampire who spends most of his time in a library researching martyrs. When a beautiful young woman named Anne (played by Suzanna Hamilton) is hired as an assistant at the library, Alex is convinced that she is his 19th Century mistress reincarnate.

The problem that most film buffs and vampire movie fans will have with A TALE OF A VAMPIRE is that it moves at a very slow pace, as director Sato attempts to establish the film as some kind of contemporary version of the elegant BLOOD AND ROSES. Considering the film's low budget and its hasty four week shooting time, A TALE OF A VAMPIRE is both elegant and stylish, and the photography of Zubin Mistry deserves a special mention.

Considering the restraints of the "all tease and no bite" script, Sands and Hamilton are adequate, nothing more. Sands was much better in ARACHNOPHOBIA, WARLOCK, WARLOCK: THE ARMAGEDDON and BOXING HELENA.

SLEEPWALKERS
1992; Columbia (Color); Producers: Mark Victor, Michael Grais & Nabeel Zahid; Director: Mick Garris; Screenwriter: Stephen King from his own novel; Camera: Rodney Charters.

A Gruesome opening scene with dead cats hung by their tails outside a Malibu house sets the pace for this rather gruesome Stephen King thriller.

Some fans would rather call this film an occult thriller, while others would prefer to classify it as a variation on the vampire theme. In any event, SLEEPWALKERS has found its way into this book for argument's sake. The film is actually a variation on another vampire/cat horror film entitled EVIL CAT (1986) from Hong Kong, about an Oriental cat monster that reincarnates every fifty years and feeds on human blood.

The premise that these "sleepwalkers" are fiendish cat-like vampire creatures who can only survive by sucking the life force out of unsuspecting virgins is quite original, though it mimics an older film known as LIFEFORCE (also covered in this book). Only in SLEEPWALKERS, these creatures are humanoid and non-extraterrestrial. These "sleepwalkers" can fade into an invisible state and also have the ability to move heavy objects about at their will. It also appears that the only thing that can destroy these creatures are

*A closeup of the nasty and vicious vampire
Radu from SUBSPECIES (1991).*

domesticated cats. In the film, domesticated felines actually rip apart the dreaded "sleepwalkers" during the climax, but it is Klovis, the wonder cat, that saves the day, as he leads his cat friends against the "sleepwalkers."

In the film, Mrs. Brady and her son Charles (Played by Alice Krige and Brian Krause) move into a sleepy old town. Soon, Charles finds himself falling for the young and beautiful Tanya Robertson (Madchen Amick), who is also a virgin. Tanya is unaware that the Bradys are ancient demons in human form whose main source of nourishment is the life-force of unsuspecting victims like herself. But it does not take too long before Tanya becomes educated to the fact that Charles is a "sleepwalker," and soon she finds herself running for her life.

The special effects are great, especially the scenes in which the Bradys transform into hideous cat creatures, but the film's gore level is very high, and in the case of this film, it is unjustifiably used without rhyme or reason. As with most Stephen King films, SLEEPWALKERS is not void of humor, particularly in Alice Krige's portrayal of the sexy and over-loving mother Mrs. Brady. One scene that is particularly funny occurs during the climax, when Mrs. Brady stabs a deputy in the back with a kernel of corn and proclaims, "....*And who says vegetables won't kill you?*"

Stephen King wrote this film directly for the screen, but SLEEPWALKERS is far from being his best effort. King has done better.

In cameo appearances are Clive Barker, John Landis, Mark Hamill, Joe Dante, Tobe Hooper and King himself.

BRAM STOKER'S DRACULA
1992; Columbia/Zoetrope (Color); Producers:
Francis Ford Coppola, Fred Fuchs & Charles

Mulvehill; Director: Francis Ford Coppola; Screenwriters: James V. Hart, based on Bram Stoker's novel *Dracula*; Camera: Michael Ballhaus.

In addition to being the most expensive, the most lavish and the most extravagant cinematic take-off on the Dracula legend, Francis Ford Coppola's BRAM STOKER'S DRACULA is a bloody visual feast. The film's grandiose style is mainly due to its exceptional design and in seeing the original story told in full.

Where most screen versions of *Dracula* borrow from the ageless but tired premise of Hamilton Deane and John Balderston's infamous play, Hart's script boasts to be the first to fundamentally follow the original 1897 novel. Still, even this multi-million dollar adaptation does not faithfully tell the entire story as Stoker had originally written it. In essence, Coppola's Dracula is an accumulation of seventy years of Dracula films, beginning with F. W. Murnau's NOSFERATU and Tod Browning's DRACULA and continuing with Christopher Lee and Frank Langella's interpretations. BRAM STOKER'S DRACULA pulls from the best parts of past vampire films, but seems most influenced by the colorful and highly dramatic Hammer pictures of the 1960's and 1970's. Even the film's soundtrack resembles a Hammer vampire movie. However, the main aspect that sets this version apart from past adaptations, in addition to its whopping $40 million budget, is Gary Oldman's bizarre and mysterious characterization of the infamous Count.

Gary Oldman, who portrays the infamous Count Dracula for the first time, projects the character as a tragic and tortured soul. From the very beginning of the film when Dracula is robbed of his true love, to the next moment we see the centuries-old vampire cloaked in full regalia, we are led to believe that the Count has been suffering since the 15th Century.

Later, in England, Oldman's vampire is shown fashionably dressed in 1920-ish attire, with smoked granny-glasses and a tall top hat. If anything, the master vampire here resembles Robert Quarry's "hippeish" vampire from THE DEATHMASTER. Still, despite the vampire's new and rather odd appearance, Oldman delivers an interesting and eccentric side of the Count that we have never seen before. In short, the actor is quite effective as the master vampire. And, even though Oldman's Dracula is purposely physically unattractive, he still possesses romantically alluring attributes. When looking back into film history, three notable performances of Count Dracula will stand out above the rest. The first,

(Keanu Reeves) is startled by Count Dracula's sudden appearance in Francis Ford Coppola's BRAM STOKER'S DRACULA (1992).

Poor Lucy (Sadie Frost), a victim of Dracula, is attacked by fearless vampire hunters in BRAM STOKER'S DRACULA (1992).

of course, will always be the late Bela Lugosi's memorable and hallmark characterization, followed next by Christopher Lee's staple and trend-setting performances in the Hammer series. The third will undeniably be Oldman's characterization in BRAM STOKER'S DRACULA.

One of the many amazing aspects of this version are the numerous physical transformations that Dracula undergoes. In this film, we see him as a wolf, while in another scene, he transforms into a hideous demon-like bat-creature with demonic green eyes. The Count also undergoes a series of age changes, from old to young to that of a rotting corpse. By far the best and most memorable scene features the vampire in mid human/mid wolf transformation as he sexually assaults poor Lucy Holmwood in the garden during a violent thunderstorm.

The film offers many memorable scenes that will undoubtedly influence future filmmakers. For example, Lucy Holmwood's descent into vampirism is cleverly captured on film. She is the first to fall prey to Dracula's charms and she is the first to actually die. There is a brilliant scene in which Van Helsing leads a group of vampire hunters into the icy cold family crypt to find Lucy as a bloodthirsty vampire. Dressed in an elaborate bridal gown, the scene shows the vampire Lucy carrying a young child snuggling on her breast. It becomes obvious that she has been feeding on this child. What follows is a beautifully mounted confrontation and staking scene that will please even the most discriminating fan of vampire movies. The scene is highly reminiscent of Barbara Shelley's staking scene in Hammer's DRACULA - PRINCE OF DARKNESS.

The plot of BRAM STOKER'S DRACULA is basically similar to what we have seen previously. Only this time, we get to see Prince Dracula in action as Vlad the Impaler, a military genius whose bloodthirsty ways are notorious throughout Europe. Prince Dracula leads his countrymen against the Turkish

Count Dracula (Gary Oldman) relishes the sight of blood in BRAM STOKER'S DRACULA (1992).

army, slaughtering fifteen thousand Turk soldiers in what is one of history's bloodiest battles. Dracula orders that all wounded and prisoners be impaled on wooden stakes throughout the countryside, a message to the enemies who dare to challenge the cross of Christ. Naturally the Turks flee in horror at the barbarous sight and Prince Dracula relishes his victory (we actually see the prince kiss a crucifix).

But tragedy befalls onto the prince. While battling the Turkish army, a Turkish arrow carrying a deceitful message finds its ways to the hands of Dracula's wife Elisabeta. Believing that her prince has been killed in battle, Elisabeta hurdles herself from the castle turret. She dies, upon which Dracula very violently renounces God. Frantically, Dracula cries out, "*.....I, Dracula, Voivode of Transylvania, will arise from my own death to avenge hers* (Elisabeta) *with all the powers of darkness.*"

The grand opening scene, set in 1462 in Transylvania, is quite an eye-opener that is both refreshing and visually stunning. For the battle scenes, Coppola first viewed the spectacular battle scene from Akira Kurosawa's KAGEMUSHA, reflections of which show up in the opening and bloody battle sequence of BRAM STOKER'S DRACULA. The scenes that follow, however, are equally visually sumptuous.

What follows next is the rather shocking and frightening tale of Prince Dracula, which picks up some four hundred years later. Dracula has already sent for a solicitor from England named R. M. Renfield to arrange for acquisition of property in London. When Renfield returns to London mad, he sends for another solicitor, Mr. Jonathan Harker (Played by Keanu Reeves).

Harker arrives at Castle Dracula, and is greeted by Count Dracula, "*.....Welcome to my house. Enter freely of your own will - and leave some of the happiness you bring!*" The real horror story begins when Harker takes that fateful step over Dracula's threshold.

Lucy (Sadie Frost) screams in pain as she is confronted with a crucifix in BRAM STOKER'S DRACULA (1992).

Our first glimpse of the vampire Count Dracula is like non other. Dracula is a tall old man, with cold blue eyes, a riveting face and long hairy hands. Most impressive, though, is the nobleman's startling Kabuki-style hair, which is long, rolled and balled up on top of his head- worn like a majestic crown. Dracula is dressed in a sweeping scarlet cloak, which undulates like a red sea of blood whenever the vampire moves around his castle. Embroidered on his cloak is the crest of Dracula, a motif of several elements (birds, dragons, wolf, snakes and fire). The vampire's four hundred year old face is a pale, stark white, like a corpse.

The tale moves very rapidly, with the vampirization of Jonathan Harker by Dracula's three seductive brides, Dracula's journey to England and arrival at Carfax Abbey, the vampire's discovery of Mina and Lucy (played by Winona Ryder and Sadie Frost) and the arrival of Professor Van Helsing (played by Anthony Hopkins).

Where Oldman's Dracula differs from previous characterizations, Hopkin's Van Helsing is far removed from those that have preceded him. Here, Hopkin's Van Helsing character is somewhat as demonic as Dracula. The professor is onery with a slight touch of madness- totally the opposite of Edward Van Sloan, Peter Cushing and Laurence Olivier's characterizations. Coppola did well in choosing Hopkins for the role, straight after his mesmerizing performance in the Academy-Award winning horror film SILENCE OF THE LAMBS. Hopkin's Abraham Van Helsing role is but one of two characterizations in this film. The second is of an old monk during the opening segment of the film.

As with previous screen versions of Stoker's novel, BRAM STOKER'S DRACULA also offers an exciting chase scene bound to Castle Dracula. This chase scene, however, is unlike any other. As Count Dracula flees to Transylvania with Mina, Van Helsing, Jonathan Harker and other vampire killers are in hot pursuit. The chase ends at the castle, where Dracula is impaled and then dies at the hands of his beloved Mina, a reincarnation of Elisabeta.

Francis Ford Coppola's BRAM STOKER'S DRACULA is a masterpiece of horror on every level. The special effects are without a doubt the most innovative the screen has yet seen. Amazingly, though, Roman Coppola, Francis' son, often used old-fashion effects techniques suggested by classic films. For example, the dramatic shadow motifs were suggested by NOSFERATU (1922), while Jean Cocteau's ORPHEUS inspired a shot combining rear projection with live action. Even Cocteau's BEAUTY AND THE BEAST helped inspire naive effects and set designs for this film. Coppola's use of shadows combined with the magnificent sets of Thomas Sanders, the visually sumptuous photography of Michael Ballhaus and the awe-inspiring costumes of Eiko Ishioka helped this film earn several Academy Awards. And so it should, since Coppola's DRACULA is perhaps the greatest screen version of the celebrated novel ever made.

Word has been circulating about a sequel planned for 1995 entitled THE RETURN OF DRACULA. Whether such a sequel will materialize will remain to be seen, however, Francis Ford Coppola's MARY SHELLEY'S FRANKENSTEIN is scheduled for a fall 1994 release.

DRACULA RISING

1993; Concorde/Roger Corman (Color); Producer: Roger Corman; Director: Fred Gallo; Screenwriters: Rodman Flender & Daniella Purcell; Camera: Ivan Varimazov.

Despite its confusing opening sequence, DRACULA RISING is really not that bad of a film. Director Fred Gallo works very hard within the confines of this film's limited budget (Corman's biggest budget next to CARNOSAUR released the same year on video). The bottom line, however, is that DRACULA RISING is Roger Corman's answer to Francis Ford Coppola's $40 million epic BRAM STOKER'S DRACULA; both films suspiciously made around the same time. Where CARNOSAUR was released to capitalize on the enormous box office success of JURASSIC PARK, DRACULA RISING was made to profit from the overflow of success generated by BRAM STOKER'S DRACULA. Both Corman films were not released theatrically. Instead, both films were issued on video only.

DRACULA RISING is a love story wrapped around a horror film. The tale begins when a historian and art restorer named Teresa (played by Stacy Travis) is visited by a peculiar young man named Vlad (played by Christopher Atkins), after which she begins to have flashbacks of a past lifetime.

Next thing we know, Teresa is on her way to Romania to restore an early Renaissance painting for a mysterious man named Alec (Doug Wert), who sports black hair, a mustache and beard. Alec is very handsome and alluring, but he's also a vampire. In fact, Alec is the film's bad vampire, who, in the film has evil intentions of putting the bite on Teresa's neck.

Vlad is the film's good vampire (and a blonde one at that) and he steps in to keep poor Teresa safe from harm's way, at least for the meantime.

The remaining half of the film revolves around both Alec and Vlad's conflict. Alec wants to convert the young girl into one of the undead, but Vlad is totally set against this action, and the two engage in a nasty cat and mouse game that seems to have been ongoing for hundreds of years. During the struggle the viewer is taken back into time via flashbacks, and we learn the trio's (Alec, Vlad and Teresa) past relationships with each other. Apparently, Vlad is the son of the infamous and feared Vlad the Impaler. As a child, Vlad was taken in by a local monastery during the late 15th Century and looked after by the then very religious and fanatical Alec. However, Vlad breaks his vows and falls in love with Teresa, who, in her past lifetime, is accused of being a witch by Alec and burned at the stake right before Vlad's eyes. At that moment in time, Vlad renounces his faith in God and in the monastery and seeks out his evil father.

Vlad the Impaler (played by Zamari Vatok) is a hideous soul who wears a mask over his mouth. In his only appearance throughout the entire film, the Prince of Darkness transforms his own son into a vampire. Prince Vlad, or Dracula, assures his son that his venomous bite is the only solution that will enable him to be reunited with his long lost love.

King Vlad's proclamation proves correct, but it takes young Vlad five hundred years to meet up with Teresa, which puts us back to the film's very beginning when the two first meet.

As predicted, there is the final showdown between Alec and Vlad, which takes place in the present. The two foes battle each other for Teresa's soul, but Vlad wins when he sends a horde of nasty vampire bats to attack and kill Alec, which they do in a scene reminiscent of the climax of THE DARK HALF.

Marie (Anne Parillaud), a beautiful vampire, breaks into a convent to escape from Joe Gennaro (Anthony LaPaglia) in INNOCENT BLOOD (1992).

Finally, Vlad, ends his life and spares Teresa's by walking into the sunlight.

Corman's DRACULA RISING, though a bit ludicrous at times, delivers some great scenes, one of which is the disturbing witch burning sequence where Stacey Travis is burned at the stake. Director Gallo actually shows the viewer her charred remains in close-up; a sight that will turn the stomach of even the most die-hard splatter fanatic. The film also offers some sumptuous love scenes between Atkins and Travis, one of which, a dream sequence, is filmed all in red. The gore level of this film does not ever go overboard,

but some of the vampire attack scenes are a bit brutal. In summary, the film is a great addition to the Dracula and vampire legend, with interesting flashback scenes and some visually sumptuous scenes. DRACULA RISING is not the inept horror film that it has been wrongly labeled, nor is it a classic. Considering its modest budget, the film falls within a happy medium between adequate and above average.

INNOCENT BLOOD
1992; Warner (Color); Producers: Lee Rich & Leslie Belzberg; Director: John Landis; Screenwriter: Michael Wolk; Camera: Mac Ahlberg.

John Landis returns to the genre of horror films which he mocked successfully with the modest box office hit-turned-cult classic AN AMERICAN WEREWOLF IN LONDON. INNOCENT BLOOD was to do for vampires what AN AMERICAN WEREWOLF did for werewolves, only this film did not do so well at the box office because it was overshadowed by the more grandiose BRAM STOKER'S DRACULA. The film, however, has enjoyed a great video life, and in all fairness, INNOCENT BLOOD is certainly a lot more fun than the Coppola film.

Fun is the key word, as Landis once again spoofs

Marie (Anne Parillaud) has a taste for Italian when she takes a bite of Mob kingpin Salvatore Macelli (Robert Loggia) in INNOCENT BLOOD (1992).

both the horror and gangster genres with this film. From the very beginning when sexy female vampire Anne Parillaud decides she's hungry for Italian, that is, Italian blood, we know we are in for some fun. She inadvertently becomes involved with crime boss Sal, or Sally The Shark - as he is known to all his friends (played by Robert Loggia), who she fails to finish-off when she gives him the near fatal-bite.

In a remarkably funny but rather gruesome scene, Loggia, presumed dead and covered in a body bag, wakens from "death," or what appears to be death, in a morgue and runs around frantically looking for a telephone to call his lawyer (Don Rickles), who he turns into a vampire as well. Don Rickles, a vampire?

In a matter of a short time, Sal has turned his own thugs into vampirized mafioso hoodlums, and now Parillaud teams up with a confused cop (played by Anthony LaPaglia) to stop Sal and his vampirized thugs.

The death scenes in INNOCENT BLOOD are highly imaginative, Landis-style, of course. Don Rickles' death as a vampire is the film's most memorable scene. In a hospital, he rises from his bed to attack a nurse from behind, who is walking towards a window. As he prepares to pounce, she unknowingly draws open the curtains and allows the bright morning sunlight into the room. As we all know, vampires will die when exposed to sunlight. In an incredibly gory but comical scene, Rickles' arms fall right off of his body and he literally burns into ashes right before our horrified eyes! As for the other vampires in this film, they are destroyed by having their necks snapped by Parillaud or by way of traditional staking.

As usual for a John Landis film, the effects are great, but the gore level will actually turn the stomachs of even the most diehard of horror fans.

There are some very funny lines, such as when Parillaud meets the obnoxious crime boss Sally the Shark for the first time and says, "*.....I should have walked away, but, he annoyed me.*" In another scene,

Parillaud, speaking of her first victim, is surprised to learn that she has made the front page of the newspaper, and comments, "......*This was the first time my food ever made the front page!*"

Much of INNOCENT BLOOD is humorous for one reason or another and the film is by far one of the more amusing and entertaining contemporary vampire movies made to date, blending humor with horror Landis style. Landis uses the familiar trappings associated with the vampire legend, such as garlic, sunlight and stakings. These trappings cast against a "gangsterish" background, give the film a fresh and original flare that most vampire movies made after 1968 have lacked. Within seventy-two years, we have seen everything from a Nazi vampire to a bloodsucking cowboy. What's left? Gangster vampires, of course!

As always, Landis uses clips of old horror films in the background on TV sets, such as THE BEAST FROM 20,000 FATHOMS, Universal's DRACULA of 1931, Hammer's HORROR OF DRACULA and even THE GORILLA! Whenever presenting fresh new material, Landis, like Joe Dante, John Carpenter and Steven Spielberg, to name a few, feels that it is necessary to remind the viewer where horror films originated.

Parillaud is brilliant as the beautiful female vampire giving a new dimension to an otherwise traditional role. She's sweet, sexy, beautiful and deadly. Contradicting tradition, Parillaud's vampire very clearly cast a reflection. She also has the ability to fly, although what we see is the camera moving about in thin air. The vampire also has the ability to enter a church at her own will and scale the side of a building. Furthermore, Parillaud's vampire is unaffected by running water. Landis has cleverly taken the traditional vampire trappings of classic films and reworked them to fit around his film.

Loggia is great as a mafioso bloodsucker, delivering what is probably one of his better recent performances. In the film, he is dramatically destroyed by fire, leaving Parillaud as the sole vampire.

Despite a few holes in the script, John Landis' INNOCENT BLOOD is well worth watching. Fans will either love it or hate it. Nevertheless, it should not be missed.

A terrified Frannie Bergman (Elaine Kagan) tries to protect herself from the advances of Mob kingpin-turned-vampire Salvatore Macelli (Robert Loggia) in INNOCENT BLOOD (1992).

TO SLEEP WITH A VAMPIRE

1993; Concorde (Color); Producer: Mike Elliott; Director Adam Friedman; Screenwriter: Patricia Harrington; Camera: Michael Craine.

TO SLEEP WITH A VAMPIRE is an interesting vampire tale based on a greater film, DANCE OF THE DAMNED. Where DANCE OF THE DAMNED offered great performances, this picture is undermined by atrocious acting.

Strangely, Roger Corman chose to rapidly remake Concorde's DANCE OF THE DAMNED, a film that the studio chose not to release in the first place. DANCE OF THE DAMNED was not released theatrically, but released on videotape by Concorde's prestige label, Classic Films. TO SLEEP WITH A VAMPIRE did not fare well at the box office, and also found its way onto video very quickly.

The remake, like the original film, features a suicidal stripper (played here by Charlie Spradling) who attracts a telepathic vampire (played by Scott Valentine). Like the vampire of the original film, this bloodsucker only feeds on hopeless wretches no one will miss. He takes her back to his apartment and promises to end her pain by sunrise. In return, the vampire asks that she tell him of the daylight he will never be able to experience.

Unlike the original film, in which the emphasis is on the strong performances of the two principal actors and the often poetic story-line, this film focuses on the busty body of Spradling and the dramatics of the rough and scroungy bloodsucker.

It is unfortunate that DANCE OF THE DAMNED, a superior outing, is often overlooked, while TO SLEEP WITH A VAMPIRE, a weak story, continues to receive more attention.

BLOODSTONE: SUBSPECIES II

1993; Full Moon Entertainment/Paramount (Color); Producers: Vlad Paunescu & Oana Paunescu; Director & Screenwriter: Ted Nicolaou, based on the original idea by Charles Band; Camera: Vlad Paunescu.

This sequel to SUBSPECIES is a surprisingly above-average effort for an independently produced Charles Band film. The film is helmed by second-time director Ted Nicolau, who delivers what is possibly the best vampire film of the 1990's. The film never pauses, from the very beginning to its climatic moments, the viewer is on the edge of their seats, especially those who are fans of Band's "Subspecies" films. The film offers fabulous cinematography, superb make-up effects and some show-stopping special effects. In addition, the sweeping music of the Aman Folk Orchestra makes this film a splendid example of how horror films should be patterned after.

Returning is actor Anders Hove as the vampire Radu, the most foul-looking vampire since Nosferatu. Radu is the embodiment of all that is evil. A true creature of the night and one of the screen's (video screen, that is) newest horror sensation. Also reprising her role as Michelle Morgan is Denice Duff, who now finds herself caught in mid-transformation as a vampire. Later during the film, she tries to fight her unquenchable desires for human blood but actually ends up putting the bite on a young man in this film.

Director Nicolaou does a magnificent job in exploring Duff's transformation from her human existence to that of a vampire.

The film offers some new faces as well. Rebecca Morgan (played by Melanie Shatner), is Michelle's sister, who flies to Romania to find her sister, but ends up meeting Radu instead. And then, of course, there's "Mommy," Radu's grotesque mother, played by Pamela Gordon covered under layers of horrendous make-up. Mommy actually ends up stealing the show in the end and is a fine addition to the assembly of ghoulish creatures in this series.

The opening scene of BLOODSTONE: SUBSPECIES II is as stunning as the original's opening sequence. Set in King Vlad's old castle in Transylvania, part two picks up right where the original left off. Michelle Morgan, the sole survivor of the first film and the mistress of Vlad's half-son Stefan, begins the narration of the sequel by recapping what had occurred during the climax of SUBSPECIES. At that moment, we see Radu's decapitated body pinned to the castle floor with a dagger straight through its chest. Suddenly, five stop-motion demonic creatures emerge. As three of the creatures pull the vampire's head towards its body, the other two pull the dagger out of Radu's chest. Suddenly, the forces of evil cause the head to merge with the body, and once again, Radu, the hideous, evil vampire is alive.

Now revived to his full capacity, Radu seeks the bloodstone. He creeps over to his brother's coffin, opens it, and drives a wooden stake through his heart. Stefan withers away into a rotted corpses, leaving the bloodstone on top of his skeletal remains. As we all know, the precious bloodstone drips the blood of saints, which keeps the vampire who possesses it from attacking mortals for nourishment.

Next, Radu moves over to Michelle's coffin. As he prepares to impale her with a wooden stake, the morning sunlight beams through the castle windows and onto Radu's face, preventing him from destroying the girl and causing him to retreat and seek shelter until sunset.

By the time Radu awakens, Michelle has already managed to beat the hideous vampire to the bloodstone, and she frantically races to the nearest train station with the prized possession, which takes her to Bucarest. But Radu is able to move through the air, as we see by his shadows, and soon he too walks the streets of Bucarest in search of Michelle and his precious bloodstone.

For Radu, Bucarest not only holds his mistress to be and the bloodstone, but also the cavern of his equally disgusting mother- a creature so foul and repulsive that when stood next to her, Radu appears as a Valentino. She demands that her son obtain the bloodstone for her. He keeps his promise, and together they kidnap Michelle to the prison of the damned, an old crypt littered with skeletons and cobwebs in Bucarest. It is Michelle's sister, Rebecca, who comes to the rescue with an old Van Helsing-like authority on vampires named Popsceu (played by Michael Bemish), and together they manage to destroy Radu once and for all with multiple dagger wounds throughout his body. As for his grotesque mother, the evil witch is burned to death, or so it seems.

During the final moments, Michelle and Rebecca attempt to flee the crypt, leaving behind them the

horror of Radu and his mother, but Michelle is unable to leave the crypt because of the sunlight. She suggests that she stay behind and reunite herself with Rebecca at night. As she renters the crypt to wait until sunset, the mother returns to life and claims her soul. All we are allowed to see is the old witch's shadow dragging Michelle deeper into the catacombs of the crypt.

Nicolau's improved use of shadows gives this film a strong supernatural atmosphere and a feeling of helplessness as if to say, no matter how far you run, you cannot escape Radu's ever-present evil. In this respect, the film never really looses its fright value. In addition, even though both SUBSPECIES films are set in modern-day Romania, Nicolau never really allows his films to fall into the cliche trap in which you have an ancient-old vampire in a modern-day setting. The film never really looses its Gothic, European flair. Nicolau proves that he is truly capable of helming what is a superb entry into the vampire movie genre. SUBSPECIES II is an incredibly great picture that should not be missed.

MIDNIGHT KISS

1993; Academy (Color); Director: Joel Bender; Screenwriters: John Weldner & Ken Lamplugh.

Not to be confused with the 1985 made-for-television film THE MIDNIGHT HOUR with Shari Belafonte and LeVar Burton, this film tells the tale of a vampire who dons different disguises to gain access

Anders Hove as the vampire Radu in BLOODSTONE: SUBSPECIES II (1993).

to female victims. Hot on his trail is actress Michelle Owens, who is very effective against battling the vampire (Michael McMillen).

In the film, Owens is bitten, and like many females before and after her, she must battle the nasty transformation. In one very effective scene, Owens, as she succumbs to her growing hunger for blood, chases her house cat throughout the apartment. Pretty creepy stuff, but vampire fans will love this scene.

As for the rest of the film, the premise is very anemic, with horrible one-liners, uninteresting characters and vapid acting, with the exception of Owens. The film is also known as IN THE MIDNIGHT HOUR.

BLOODLUST: SUBSPECIES III
1993; Full Moon Entertainment/Paramount (Color); Producers: Vlad Paunescu & Oana Paunescu; Director & Screenwriter: Ted Nicolaou, based on the idea by Charles Band; Camera: Vlad Paunescu.
Camera:

This dissatisfying conclusion to Full Moon's superior "Subspecies" trilogy was made immediately after the completion of SUBSPECIES II much in the same manner in which the last two BACK TO THE FUTURE films were made. BLOODLUST: SUBSPECIES III is inferior to its two predecessors for one simple reason: boredom. This film is boring, that is, boring compared to the more visually exciting and innovative originals. The script has too many holes, the events are uninteresting and by this point in the series, the vampire trappings are old. Even the Transylvanian setting, which was considered fresh and innovative with the first two films, has become tired. Executive producer Charles Band could have wrapped parts two and three into one film and pleased a lot more fans. Still, despite these and several other flaws, three-time "Subspecies" director Ted Nicolau has managed to turn out another entertaining installment that revolves around vampire Radu and his precious bloodstone.

BLOODLUST: SUBSPECIES III picks up right where part two ended. The fans of this series will be disappointed with Radu's resurrection in this film, with his previous and more elaborate revival in part two freshly remembered. Following an old formula used in many older vampire films, Radu (once again played by Andres Hove) is given life by his grotesque and evil mother when he is fed Michelle's (once again played Denice Duff) blood (either producer Charles Band could not afford to use the stop-motion demons of the previous film, or the screenwriters decided to avoid familiar material so soon after the second part).

Again, Radu wants Michelle as his disciple, and in this film, he actually manages to keep her a prisoner in his old family castle back in Transylvania. The foul creature of the night walks the city streets at night in Bucarest to collect victims for poor Michelle in his attempt to force her to develop a fresh craving for warm human blood. His reasoning is that, like a pet animal, if you bring them food, they will become subservient and loyal to their master. In this case, Radu is the master and Michelle is his fledgling pet.

After forty-five minutes of meaningless events and inferior dialogue, Radu's plans are ruined when Michelle's sister Rebecca (played again by Melanie Shatner) and her handsome friend from the American Embassy (played by Kevin Blair) team up with Michelle against Radu and steal his precious bloodstone. As Radu, mortally wounded by multiple gun wounds that would not otherwise hurt a movie vampire, chases the trio through his castle and onto the roof, he is momentarily hindered by the sun's rays. Michelle throws the bloodstone over the castle wall. As Radu frantically races to capture it, he exposes himself to the morning sun, which causes him to burn and topple over the castle roof. The dreaded vampire falls into the valley below where he is impaled to death by wooden tree branches.

Of course, the film's ending still leaves unanswered questions. For example, Michelle is still alive. What will happen to her? Furthermore, during the final seconds of the film, droppings of Radu's blood once again materializes into little demonic minions (via stop-motion photography), who find their way over to the bloodstone to find that it has been destroyed. Are we to assume that the precious and ancient artifact is no longer useful to the vampire? If so, this would mean that poor Michelle will suffer an eternity drinking human blood from innocent victims; the type of suffering Radu wanted her to experience in the first place. So who really wins here? The ambiguous ending leaves us to believe that a fourth film will follow.

Radu (Anders Hove) consoles his fledgling Michelle (Denice Duff) in BLOODLUST: SUBSPECIES II (1993).

NIGHT OWL
1993; Franco Film Production (B&W); Producer, Director & Screenwriter: Jeffrey Arsenault; Camera: Pierre Clavel, Howard Krupa and Neil Shapiro.

This obscure film crept into select movie houses and quickly disappeared, which is just as well, since this modern take on the familiar vampire mythology is neither scary nor funny. The amateurish film fails to develop a clear structure of ideas, such as the interesting link between sex and blood-thirst. Even the characters and basic premise is incoherent.

NIGHT OWL is set in New York's East Village where an attractive vampire named Jake (played by James Raftery) targets his female victims in a sleazy neighborhood bar (it is apparent that filmmakers of modern day vampire movies associate these bloodsucking species with sleazy bars and seedy hangouts).

The film begins rather promisingly with an intense sex scene between Jake and his first victim, Zorha (Karen Wexler), followed by numerous murders and a tender romance with Anne (Played by Ali Thomas). Jake resists killing beautiful Anne, and tension is injected into their romance when Zorha's brother decides to look for her missing sister.

NIGHT OWL fails to deliver anything new to the legend. The film feels more like an exercise in noir-style and mood rather than a vampire film that goes straight for the throat!

CRONOS (CHRONOS)

1993-1994; Iguana Productions (Mexico) (Color); Producers: Bertha Navarro & Arthur Gorson; Director & Screenwriter: Guillermo del Toro; camera: Guillermo Navarro.

Produced in 1993, but not released in America until 1994, Mexico's CRONOS is the first vampire movie to come out of that country in years. The film is actually not bad, considering Mexico's infamous reputation for producing horrid vampire movies. Despite a few loose ends in the script - such as characters speaking half English/half Spanish - CRONOS offers an overall healthy measure of originality and interest.

The film begins with a preface chronicling the flight to Mexico of an alchemist from the hands on the Inquisition in 1536. Obsessed with immortality, he invented the "Chronos Device," an ornate clockwork apparatus with the power to grant eternal life. The device, when used, gives its user a thirst for life-sustaining human blood.

Years later, in the 1930's, the alchemist dies in a freak explosion in an ancient building in downtown Mexico City. The device turns up at the base of a statute at an antique shop run by Jesus Gris (Federico Luppi). Intrigued by the device, he winds it up and pays the price.

Things become complicated when an aging and dying millionaire industrialist (Claudio Brook) comes into possession of the alchemist's original diary and he sends his cold-blooded nephew (played by American actor Ron Perlman) to search for the device. Naturally, the nephew has his own greedy plans for using the device on himself.

CRONOS, produced at just over $2 million by the film's creator Guillermo del Toro and the Mexican government, will certainly surprise those who are expecting a film like SANTO AND THE BLUE DEMON VS. DRACULA. As one of the most expensive films to come out of Mexico, CRONOS has earned itself high honors at the last Cannes Film Festival. CRONOS may be the film responsible for rejuvenating the genre in Mexico.

Peter Cushing in BRIDES OF DRACULA (1960).